Seasons of the Sun

Seasons of the Sun

Celebrations from the World's Spiritual Traditions

PATRICIA TELESCO

SAMUEL WEISER, INC.
York Beach, Maine

First published in 1996 by
SAMUEL WEISER, INC.
P. O. Box 612
York Beach, ME 03910-0612

Library of Congress Cataloging-in-Publication Data

Telesco, Patricia
    Seasons of the sun : celebrations, festivals, and obser
vances / Patricia Telesco.
        p. cm.
    Includes bibliographical references and index.
1. Magic. 2. Witchcraft. 3. New Age movement. 4 Seasons —
Folklore. 5. Festivals — Calendars. 6. Holidays — Calendars.
I. Title.
BF1623.R6T45   1996
291.3'6 — dc20   96-15607
                                                          CIP

ISBN 0-87728-872-0
MV

Cover art and interior illustrations by Colleen Koziara
Text design by Kathryn Sky-Peck

Typeset in 10.5 Cochin

Printed in the United States of America

04 03 02 01 00 99 98 97 96
10 9 8 7 6 5 4 3 2 1

The paper used in this publication meets the minimum requirements of the
American National Standard for Permanence of Paper for Printed Library
Materials Z39.48-1984.

Table of Contents

PART I
CONDUCTING THE CALENDAR

PART II
THE CALENDAR YEAR

The Spring Calendar

PART III
THE DAYS OF OUR LIVES

List of Illustrations

To all the people in my life who make holidays something to look forward to, and every day a reason to rejoice.

To Steven and Dorothy, for selflessly offering to help me over editorial "bumps."

To Blyth and David, who lent me some terrific research material for this book, without a return due date attached.

To my daughter for changing my identity from "Author" to "Samantha's Mom."

To Paul and Karl, special hugs—just because.

To Elizabeth, the new little shining spirit born to Jody and Dave, welcome to our world! Your parents are dear friends without whom our lives would be much less filled with joy.

An additional welcome to Tyler, born to Judy and Kevin in June 1996.

To Colleen, my ever faithful and patient illustrator whose vision fills these pages with beauty.

To all the folks at Weiser—thank you for making me feel so welcome.

Acknowledgments

The quoted material used at the chapter openings of this book have been reprinted from the following sources: John Bartlett, editor, *Familiar Quotations* (Boston, MA: Little Brown & Co., 1938), p. 363, for Samuel Gilman, stanza 1, "Ode," Bicentennial, Harvard University, Sept. 8, 1836 [1]; p. 790, William Butler Yeats, "The Song of Wandering Aengus" [23A]; Tyron Edwards, editor, *New Dictionary of Thoughts* (New York: Standard Book Co., 1934), p. 299, Benjamin Franklin [viii]; p. 299, Jean Paul Richter [24]; p. 535, Richard Baxter [325]; p. 418, Edward Young; W. O. E. Oesterly, editor, *Sacred Dance* (Brooklyn, NY: Cambridge University Press, 1923), p. 123, for Aristophanes, *The Frogs* [1A].

Preface

If a man empties his purse into his head,
no one can take it from him.
— Benjamin Franklin

A common question received about my books is why I place such a strong emphasis on history, and adapting that history for our modern world. Having spent the last fourteen years participating in a historical recreation group, I have developed a gratifying appreciation of human chronicles. While much of history has been unpleasant, it is also permeated with examples of the human capacity to discover, learn, grow, adapt, and to periodically shine with genius. It is this side of history, its empowering and useful aspects, that I share with my readers.

When we consider the human animal moving from primitive behavior to reaching for the stars, it's hard not to feel a little awestruck. The unquenchable zeal that drove us to such discoveries, and the compelling energy that keeps stretching our reach, is a very distinctive part of the human experience. It is an important aspect of spiritual development as well.

The learning and wisdom of our forefathers is rarely outmoded or without usefulness today. It helps to keep us from repeating past mistakes. The atrocities acted out in the name of God or greed, and the tremendous loss resulting therefrom, is not easily measured by modern standards.

The burning of the great library at Alexandria and the "disappearance" of many historical treasures during the Crusades stand out as two glaring examples of such waste. We will never know what knowledge was lost forever during these and similar events. We can, however, keep the memory of that knowledge alive. Such accounts dramatically illustrate what happens when one group or faction decides it alone should be the controlling power over peoples' lives and thoughts.

On a less somber note, our ancestors' lives were not technologically driven as are our own. Our forebears' simple approaches, brimming with ritual and tradition, still have much to offer in today's world. Specifically, reemerging arts like herbalism have proven themselves healthful and ecologically friendly. Thus, one guidepost to an earth-aware future exists in the past!

Another area where history offers tremendous insight is in our own magical "backyard." Many people have no idea how rich the chronicles of metaphysical philosophies are. It often comes as a shock when they discover that magic is far older than Christianity. Actually, basic magical concepts have surfaced in almost every country around the globe. The prevalence of animism in ancient tribal cultures is one good example. It was here that an abiding respect for the divine spark in all things had its inception.

More revealing still is how magic has adapted and changed to meet the transforming facets of our world. Keeping the craft alive required tremendous sacrifice on the part of many dedicated individuals. Despite the Church's attempts to dethrone the gods of old by applying labels of heresy, and even indulging in the horrors of witch hunts, magic has survived. As a testimony to the old saying, "What doesn't kill us makes us stronger," Wicca, Paganism and related religions are among the fastest growing faiths in the world today. Modern magicians bear witness to this, and to the memory of those who gave their lives that we might worship freely. They do this not just by deed or word, but by living every moment in a uniquely magical way.

With this in mind, history becomes a mirror for us to examine. Within her pages are lessons and treasures to rediscover. As we research and review, we should also gently remind ourselves that today's actions potentially become the history, celebrations, and spells of tomorrow. What wisdom will those future generations find when they peruse our tomes? That question is one only time can answer.

Introduction

*To everything there is a season,
and a time to every purpose under heaven.*
—Ecclesiastes 3:1

Every day is a holiday. Somewhere in the world right now, at least one group of people is commemorating a specific occasion. Perhaps it is to welcome the birth of a child among them, to mark the time of the year, to honor a great person in their history, or to venerate some special event that shaped that society. Perhaps it is just to celebrate the spirit of life itself.

No matter the reason, humankind has always marked distinctive occurrences with all kinds of mini-rituals in which we gather, perform various activities known as "traditions," and pay our respects to whatever moment (or person) is being revered. These minirituals provide structure within communities, uniting them on a regular basis to rejoice in their common bonds.

During the Middle Ages, for example, a whole village would assemble to celebrate occasions such as Yule, Plough Monday, and harvest festivals with wrestling, archery, and staff competitions. Periodically, the townfolk also held a carnival where they became their own kings and queens, poking fun at the resident royalty. These activities granted the commoners a well-earned, momentary relief from their harsh toils.

Ritualistic observances like these tied the year together into a cohesive cycle that continues into our modern world. The structure of annual holidays gives us something to look forward to. It also adds a unique cultural rhythm to every moment of living. Knowing this pulse improves our affinity with natural cycles, encourages an understanding of our ancestry, and brings us closer to the world of magic itself. But exactly how and why do these important connections take place?

The power of tradition, custom, myth, and ritual should not be underestimated. Each time a person or group repeats a specific phrase or action for a designated purpose, it reinforces the energy of that purpose. As a case in point, if I walk into my home and smell a roast beef dinner, I immediately think of happy Yule gatherings with my family. Why? Because my mother *refused* to serve any Christmas dinner without roast beef, no matter what!

There was nothing remotely magical about that roast, other than the love baked into it. Yet, you could almost taste the warm emotions in every bite. To this day, I continue the tradition of Yule roasts, thinking all the while of mother puttering merrily in the kitchen. I truly believe the same good feelings she inspired in me are being transferred into that meal for my family to remember.

This simple illustration demonstrates how the human mind sorts all experience into specific categories. Each category has anticipations and emotions associated with it. The more often each episode is experienced, the stronger the associations become, until eventually one without other is almost inconceivable. The energy of a given activity is in symmetry with a specific feeling, and you *expect* that feeling. All this equates to an amazing amount of thematic universal power to draw on for positive ends.

Let's look at one common holiday as a prototype. Superficially, St. Patrick's Day appears to have no mystical aspects. Yet, there are ways to transform the latent energy of March 17 into a spectacular celebration for yourself and guests. In this instance, the phrase "luck of the Irish" comes immediately to mind. To prepare, bless green foods and decorations by a waxing Moon for growing good fortune. For after-dinner fun, enchant pennies and wrap them, adding sprigs of parsley and shamrocks, into ornamental bundles as party favors. These portable charms then allow the "lucky" disposition of this holiday to flow unfettered into your life, and the lives of those you care about.

This example is doubly effective in that it takes a celebration extolling a Christian hero and transforms it into something positive for the eclectic New Age. Since the Church used this adaptive approach to Christianize many pagan holidays, turning the tables seems apt. In this manner, mystical traditions can begin reclaiming holidays throughout the year by adding their own unique perspective to them.

This basic technique is not limited to religious observances. Instead, this approach suggests that every special occasion be appraised for its magical potential. In this way, when the mundane world keeps us away from gatherings, we can find an alternative date with a similar tone on which to celebrate. Or, if there is a special need in our lives (such as love), we can decide the best time to direct activities toward that need, like St. Valentine's Day.

Personally meaningful days are also included in this method. Birthdays are a perfect time to rededicate and bless yourself for the year to come. Anniversaries are times to perform rituals for romance and the refreshment of relationships. The death of a loved one inspires projects to help allay grief, while the birth of a child commemorates the cycle of life and joy. All of these moments should be remembered in a distinctive way which emulates our Path, reflects our feelings, and satisfies the prevalent conditions in our lives.

We are moving into an era when the world is stretching beyond its boundaries in many senses. Such rapid growth means that New Age traditions will have to experience expansion, renovation, and novelty to endure. One way to keep up with the pace is by adapting and enjoying the annual festivals handed down to us. This allows innovation and tradition to coexist in a harmonious, flowing form.

The question for many people up to this point, though, has been how to accomplish this. How do we adapt a holiday? What are some ideas for traditional or adapted holiday activities? This book attempts to answer these questions by applying a hands-on approach to every portion of a celebration.

The first chapter of Part I gives a brief overview of the history of the calendar and demonstrates that you can effectively observe a special event on your choice of several days—the modern date, a date by the old calendar, or the date considered historically correct. Each of these dates is totally fitting, depending on your point of view!

For instance, there are some esoteric traditions which incorporate Christ as a master-teacher image. If you wish to honor him in a ritual, it can be done on December 25 with the rest of the world. Or, you may choose a random date in late August, which is generally regarded as the true month of his birth. The timing of the Christian holiday merged the Pagan observance (Winter Solstice) with the new god on the scene, thereby encouraging conversions. The symbolism of a reborn Sun was certainly not lost to the early Christian theologians! In essence, timing discrepancies like this support a flexible framework for how, when, and why we choose to celebrate any notable happening.

In Part II, you will find a catalog of holidays, organized by the season in which they occur. Many of these celebrations have ancient derivations, and some of their associated traditions have spiritual overtones. Because of this, information on folklore, legends, and superstition is presented for each observance. This material serves to clarify and classify the mystical aspects of a holiday. It also provides themes to contemplate when devising meditations, prayers, spells, and rituals of your own.

Part III provides an overview of how to adapt *any* celebration for personal goals. There is a diversity of holiday ideas in these pages, and countless more to consider from your own culture, locale, or the country in which your tradition originated. Ultimately, the goal is to create a Wheel of the Year as splendidly unique as your own vision.

Putting all this information together facilitates whole new dimensions in our worship, be it personal or with a group. From decorations, foods, and guided meditations to dances and games, each moment of any chosen day can inspire "supernatural" results. All that remains is to venture forward and seize the moment.

Start considering every day of existence as a reason to rejoice. Weave magically enhanced observances into your personal Wheel of the Year more often. In the process you will find the power of, and an appreciation for, your path growing proportionally.

The more we live it, the more we "become" the magic, in word and deed. Spirituality is not limited to a tiny corner of our reality. It does not suddenly appear during a gathering, then quietly recede while we go about our daily business. Instead, metaphysical practices aspire to give shape and contour to every moment of our lives. They should ignite the power of our heritage in everything and everyone we touch.

Employing magical attitudes in our observances every day throughout the year is one means to that end. Celebrate each Season of the Sun. In Winter, rest with the earth. In Spring, be reborn. In Summer, sow the seeds of character, and in Autumn, gather your harvest. Your efforts will be rewarded with one wonderful result. New Age ideals will expand to permeate your life on a regular basis... and so too, your magic!

Note to the Reader

used both contemporary and ancient sources for reference to assemble this book. When reading this text, and the dates ascribed to each holiday, bear in mind that Hindu, Moslem, Chinese, Jewish, Ancient Greek, Roman, Mayan, and Christian calendars all have different bases. Their approach to astronomical systems, cycles, and the Seasons of the Sun are diverse.

Every effort was made to place a celebration in its proper time frame. Some of these may experience slight shifting as years pass, due to lunar and solar sequences. Usually this shift is no more than a day or two.

Similarly, I have depended upon the research of many authors to coordinate exactly which traditions were pertinent to each holiday. Since we did not witness these events, certain assumptions must be made about origins, changes that occurred over time and distance, cultural influences, etc. Wherever such hypotheses are drawn, they are noted, and it is left to your discretion to determine their validity.

Finally, remember that each observance was commemorated in a slightly different way, depending on the family or township celebrating. These abundant personalizations and revisions must not be overlooked. I have tried to provide an inclusive treatment of unique approaches that are specifically helpful to the magical practitioner. Other tidbits that you find on your own should be added to your own Book of Days to accentuate your efforts further.

Good Celebrating!

PART I

Conducting the Calendar

By these festival rites from the age that is past,
to the age that is waiting before.
—Samuel Gilman

The Calendar and Modern Life

Let the mystic measure beat:
Come in riot fiery feet;
Free and holy all before thee . . .
— ARISTOPHANES

s life in the work-a-day world becomes increasingly complex, there is less time to devote to spiritual pursuits. How frequently have you planned to attend a special gathering only to be dissuaded by your budget, your work schedule, a car in disrepair, the lack of a baby-sitter, or some other mundane glitch? I suspect that the answer to this question is "yes" far more frequently than makes anyone happy.

The inability to participate in these special activities can leave you feeling frustrated, out-of-touch, and isolated. Some feel guilty for not remembering a specific event, even though they may have been struggling with serious personal matters at the time. Then there are those, like myself, who want to bring more positive energy into their lives without having to turn their routines inside out.

If your life fits any of these scenarios, then this book should be refreshing. For a moment, consider the calendar year as a symphony score. To the untrained eye, the splotches of ink on the paper seem like refined doodles. Yet, to a skilled musician, written music is a tool for creating tremendous beauty. The idea behind this section is to help you direct annual observances as a talented conductor guides and inspires an orchestra. This direction includes, but is not limited to:

Choosing the dates and times for celebration;
Considering decorations;
Creating other appropriate accents for the occasion;
Writing spells, rituals, prayers, meditations, and
    invocations accordingly;

Creating (or participating in) activities to accentuate
   your theme;
Preparing edibles for the occasion with a thematic
   flair;
Finding symbols, colors, songs, and other props to;
   round out the ambiance;
Opening and closing rites;
Keeping your own book of days to record each celebration.

You should no longer have to wait for a specific date to make any
day into a magical celebration. If you can't participate in a specific observance, these techniques will provide you with the fun-
damentals to create one of your own, right where you are, inex-
pensively and creatively. You will learn to devise or augment an
event calendar which portrays your own particular vision of
spirituality, one that is realistic considering your time constraints. These techniques are totally flexible and will respond to
spur-of-the-moment inspirations or needs.

Each holiday presented in Part II includes illustrations to
get you started. However, I heartily encourage you to personal-
ize the examples to make them more meaningful. This step is
vital to the effectiveness of *any* metaphysical endeavor. If something doesn't make sense, if you think it should be done differently, or if you feel uncomfortable with the exercises given, then
revamp the approach until it is right for you. The reward for
your efforts will be a deeper understanding of specific spiritual
principles as they pertain directly to your life. Don't be afraid to
get innovative!

The Calendar and History

he calendar as we know it has undergone tremendous change since the dawn of time. The first functional calendar was based on old-fashioned observation. People watched the signs from nature to know when to sow crops, prepare for Winter, or go to market with their goods. Each season of the sun provided a measuring system in which the end of an extended, consistent pattern of weather conditions denoted the end of a year.

The position of the Moon or the Sun marked time's passage. This particular method became important for hunter-gatherers, who depended on specific cycles to insure their survival. Later, this idea was applied in Babylon to chart celestial objects, as an aid to travelers and merchants. Certain constellations, when compared to the Moon's location, portended what kind of conditions to expect on a journey. Basically, these astronomical observations became the first functional road maps!

As understanding of the natural world grew, distinctive calendar systems flourished according to region and culture. Be it the French monks, Mayan Indians, or Asian astrologers, key individuals in each civilization devised calendars that honored their gods and the cycle of life.

In China, the lunar month was marked, each one of the twelve months being depicted by an animal. As in Western astrology, the prevalent belief was that each creature set characteristic themes for anyone born beneath its sign. Likewise, symbols for the year, month, and hour of birth all combined to establish expected personality traits.

The Animal Calendar, with its unique Eastern flavor, is still being used today. To adapt this calendar to your own life, apply

Table 1. Associations of the Animal Calendar

MONTH	ANIMAL	ASSOCIATIONS
January	Rat	Charm, opportunity, wealth, confidence, socialization
February	Buffalo	Family, leadership, patience, precision, courtesy, the mind
March	Tiger	Meditation, command, success, charity, individuality
April	Cat	Joy, talent, discretion, peace, security, recovery
May	Dragon	Health, vitality, power, courage, conviction, ideals
June	Snake	Luck, wisdom, humor, romance, intuition, decision making
July	Horse	Sympathy, happiness, keen wit, practicality, determination
August	Goat	The arts, nature, whimsy, adaptation, security
September	Monkey	Energy, rapport, playfulness, memory, innovation, learning
October	Rooster	Frankness, boldness, bravery, conservation, confidence
November	Dog	Service, loyalty, protection, alertness, faithfulness
December	Pig	Chivalry, purity, trust, will, tolerance, impartiality

the most positive symbolic aspects of each animal-month as a focus for activities executed during that time frame (see Table 1).

When devising a ritual to help with religious studies, execute it in the month of May to bring amplified power along with solid convictions. Or perform the rite in June to improve your discernment for spiritual matters. Another illustration would be to enact a spell for household leadership any day in February, whereas authority in a social setting is improved by scheduling the observance for March.

Another civilization that had a representative month structure was that of the Aztecs. Their year encompassed eighteen periods of twenty days (comparable to our months), with five unlucky days left over. Each day of each period was named after an item, an animal, or a phenomenon that was considered emblematic. Each day also had a corresponding deity. Unfortunately, it is difficult to accurately convert this calendar for modern use.

One of the best-known early calendars was developed by Julius Caesar in 46 B.C. This calendar contained 365 days, with every fourth year gaining one day. Caesar was probably following the Egyptians on this, who also had a 365 day year, adjusted according to the Nile's flood cycle. This calendar set a defining tone for our contemporary dating system.

The length of a week, however, was often subject to local legend or the social activities of an area. In the Orient, the week related to market cycles. The Israelites assigned seven days since seven was a holy number. In Mesopotamia, the seven days of the week corresponded to the seven major objects which could be viewed in the sky. Eventually, the Romans and Saxons settled on the seven-day cycle (A.D. 321), naming the days mostly after gods (see page 11), and basing their model on the changing Moon cycles, which averaged seven days.

The Julian system, although somewhat flawed, remained in use until 1582, when Pope Gregory decided to correct its inherent problems. He deleted ten days, and declared leap years to be those divisible by four. Even though this new calendar, which is now known as our modern Gregorian calendar, was more accurate, people were slow to convert, with widespread use coming only in the late 1700s. In fact, New Year's Day was celebrated on March 25 until 1752, when it was officially changed to January 1.

These cultural transformations in our concepts of time and its measurement have had an impact on how we decide which timing is best for an event. They have introduced a factor of adaptability into our thinking about time. Take, for instance, Daylight Savings Time, which was signed into law in 1967 in the U.S.A. Consider the impact of this change, which made all times during the day relative to location. For example, not all countries observe Daylight Savings Time. With such differences in mind, if a spell's instructions call for a casting time of 2 A.M., there is always somewhere in the world where it is 2 A.M. at any given moment.

Magic, by definition, works outside conventional modes of thought. Therefore, it does not have to be limited to particular time zones and the constraints of linear thought patterns. By learning to perceive time in a universal manner, the turning Wheel can be honored at meaningful junctures, without having to perform a juggling act with your other responsibilities.

Choosing Dates and Hours

The choice of days and hours can greatly affect the results of any undertaking. By choosing propitious days and hours for different observances, you can draw on the energies of deeply rooted correspondences and long-held associations to augment the power of your wishes and thoughts. In choosing times, basically look for one of the following:

- A holiday whose date is accessible to your schedule, and whose theme is appropriate to your magical intentions;

- A date that can act as a substitute for another traditional observance because the central focus is the same;

- An upcoming holiday to celebrate, but personalizing the observation to mirror your path and meet any other needs you presently have;

- A meaningful date and time to schedule a personal event. This timing should also somehow empower the magic being performed.

I have always felt that *anytime* is the right time for magic. Yet, from a more traditional vantage point, timing has been an important element in magical procedures (in the broadest sense of the term) through the ages. The early mages looked to omens portended by the position of stars, the Moon, the Sun, the hours of the day, and the days of the week to discern the most constructive time to perform their spells. This time-oriented approach is far from obsolete, and is most commonly evidenced today in ceremonial magic.

But the precision of these methods need not dissuade folk magicians, or people of alternative paths, who frequently work on gut instinct. Exactly how detailed you get with each of your holiday observances is completely up to you. Listen closely to your intuitive senses, and allow them to steer you in the right direction. If you feel special timing is important, follow that instinct, using the information in this section as a guide. If not, look to other symbolic levels to make your celebration just as meaningful and potent.

To determine the Sun sign or Moon sign of a specific date, and its associated energies, your best resource is an astrological almanac or calendar (the first is preferable). While generalities can be drawn for every astrological sign, there are many other factors to be considered. The job of a good astrologer is to know how diverse influences fit together during any particular year. Thus, astrological almanacs and calendars are the best guidebooks to help in planning your ceremonies.

Undertakings of a simple or ongoing nature can usually be deferred until a symbolic time, if you wish. To illustrate, perhaps there is a habit in your life which annoys you. You have made frequent attempts to rid yourself of this tendency, but without success. In choosing a date for a special effort toward change, which common holiday comes to mind? How about New Year's Eve at midnight, when many people are rededicating themselves to overcoming similar habits?

While you need not abandon regular efforts before then, on the next New Year's Eve, have a special spell, meditation, or ritual prepared. The occasion itself releases a powerful symbolism of the fading away of the old order, which in turn enhances the magic. It also encourages determination and refreshed spiritual energy toward success in your goal. If you don't want to wait that long, an alternative would be to perform the rite on Samhain (Halloween), the Celtic New Year.

Looking at it another way, assume that May Day is next week. Perhaps you would like to honor this holiday on your personal Wheel of the Year. But what exactly will you be venerating? First to come to mind is the season of Spring, with its emblems of birth, growth, fertility, abundance, and beauty. But May Day (Beltane) is also a fire festival, full of frolic and romance. I know of no home that would not enjoy a little extra loveliness or pleasure on a regular basis. These then are some of the themes from which you have to choose. Once you decide which focus will be central, everything else becomes a matter of selecting activities to highlight that theme and putting those activities into a cohesive order.

The following is a brief, general listing of correspondences that will help you choose dates and times for your celebrations. These should act as guidelines only; your own resourcefulness in adding original touches will insure truly profound and powerful results.

WEEKDAYS

Weekdays were named after various gods, goddesses, and celestial objects, each of which influences the positive energies of these days.

Monday—All Moon- and goddess-related magic; matters of inventiveness, intuition, fruitfulness, and spiritual growth. Monday was named after the Moon.

Tuesday—The conscious mind and skill; matters of activity, legality, vitality, and logic. Tuesday takes its name from the god Tiw, who governs athletics and legislation.

Wednesday—The muse and creative energy; matters of fancy, ingenuity, resourcefulness, and mystical insight. Wednesday is named after Woden (Germanic), who is identified with the chief Norse god, Odin.

Thursday—Power, energy and enthusiasm; matters of dedication, faithfulness, loyalty, and endurance. Thursday is named after Thor, who governs contractual obligations.

Friday—Relationships and productivity; matters of love, communication, efficiency and fertility. Friday is named after Frigg, a goddess known for protecting marriage.

Saturday—Outcomes and effects; matters of growth, change, motivation, and understanding. Saturday takes its name from Saturn, a god of the harvest.

Sunday—Solar and god magic; matters of instruction, learning, administration, authority, reason. Sunday takes its name from the golden solar disk.

HOURS

Many celebrations in history began or ended at a specific time because of the potent symbolism that time evoked for the participants, or because of other associated astrological influences.

Morning—Daylight hours are best for matters of the conscious mind, including magic for leadership, intelligence, and all cognitive functions. The Sun is a welcome friend to chase any shadows that may be hiding in our lives. It is regarded as a beneficial sign of divine blessing when it shines on any special occasion. Mystical pursuits during daylight hours can be empowered when combined with a southerly wind.

Night—The intuitive, emotional self, maternal nature, healing, fertility, and Moon magic are all part of the charm of the night. Wishing on stars, dreams, the eternal nature of the spirit, and ancient mysteries come into play once the Sun has set. If your observance can incorporate the west wind, all the better. This breeze is filled with flowing water and peacefulness.

Dawn—Beginning any ritual, spell, or celebration at dawn commemorates a new beginning, freshness, warmth, and renewed hope. An especially potent time for Spring observances. Magic performed at dawn can also be accentuated by working with an easterly wind, blowing from the horizon where the Sun rises.

Dusk—Closing and ending are the messages dusk brings. But this finality is not without promise. Dusk marks a temporary change toward darkness. It is a time to look within oneself and ponder universal truths. It is an excellent time to perform rites which mark the passage of a loved one, intense personal transitions, or to mark the end of any cycle. Magic performed at dusk is aided by the northerly wind, which is cool, bringing heated matters to rest and an opportunity to reconsider our actions.

Midnight and Noon—Commonly called the "in-between" hours, hanging between night and day. The most active times for elemental creatures such as the fairy folk and disincarnate spirits. Excellent for all magic pertaining to positive modifications in your life, endings and beginnings.

The specific hours of the day also have magical associations in many cultures. Following is a brief summary of some of these:

1 A.M.—The first hour of a new day. Focus is on wholeness of self and the banishing of any shadows.

2 A.M.—Ridding partnerships or relationships of negativity.

3 A.M.—Determination, especially in matters that seem to hold you back.

4 A.M.—Improved luck or victory over a specific set of deterring circumstances.

5 A.M.—Encouraging growth of the psychic self.

6 A.M.—Tenacity and perseverance, especially with something you have been putting off.

7 A.M.—Hope, improved insight, and perspective.

8 A.M.—Personal change aimed toward the conscious mind.

9 A.M.—Assistance for others, focusing on concrete matters.

10 A.M.—Improving personal convictions and resolutions.

11 A.M.—Energy directed toward transformations which may have seemed impossible.

1 P.M.—Self-image and personal security.

2 P.M.—Building relationships, encouraging understanding and love between people, sexual symmetry.

3 P.M.—Balancing matters of the body, mind, and spirit.

4 P.M.—Harmony of elements, sticking to schedules, magic to accentuate goals.

5 P.M.—Insight into the self. Communicating with spiritual guides.

6 P.M.—Matters of safety, protection, and completion.

7 P.M.—Diversity, blending or healing differences, gentle care toward others.

8 P.M.—Leadership, command, and guidance.

9 P.M.—Comprehension of universal truth.

10 P.M.—Improving the rational mind, sensibility, and clear mindedness.

11 P.M.—Coping with drastic change in a positive manner.

MONTHS

Like the days and the hours of our lives, the months have mystical, astrological, and magical associations. Some have already been mentioned on page 6. The following is a partial list of some other common correspondences:

January—Protection, security, defense. The name derives from the god Janus who cares for heaven's gate.

February—Mercy, grace, motivations, health. The Roman month of repentance and atonement.

March — Victory, mastery, overcoming. The name derives from the god of war, Mars.

April — Fortune, fate, opportunity. From a Latin word which means "open."

May — Progress, maturation, the blossoming of an effort. The name is taken from the goddess Maia, who cares for all plant life.

June — Relationships, devotion, faithfulness. From the goddess Juno, who presides over marriage.

July — Leadership, self-control, composure. Named after one of the greatest rulers, Julius Caesar.

August — Harmony, agreement, unity. Refers to the Roman Emperor, Augustus, an avid supporter of the arts and peace.

September — Mystical growth, understanding deeper mysteries. Named after the Latin number seven.*

October — Transformation, change and personal development. Named after the Latin number eight.*

November — Psychic awareness, compassion, universal law. Named after the Latin number nine.*

December — Insight, sagacity, good judgment, prudence. Named after the Latin number ten.*

---

*So named according to the order of their appearance on the Roman calendar.

The Atmosphere of Celebration

Every observance has its own unique ambiance. Part of this comes from the season in which the holiday accurs. For the most part, however, the tenor of the occasion is determined by the reason for the celebration and by the participants themselves. From these two sources, a combination of elements emerge, creating appropriate embellishments and moods. Sometimes the accents are culturally or socially determined, and sometimes they come from pure caprice.

Within the circle, and on altars dedicated to magical traditions, we take this basic idea one step further to give flavor and fullness to a special observance. For example, what birthday ritual for a child is complete without balloons and dessert? In this setting, the balloons can mark the perimeter of the circle instead of just decorating the walls. The birthday cake then becomes the post-ritual feast!

If the birthday happens to correspond with a rite of passage into adulthood, pictures of the child at younger ages can adorn one side of the room, while gifts symbolizing their new adult role await them on the other. In this manner, everything within the magical sphere has a specific meaning that empowers the rite. These props enhance the enjoyment of all participants because they reflect the emotions, desires, and general atmosphere befitting that occasion.

In all cases, the components you assemble will be very different depending on the observance in question. In addition, the desires of the individuals participating should be of primary concern. This is especially true for deeply personal moments such as eldership, marriage, and wiccaning rituals. For these celebrations, the dominant "character's" choice of emblems, wording, etc. should be foundational to all your efforts.

One subtle and easy way to embellish a ceremony is through color. Psychology has shown us that specific pigments contribute to specific frames of mind. Because of this, minute accents of color can amplify the magic at hand. In the case of a birthday party, this would mean bright, festive colors (especially red) to celebrate life's continuance. Representative pigments can be part of flower arrangements, any number of decorations, altar cloths, robes, lighting, candles, etc. Here is a brief list of color associations:

Red — Life's energy, the element of fire, vigor, courage, power, zeal, vitality;

Orange — Sympathy, cordial feelings, growing energy, fruitfulness, kinship, the harvest;

Yellow — Creativity, fertility, element of air, movement, oracular attempts, whimsy;

Green — Healing, beliefs and convictions, financial matters, progress or growth;

Blue — Harmony, rest, the water element, happiness, the contemplative nature, unity;

Purple — Metaphysical topics, the soul, dedication, insight, the higher self, wisdom;

White — Peace, safety, cleansing, purity, truce;

Black — Turning negativity, repose, the unknown;

Brown — Nature, grounding and foundations, beginnings;

Pink — Friendship, relaxation, improved emotions, moods, and physical well-being.

Personally Created Spells, Rituals, and Invocations

Like the props to the holiday plays you put together, the script is very important to your effort. The spells and prayers that appear regularly in your liturgy are sometimes unsuitable outside their normal setting. The words and feelings just don't fit every circumstance, nor should they. The more specialized the wording, the more dynamic it will be for empowering your goal. This is why personally devised spells, rituals, prayers, and invocations are important ingredients in your annual observances.

Everyone's approach to creating these components is a little different. Some use rhyme and meter, others prefer free-verse composition, and yet others like to be spontaneous. Depending on the setting, each one of these tactics has its benefits: spontaneous verbiage flows with the emotion of the moment; prepared verses tend to be eloquent and precise; rhyme and meter aid in memory retention, freeing you to focus ardently on directing your magic; free verse is comfortable on the lips, but not as easily recalled. The choice depends on what puts you at ease. Choose the style in which the intentions, not the words which convey them, become the primary focus. Ultimately, each ingredient of your observance should fit together in form, tone, theme, etc., for a feeling of wholeness. Once this is achieved, everyone involved will notice the difference.

For those who feel uneasy about inventing verbal components, try browsing through books of good literature and poetry, or various magical texts. Also, seek out respected people in your spiritual community for recommendations. If you are working alone, then relax! The only two who will hear your supplications are yourself and the Divine. Somehow I doubt that the god or goddess is more impressed by fancy language than she or he is in the true intentions of your spirit. Keep these concepts in mind as you begin to formulate your ceremonies.

Spells should be specifically phrased to indicate the needs at hand and the applicable time frames. They are then released and directed toward those specific ends. Spells are similar in form and function to prayers, except that you may, or may not, choose to request Divine aid.

Rituals are basically elongated spells that incorporate increased detail: movements, props, libations, and so forth. Each section of the ritual accentuates, builds, and guides energy toward a distinctive goal.

Invocations are fundamentally a way to offer welcome to elemental or Divine powers. When your work is completed, some type of thankful dismissal for these beings is also fitting.

Blessings sanctify people or objects through an outpouring of Divine energy. The most common method is the laying on of hands, as a conduit for the Great Spirit.

Samples of all these magical techniques follow for each holiday discussed. Use these as guidelines, adapting the language to fit the circumstances at hand. Find phrases which are normal to your way of communicating, and that express what is in your heart, and you should be very successful.

Activities to Accentuate
Your Theme or Goals

When you have decided on the date and time for your celebration and created appropriate verbal components to round out the observance, the next step is to plan the order for your celebratory program. This sequence of events needs to be in harmony with the observance itself. Here are some factors to consider:

Decking the Halls: This enhances the atmosphere and can also become a project that gets people involved with, and expectant about, the festival. Making and setting up decorations is a great treat, especially for children, who feel displaced by other adult activities. Further, the hands-on approach saturates all your ornamentation with energy to enhance the sacred space.

Opening the Festivities: Almost all holidays have something that marks their beginning: fireworks, a rising Moon, or perhaps a parade. In the earlier illustration of a birthday party, the festivities are suitably begun by singing to the celebrant! Whatever you choose to do, this moment defines the line between the mundane and magical worlds. It should be designed to put participants in the right frame of mind.

Dances, Music, or other Accompaniments: Circle or line dances, and the playing of music, add tremendously to a celebration. Patterns for simple dances can be adapted from any that you already know. Also, check the library for dance books. Some will have floor patterns to try, and will tell you about a folk-dance's history so you can tie it into your theme.

Music is simple to come by, thanks to the wide variety of New Age artists now on the market. Beyond this, anyone with a good voice or a little musical talent can bring tremendous feeling to a special moment. Homemade rattles, drums, or even kazoos are effective in a celebratory setting. So have a little fun!

Sharing a Cup: Passing a cup or sharing in a toast unites everyone toward a common cause. It is nice to have participants share something pertinent to the occassion when the cup comes their way. The toast voices the sentiments of everyone, and participants literally "charge" their glasses (and the moment) by way of agreement.

Foods: A favorite pastime of mine is designing and preparing thematic foods. Every occasion has certain foods or beverages that naturally accompany it. Easter is one illustration, where egg dishes adorn the feast table to symbolize fertility and the aspects of Spring.

In choosing your menu, consider each component for its magical associations. Find those items that you enjoy the most, and which best suit your overall focus. Prepare the edibles, adding some chants, spells, or symbolic timing to increase their effectiveness; then serve to hungry guests! More ideas along these lines can be found in my other books, *Kitchen Witch's Cookbook*, and *A Witch's Brew*, and in Scott Cunningham's *The Magic in Food*.

Games: Games can take place before, during, or after a holiday ritual, and are definitely not limited to just children. Anyone young at heart enjoys an Easter egg hunt, where they symbolically gather hope and abundance for the coming months. Or, at Samhain, try bobbing for apples—biting them for health through the Winter.

There are many books of games and pastimes available at your local library. Nor should you overlook traditional childhood frolics like jumping in leaves in the Autumn, or cavorting around the May Pole in Spring. If the meaning of your chosen diversion isn't obvious to the participants, take a moment to explain its significance; then let your inner child prevail!

The "Main Event": This constitutes a central activity that focuses the energy of your gathering. Good examples include guided meditations and the creation of amulets or charms. This exercise takes up more time than any other component because of its importance in directing the magic you've created. An example comes to mind in Earth Day. Recycling projects, litter pickups, and tree planting are common to this day, but the spirit of Gaia also needs atttention.

To these ends, your main event might be a guided meditation. Here, everyone gathers together in a natural setting and directs metaphysical energy toward Earth's renewal. This is followed by songs that promote the image of a whole united Earth (example: Starhawk's *The Earth is our Mother*[1]). The musical healing can continue until sunset marks the end of your ritual.

Closing the Festivities: Nearly every celebration I have researched has a meaningful way of closing the day. Closing festivities leave one final thought with the participants, and provide a definite conclusion for the observed cycle until the following year. Some of the most common closings employ prayer by a leader, removal or blowing out of the light source, benedictions, grand finales (like fireworks), or awaiting sunrise or sunset.

In a magical setting, releasing the circle is one fitting way to mark the end of your celebration. Whatever you choose, the lasting impression for the gathering should be positive and bountiful in memories.

---

1. Starhawk sings a song, *The Earth is our Mother.* This song is sung regularly in magical circles.

Your Personal Book of Days

It would be misleading for me to tell you that putting together the "perfect" holiday is an effortless task. Initiative, contemplation, and creativity are all necessary for a truly successful observance. This means giving yourself an adequate amount of time to plan, so that you don't feel rushed or pressured. It also means asking for help when you need it. Your energy and fortitude will not go unrewarded.

With experimentation and refinement, you will compile many notable observances to repeat each year (or as the occasion comes up). This is where a personal Book of Days comes in handy. Keep all your celebrations, in the order in which they occur, carefully documented in some kind of binder. Take care to describe all the details that made that date something really exceptional. Describe your personal feelings after the holiday has ended. These will bring warm memories back in coming years. Make additional notes each time you use the ritual, showing how you improved or adapted it.

In the end, what you possess will be a completely individualized Magical Calendar that celebrates the Seasons of the Sun, all the important moments in your life, and those of your friends and loved ones. It will be a celebration of spirit, chronicling the mystical efforts you extended to others, to the Earth, and toward remembering your place in the universe. Once completed, this tome will be a book to be treasured, shared, and handed down through the generations.

PART II

The Calendar Year

And walk among long dappled grass,
And pluck till time and times are done
The silver apples of the moon,
The golden apples of the sun.
—William Yeats

The Seasons

Time is the Chrysalis of Eternity.
—Jean Paul Richter

n the interest of consistency and simplicity, a season's beginning is defined throughout this book by its Equinox or Solstice. Its holidays will include all dates from that point until the next Equinox or Solstice. This system closely adheres to changes in the natural cycles evidenced by where the Sun is in the sky, and the corresponding transformations this brings to life on our planet. Here are the approximate dates used for this structure:

Spring—March 20 through June 19;
Summer—June 20 through September 19;
Autumn—September 20 through December 19;
Winter—December 20 through March 19.

This system has limitations, especially for people who do not have a four-season climate. Please adjust each section to suit your idea of, or timing for, each season. Allow the signs from Gaia to be your guide. In warmer regions, a rainy period marks the ending or beginning of a cycle. In wintery areas, when animals start growing a thicker coat an early Winter might be anticipated. Or when you see the first shoot of new grass, make that morning your first day of Spring!

Some holidays change their date of observance from year to year. Consequently, each season includes a brief listing of general or undated observances. These can augment your Book of Days by being totally flexible within that season. In addition, they can act as a basis for similar activities at other junctures.

The main idea is not to become so restricted by set dates that you overlook signs from the Earth or your own moments of inspiration. In a metaphysical setting, indications from the Mother are very important to reconnect you with the nontechnical world. They are also meaningful in your quest to become more aware of natural rhythms and their associated symbols. Likewise creativity, when guided by a loving heart, can originate the most sublime spiritual experiences you will ever have.

As you begin to assemble your Book of Days, listen carefully to the songs of your heart, the Earth, the Universe, and the Great Spirit. The music is subtle; it beats and swells with your own life's blood. It has many melodies for those willing to listen, at least one of which will echo the sonnet within your own soul.

The Spring Calendar

pring's theme is one of birth and resurrection. Harsh snows and rainy intervals are passing, animals begin to give birth, and all that dwell on the Earth show signs of reawakening. So it is for Spring celebrations. The observances during this season rejoice in the warmer weather; the more ancient ones revel in the natural fertility being evidenced all around.

Spring's motif is one of pale but lively coloration. Pastels, especially green for growth, yellow for creativity, and red for the returning Sun, are appropriate. Accent your sacred space with all types of seedlings, buds, wild flowers, grass, gathered rain, and early-blossoming plants. Scents for the season include aromatics such as hazelnut, apple, cherry blossom, and peach, to be carried on the fresh winds.

Since nature herself seems to be bearing young, consider decorations that depict baby animals, children, or soft toys. These encourage a youthful spirit. Colored eggs or jars of seeds can be placed at the four quarters along with images of the pregnant goddess. Possible deities to bless your efforts include:

Acat—Mayan god of fruitfulness;
Aima—Hebrew goddess of fertility;
Amaterasu—Japanese goddess of the Sun and joy;
Aphrodite—Greek goddess of love and fertility;
Apollo—Greek and Roman god of creativity, abundance, health;
Baldur—Scandinavian god of goodness and happiness;
Bonus Eventus—Roman god of luck;

Brighid—Irish goddess of inventiveness, well being

Dionysus—Greek god of fecundity, celebration and resurrection;

Eos—Greek god of the sunrise;

Eostre—Anglo Saxon goddess of Spring (rabbits are sacred to her, and she is often given offerings of colored eggs);

Freya—Teutonic goddess of fertility;

Isis and Osiris—Egyptian couple whose union brought the birth of the Sun god (Horus);

Kama—Hindu god of romance;

Lakshmi—Hindu goddess of fortune;

Liban—Irish goddess of vitality;

Lono—Polynesian goddess of productivity;

Maya—Hindu goddess of growing things;

Ptah—Egyptian god of Originality;

Tien Kuan—Chinese god of gladness and good health;

Wajwer—Egyptian god of fruitfulness;

Springtime birth-gems are as follows: for March the bloodstone, which provides courage, fame, and longevity to its wearer; for April, the diamond, which brings peace, love, and durability; for May, the emerald, for good fortune and ease in childbirth; and for June, pearls, to encourage success and attract honor.

Spiritual efforts enhanced by Spring timing include spells, rituals, and celebrations centering around luck, change, growth, playfulness, fertility, young love, and new beginnings.

GENERAL SPRING CELEBRATIONS

Many societies developed general holiday rituals with common themes tied closely to geographical and cultural factors, but not tied to any specific date. These "seasonal" holidays were often observed to mark agricultural cycles, historical traditions, religious beliefs, or rites of passage. They were usually closely associated with the land and its local traditions. Spring being the season of rebirth, the common celebrations associated with it tend to focus on beginnings, growth, and transitions. The following is a sampler of some of these.

BLESSING THE LAND AND SEEDS

This festival frequently occurs just prior to the planting season or after the first thaw. Found predominantly in farming communities, this celebration is one of thankfulness and hopeful supplication for divine favor for the land and forthcoming crops. In China, for example, officials proceed to their local fields to leave offerings on southern facing altars. These offerings include grain (specifically rice), meat, wine, and fresh fruit. Once the offerings are presented, the highest official humbly addresses the gods. This individual then makes several furrows in the fields, spades the ground nine times, and then returns to town.

A similar festival which occurred in Rome was called the Ceralia, which honored Ceres, the goddess of fields and grain. Roman farmers danced their fields on April 13, robed in white and bearing torches. As they moved, prayers and songs invited Ceres' blessing. Later on, the farmers' movements became regional folkdances.

Similar celebrations from other parts of the globe entail circling the parcel of soil at the first sign of dawn while reciting benedictions or asperging with a special herb tincture. The benefit of asperging is doubly meaningful if the tincture has ingredients that keep insects away, or that help fertilize the land. Here is one sample recipe which covers an area four feet wide and nine feet long:

Blessed Bug Repellant

1 1/2 gallons water
1 cup tomato-leaf solution
1 cup cucumber-peel solution
1 cup tansy solution
1 cup marigold solution

1 cup garlic juice
1 cup onion juice

Directions: The four solutions in this recipe can be prepared late in the harvest season of the preceding year and frozen until Spring. A good proportion is 2 cups herb or vegetable to 1 1/2 cups water, to make a strong, tea-like infusion. Warm over a low flame until the liquid is reduced to 1 cup, then strain and add to the other ingredients. Use any garden hose or sprinkler (old spray bottles work) to apply the mixture to the soil and leaves.

Additives: Strong aromatics like pennyroyal, eucalyptus, and bayberry will help keep the insects away. These are most effective if added in the form of essential oil (approximately 15 drops each). Shake well before using each time.

Magical techniques: Prepare during a waning Moon to help deter infestation. Even more potent if readied on a Thursday.

For group work: To do a soil blessing for a large number of people, create a small amount of this tincture and add it to a cauldron full of soil, central to your sacred space. Lay your seeds on the altar to absorb positive energy. Participants take these home later, along with a scoop of the earth, to bless their own garden or planters.

EARTH DAY

Observed some time late in March, Earth Day began in 1970 as a modern version of Arbor Day. Both have strong ecological overtones. Use this day as a chance to reconnect with nature by planting trees or flowers in a nearby park, having litter pickups, and by sharing practical ways to heal the Earth with other concerned community members.

Add songs, visualizations, and meditations that direct healing energy throughout the globe for the welfare of Earth and its residents. Other activities might include painting a sphere named "Earth" with medicinal salve, individual and group pledges for Earth-centered efforts, and tree blessings.

CHOES FESTIVAL

Known as the Jug Festival, this is performed on a randomly chosen Spring morning in Greece, as part of Anthesteria (a festival of Dionysus). The Choes Festival commemorates Spring and the transition into adulthood for Greek boys. Between roughly 800-300 B.C., young men gathered at dawn outside the Acropolis to receive their first draught of wine from the priests.

In our circles, a Jug Festival equates to rites of passage for children, celebrating their adult roles at home or in the group. Teens can share a sip of wine (possibly prepared a year and a day beforehand) and receive symbols of their new adult capacities after the celebration. Here are some spiced wine recipes to brew for this event:

Rite of Passage Spiced Wine

For Women	*For Men*
1/2 gallon apple wine	1/2 gallon apple wine
sliced lemon	12 whole cloves
sliced orange	2 cinnamon sticks
dash thyme	1 inch bruised ginger root
dash comfrey	1 cup pineapple chunks
elder flower garnish	dandelion or marigold garnish

Directions: Apple wine was chosen here as an emblem of wisdom, peace, and growing knowledge. Other wines can be substituted as inspiration dictates. For the women's punch, I suggest pouring the wine over a large block of round ice. This gives the appearance of a Full Moon rising out of the liquid. Float the herbs, fruits, and garnish on top of the punch bowl and serve via communal cup. Elder flowers are sacred to the goddess.

Enhance the men's beverage by serving it hot, since the fire element is connected with the masculine nature. Warm all the ingredients over a low flame until the punch is heady with the spices. Serve with garnishes that look like a noonday solar disk.

Alternatives: Apple juice can be substituted for people who prefer nonalcoholic substances. Local laws regarding drinking ages may also require this change.

Magical techniques: As mentioned before, create enough of this mixture a year and a day before the actual event is supposed to take place. This reflects the traditional novice training period for many magical groups.

To prepare, warm the wine over a low flame with your fruits and herbs. Strain and place back in a sterilized, airtight container and store in a dark, cool area. Accent this effort further by preparing the wine during a Full Moon—the sign of wholeness and maturity.

MINOAN BULL LEAPING

While the actual date for this festivity is unknown, I believe it may have taken place in the Spring because of its connection with fertility rites. This celebration dates from the years 3000-1100 B.C., honoring the Minoan goddesses of the hearth, pasture, herds, and fields. The celebration was observed in a joyous, aerobic fashion known to the Minoan people. Originally, the gymnastics were performed by the prince and princess who were later replaced by trained athletes.

Bull leaping participants lined up to do handsprings over the bull's back. A companion waiting on the other side steadied them after dismounting. The modern aphorism "seize the bull by its horns" originated with this unusual acrobatic adventure.

Adapting the abundant symbols here for your celebrations is not difficult. Say, for example, you have been plagued by procrastination. Try visualizing bull horns in your spellcraft to inspire impetus and improved drive. Alternatively, make a stuffed set of horns to serve as the object of a blindfolded quest, in which you focus all your attention on an elusive goal while hunting for the horns! A friend or magical partner can act as a spotter, as the Minoan acrobats did, to keep you out of harm's way and provide small amounts of guidance.

Another option is to use metal or stone carvings of bulls near your garden, threshold, windows, and fireplace. This strate-

gic positioning blesses your pets, plants, and the general sancti-
ty of your home. These can be set out during one of your traditional Spring holidays as part of the ongoing observances, then
taken in in early Winter. Check a lawn and garden shop for
images that are made to endure changing weather conditions.

PASSOVER

Generally falling in late March, Passover commemorates the
Israelite's successful struggle to win their freedom from cruel
Egyptian domination. In its earliest form, the faithful observed
Passover by sacrificing a lamb to god to show their gratitude.
Later, the Seder narratives, filled with prayers and benedictions,
replaced the sacrificial lamb as the offering.

In strict Jewish sects, Passover lasts seven days.
Throughout this period, families prepare special foods that symbolize the great epoch of the Israelites. They eat bitter herbs to
honor their ancestors' hardships, and a tasty mixture of nuts,
wine, and apples, to symbolize the bricks made in Egypt by
Israelite slaves. Unleavened bread (*matzoth*) is also consumed in
memory of the fact that the Israelites left Egypt so quickly that
the bread did not have time to rise.

In a modern setting, this holiday represents a time of meditation and thoughtfulness. Devise rituals, spells, prayers, and
positive activities that emancipate you from anything which
holds you captive. Also, remember those things for which you
are thankful. If you decide to prepare any of the customary foods
to accent your personal version of Passover, the matzoth spiritually emblematizes prudent, speedy settlements, the bitter herbs
represent your ability to overcome tribulation, and the apples
themselves symbolize strength and endurance.

Passover Endurance Apples

Directions: To make one version of the apple dish, take 7 large
apples (one for each day of Passover, and also the magical number of completion) and peel them. Slice the peeled apples thinly

into a mixing bowl. Add 1/2 cup chopped walnuts for the conscious mind, 1/2 cup wine for the promise of joy, 1/2 cup sugar for the sweet things in life and 1 teaspoon of cinnamon for strength and victory. Mix this thoroughly, then pat it down into a small, greased loaf pan (to make it appear like a brick when cooked). Dot the top with 1/2 stick of butter. Cover with aluminum foil and bake at 350 degrees for one hour. Turn out onto a plate and serve.

EASTER

Occurring in late March or early April, the date on which Easter falls is determined by finding the first Sunday following the Full Moon after the Vernal Equinox (March 21). This festival, although known for its Christian connotations, is very pagan in origin, taking its name from the Teutonic goddess of Spring, Ostern, or the Anglo Saxon goddess, Eostra (Eastore).

Regardless of its origin, this celebration is central to the season, honoring nature and fertility. A favorite treat still enjoyed, the hot cross bun, probably had its origins with the Anglo Saxon cakes prepared for the occasion. For them, the cross symbolized the solar wheel.

Besides wearing new clothes for good luck, participants in many ancient and modern observances revel in the use of eggs as the focus of games, foods, and decorations. There is no reason not to follow suit in your personal festival. Decorate your eggs using powerful emblems, like runes. Use wax and commercial dyes, or glue cut-outs on the hard boiled eggs to form appropriate patterns.

Once completed, add these eggs to thematic gift baskets for health, joy, or prosperity. In the first scenario, fashion eggs with green dyes and decorate them with a circular design for wholeness. Lay the treasures on an herb pillow stuffed with dried apple peel, thyme, sage, and pine needles to encourage well-being. Other healthful gifts for this basket include herb teas, fresh fruit, and chicken soup!

A game called Canigeln adds tremendous fun to Easter celebrations. This is basically an egg roll, where raw eggs are aimed

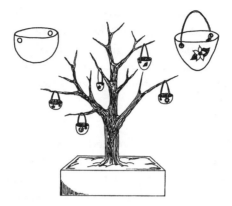

Figure 1. Eggshell tree.

toward a hoop. The distance from the starting line to the hoop is determined by age groups. The person to roll the most eggs through the hoop without breaking them wins the game.

For a magical flair, individuals who need improved fertility and productivity in their life can enact this game. The person rolling the egg holds it with both hands first, concentrating on a specific area of need. Then, as they release the egg, energy is directed toward that ambition (symbolized by the hoop). Each success adds positive power and guidance to the visualization.

One other activity for children, which results in a lively decoration, is making an eggshell tree. For the weeks before your celebration, carefully save the halves of all eggs used in cooking. Dye these with nontoxic colorings and decorate in any way you like. Then, make two small holes on opposite sides of the open end of the shell using a sharp needle (see figure 1). Create a handle by attaching string through these holes on each shell piece.

Next, find a fairly large fallen branch and secure it in a pot of soil, cement, or modeling clay (see figure 1). Have the children hang the egg baskets from the branches and fill them with candies, seeds, flower petals, or whatever suits their fancy! Then, each of your holiday guests (or the circle's participants) take one cache home to transport the magic of the day with them.

An even better foundation for this project is a young sapling purchased at a nursery. These usually come with a large base, and can be planted as a gift to the Earth after your observance. This will remain as a permanent marker for your site, and one which may be decorated to suit every occasion!

SACRED WELL CELEBRATIONS

This tradition comes from England. It was observed any time during the month of May. Well celebrations may partially owe their origins to the Roman festival of Fortunalia (May 26), where all the water gods of the empire were appeased.

In both traditions, people decorated the various holy wells throughout the region with floral garlands and other embellishments. Each holy well had beneficent, indwelling spirits. A petitioner could secure aid from these spirits, if the spirits were properly appeased. To this end, offerings of grain, flowers, and even gold were tossed into the well, along with a wish. This is probably how our modern tradition of dropping pennies in fountains got started.

For your own spring festival, it's fun to make a special wishing well to use in the circle, or as a permanent adornment to your home or yard. Larger, prefashioned wells, manufactured of resilient materials, are available at lawn and garden shops, or

Figure 2. Sacred wishing well. Left: an illustration of what the bowl you use for the base looks like when you work on it; Right: the finished well.

nurseries. You can make smaller wells using stoneware or glass bowls as a base.

For the latter, affix flat-sided stones around the central fixture chosen to make an external wall. Leave a space around the rim to add a handle fashioned from twigs. Hang a small cup from the handle (see figure 2). On the day of your celebration, have each member of your home or coven toss in a token and make their wish. During the remainder of the year, the well makes a handy change jar. Use the contents for little frivolities on which you might not normally splurge, or donate the change to a worthy charity so that positive energy returns to you.

WAPYNSHAW

This festival was held in medieval Scotland beginning in 1424. In the Highlands, Spring marked the beginning of many minor skirmishes between clans. Men were restless after the long Winter months, and the need for ready warriors was not uncommon. To be certain all able-bodied men were prepared to fight, everyone displayed their weapon of choice, in its best condition. This meant weeks of polishing, sharpening, and replacing any items lost the previous year. Once everyone had gathered, the Wapynshaw celebrated Scottish tradition by highlighting the event with drums and pipes.

In a contemporary setting, I see several applications for the Wapynshaw. It can be a day set aside to cleanse, bless, and rededicate all your personal sacred space and tools. Alternatively, focus on spells or rituals that enhance the warrior spirit (the rune ↑) for any personal crusade that needs energy and guidance.

GREEN PLAYS

Early tribal cultures with animistic faiths sometimes celebrated Spring by bedecking themselves in greenery made from flowers, leaves, and other organic items. This ritual was devised to demonstrate an appreciation of the nature spirits in the hopes that abundant crops would follow.

In New Guinea, young couples are married in the rain forest during this festival, the forest being a potent symbol of fertility. In other regions, the celebration is often ushered in by the collection of money for the poor. This probably dates back to when village shamans demanded offerings to satisfy the natural spirits before the growing season began.

There are several ways to adapt the Green Play today. For children, the chance to dress up as plants can be an entertaining and educational diversion. Teens and adults might produce a ritual theatre program centering around the plant kingdom and its lessons. Once planned, perform the play for friends, family, or coven members.

Finally, taking up a collection for a worthy cause is a marvelous idea any time of the year. In this setting, the money can be put into a special account for times when members of the circle have financial need, or donated to an accredited charity.

March

March 22 and 23

FESTIVAL OF MINERVA (ROME)

Magical Themes: Improved wisdom; learning or refining an art or science.

History/Lore: A holiday that honored the patron goddess of commerce, industry, and education. Minerva was the wife of

Jupiter. Her earlier Etruscan form was the goddess of discernment, who wielded lightning bolts at the Spring Equinox.

Decorating Ideas: Minerva favored tiger lilies, and they make a lovely altar decoration. You can also string the long stems together to create garlands for doorways and windows (see figure 10, page 68).

Garments: To honor the electrical aspect of this goddess, don gold-colored attire or jewelry.

Ritual Cup: I suggest a geranium punch. Geraniums were used for offerings to Minerva at the temples. To prepare this, warm a gallon of ruby red wine over a low flame. Add a pinch of sage for wisdom and rosemary for improved mental awareness. Pour the warm liquid over petals from a dozen rose geraniums. Let this mixture sit for fifteen minutes, then strain it and chill. Serve in glasses with a fresh, whole flower as a garnish.

Ritual Foods: Anything with peaches for sagacity. Alternatively, make apple turnovers with a hint of vanilla and nutmeg to improve your perception. Here is a recipe:

Perception Apple Turnovers

2 packages of dairy-case crescent rolls
5 medium apples, peeled and diced
1/4 stick of butter
sugar to taste
1 teaspoon vanilla
1/2 teaspoon nutmeg
1 tablespoon flour
2 tablespoons apple juice

Directions: Place the diced apples in a large mixing bowl. Melt the butter over a low flame, and drizzle it over the apples. Add the remaining ingredients, taking care that the apples are well-coated. Turn this into a saucepan and cook over low heat until the apples are tender.

Next, lay out the crescent roll dough. Place 2 tablespoons of apple mixture in the center of one triangle, then cover it with another piece of dough. Seal the edges by dabbing the closure with a bit of water and pressing the dough in place. Bake in the oven according to the directions given on the roll package. Average yield is 8 turnovers.

Incense: For wisdom: sage, hazelwood, and pansy; for creativity: angelica with bay. This also enhances psychic alertness.

Activities: Go to a museum to admire the art forms you enjoy. Consider a special ritual to empower your own crafts, hobbies, or areas of study. Call on Minerva to bless your efforts.

Sample Invocation: To specifically energize this invocation for insight, repeat it five times, once at each elemental point of the circle and once in the center.

> *Minerva come, see my need;*
> *Your wisdom and inspiration, I shall heed.*
> *Touch my life, my crafts, my trade;*
> *Remove obstacles; new inroads lay.*
> *Clear my vision; empower my art;*
> *Minerva hear the cry of my heart.*

Other Accents: Minerva's color is ruby, so include some red candles or other decorations in your sacred space. Rams and owls were animals sacred to her, so any depictions of these would be suitable.

March 25

HILARIA (ROME)

Magical Themes: Improving your sense of humor; joy, lighthearted pleasures; the Fool card in tarot.

History/Lore: This holiday has its roots in the celebrations held for Cybele and Attis. It is, in fact, a laughing day when happy outbursts bring renewed health and well-being.

Decorating Ideas: Bright colors, streamers, caricature sketches, and any other embellishments that lift your spirits.

Garments: Something fun and frivolous. If there is an outfit you keep specifically for "play clothes," now is your chance to dust it off!

Ritual Cup: Anything with bubbles to tickle your nose! For children, mix ginger ale with a little blueberry juice (for abundant happiness). Adults can enjoy champagne or sparkling wines.

Ritual Foods: Keep the feasting pleasant but simple. You're not supposed to be working today! How about grilled hotdogs, laid out on your plate with carrots to look like a smiling face? Gelatin or ice cream make amusing desserts if fashioned in molds.

Incense: Combine some anise with catnip and zinnia petals to keep your repartee and wit upbeat.

Activities: Go to a comedy club, rent lighthearted movies, play games with your children. Take a day trip to an amusement park or playground.

For a special treat, perform auric cleansing on each other, using feathers as an implement to move positive, giggling energy into your life. To do this, make sure to move the feather in a clockwise manner around the energy field. Visualize bright, smiling bubbles being sprinkled in like glitter.

Sample Invocation:

Humor be quick; humor be keen;
Laughter's the best medicine I've ever seen.
Puck, come and be my guide;
Joy and wit, in my heart abide.

Other Accents: Work during daylight hours. Play cheerful, enthusiastic music. Surround yourself with pictures of rollicking creatures.

Alternative Timing: April Fool's Day

March 27

SMELL THE BREEZE DAY (EGYPT)

Magical Themes: Fortune, luck, well-being, and kinship; working with the element of air or directional winds for symbolism.

History/Lore: Close to the Easter holiday, this is a favorite day in Egypt to dress in festive colors and go on outings with the family (especially picnics). It is believed that smelling a fresh-cut onion at dawn will bring good luck, and that the time spent outdoors insures the participant's health.

Decorating Ideas: Wind-sensitive items all around your celebration space. This includes streamers, chimes, banners with magical emblems, strings of bells, balloons, feathers, or loose flower petals.

Garments: Consider fabrics like chiffon, which are light and airy. Any piece of jewelry depicting feathers is also fitting.

Ritual Cup: Onion wine is one possibility.[1] Another is any beverage made with corresponding air herbs like anise liqueur, dandelion wine, and mint or sage tea.

Ritual Foods: Edibles which have a buoyant, almost weightless texture have potential. Included in this list are meringue pies or cookies, angelfood cake, puff pastry, and soufflés.

Incense: A combination of pine needles for health, dried parsley for serendipity, and lavender to bring peaceful joy into your day. Prepare this mixture using 1/4 cup sandalwood powder (or other aromatic wood), to which 3 teaspoons of each ingredient, except parsley, is added for symmetry in body, mind, and soul. Reduce the parsley to 1 teaspoon so the aroma is not overly pungent.

Activities: Any object which can carry your magic on the winds makes for an enjoyable part of your holiday observance. One good example would be releasing a handful of clover to encourage serendipity in your life. In this case, sprinkle the leaves so they move *toward* you.

---

1. See the recipe in my book, *A Witch's Brew* (St. Paul, MN: Llewellyn Publications, 1995), p. 84.

Another pastime which children enjoy is making a wind rope. These originated in Arabia. Begin by holding a good length of rope in the air. Visualize the wind as a colored light that gets absorbed into the rope. When you see this clearly, tie one knot saying, *"This rope I wind, the wind to bind."* Repeat this procedure, leaving a little space between each knot until the length is completed. I suggest seven knots total, the number of fruition. Hang this rope just outside your home somewhere. On hot Summer days, release one knot to liberate a refreshing breeze.

Sample Invocation:

Winds of health and luck and fate,
Come and help us celebrate.
Your breezes fair this day reveres;
Come and waltz with all those here!

Other Accents: Music with bells or pan pipes. Pastel or pale colors, weightless as the wind itself. If your celebration is taking place indoors, have paper or electric fans for accent pieces. Open windows in your sacred space at some point (even briefly) to allow rejuvenating winds to enter.

Also This Date: This is also the Festival of Liberalia in Rome, a holiday that marked the transition into adulthood for young men. Traditionally, the boys changed out of their purple togas into the white ones worn by adult males. At this point, they assumed all the duties and rights of citizens. Therefore, this date would be a good choice for men's mystery rituals.

March 31 — April 2

BORROWED DAYS

Magical Themes: Thrift; wise use of time and money; sensibility and abundance.

History/Lore: Folklore tells us that the month of March (named after Mars, the god of war), borrowed its last three days from April because one old woman dared to challenge the month's blustery authority. When she showed her antagonism on March 31, Mars rallied by "borrowing" three days from the next month and sending traditional snow, sleet, and frost to kill the woman's prized goat. Because of this story, the Scots believe no borrowing or lending should be done during this period to insure prosperity.

Decorating Ideas: Frosted windows with snow flakes; any depictions of snowy scenes; images of Mars.

Garments: A Celtic-style robe in white or silver and any silver jewelry. Alternatively, winter apparel to prepare yourself for March's last hurrah!

Ritual Cup: Place 1 cup of milk and 3 ice cubes in a blender together. This makes a white, snowy beverage for sharing around the circle. If you are lactose-intolerant, use ice chips flavored with white grape juice instead.

Ritual Foods: Prepare a salad from iceberg lettuce, alfalfa sprouts (prudence), white onion (protection), blanched almonds (moderation), croutons (sustenance), and caraway dressing (to safeguard your finances). For main dishes, think in terms of stews and casseroles to accent thriftiness.

Incense: Mix 2 tablespoons powdered apple peel (run dried peel through your blender) with 1/4 teaspoon basil, and add 2 drops vanilla extract. Allow to dry before burning. This incense is for wise decisions, financial stability, and increased awareness.

Activities: Find a small box or other waterproof container large enough to house a silver coin. Fill the container half full with water and freeze. Once solid, place the coin on the ice, add more water on top and a little of the milk snow you made before. Focus your magical energy by adding an incantation like:

> *Protection 'round this coin of mine,*
> *Prosperity in this house to shine.*
> *Beneath the snow my hope encased;*
> *Moderation born, waste erased.*

Leave this in the freezer to act as an ongoing amulet for financial stability in your home.

For children, arrange a coin hunt in the snow (sand or hay can substitute if March doesn't prove blustery). Older children can likewise enjoy a more complex treasure hunt. The adults of a group, following this theme, could organize a scavenger hunt, the prize of which should be a money tree or something else pertaining to prosperity.

Sample Invocation:

From out the ice and blowing snow,
Let now a new wind rise and blow;
One filled with wisdom, reason, and care,
So pockets and cupboards will never be bare.

Other Accents Colors are best in shades of silver, white, and white-blues to honor March's chill. Music can include the theme from *Dr. Zhivago* or George Winston's *December*, both of which have haunting melodies reminiscent of the vestiges of Winter still evidenced in the land.

If you can coordinate your activities when the Moon is in Sagittarius, this will increase the energy of your spells and rituals for economy or savings.

April

April 1

APRIL FOOL'S DAY

Magical Themes: Youthful energy and adventure; the Fool card of the tarot; divination by omens and signs.

History/Lore: In Rome, April 1 was called Veneralia and was one of the holidays that honored Venus. Various images of this goddess of beauty and romance were purified and adorned by women throughout Rome on this day. Such actions were a form of worship that could bring fertility, happiness, and beauty if the goddess showed her favor. Since love tends to make even the sage into a fool, this may explain the silly pranks eventually arising from this ancient rite.

Another hypothesis proposed by historians is that April Fool's Day originated when New Year's Day was modified from March 25 to January 1. Many people did not like this change, and some even refused to honor it. Consequently, these people's foolish stubbornness was emphasized by other people playing jokes on them.

The French call April 1 Fish Day. At this time of the year, the number of young fish in the water increases drastically; many of them are caught by clever fishermen. On April Fool's Day, however, fish aren't the ones that end up on hooks—instead, it's unsuspecting friends and family members!

Wherever April Fool's Day originated, shenanigans and pranks reach their pinnacle on April 1, along with the observance of weather omens. According to folklore, hay and corn crops will fare well if there's a strong wind on that day. Similarly, the following Autumn's harvest will be abundant if the day is crisp. Finally, if there's abundant rain, this weather is sure to bring "May flowers."

Decorating Ideas: Extol the spirit of whimsy. Comical frills that are also visual puns or jokes are one good option.

Garments: Comfortable! This is a day of nonchalant silliness.

Ritual Cup: Any beverage that lifts your spirits, perhaps those which are carbonated. Purchase some small silk flowers that can be frozen in ice cubes so it appears that they fell unwittingly into the chalice. Liquids spiced with anise, almond, or catnip can accentuate your sense of humor.

Ritual Foods: During the Middle Ages, a favorite cooking art was that of creating the "soteltie," any dish presented in such a manner as to look like something it is not. For our purposes, this might equate to a potpie shell filled with toys or candies for children (the top is baked separately, then carefully attached), and other witty side dishes.

Incense: Try making an acronymic aromatic! This is done by choosing the base ingredients for your incense by the first letters of their names, or the first letters of their magical associations. These letters, in a certain order, create a word befitting the mood of the holiday:

Frankincense	OR	Allspice	=	Fortune
Rose		Apple	=	Unity
Orris root		Basil	=	Negotiation
Lavender				
Iris				
Carnation				

Activities: This holiday, while enjoyable for adults, is sometimes best left to the children of our families and circles. Allow the young ones to delight in "pulling the wool" over your eyes, and appreciate watching their pleasure in the ruse.

Plan a walk outside to observe the signs in nature as our ancestors did, or just to enjoy some fresh air (and hopefully a happier perspective too). If you work with the tarot, April 1 is an excellent opportunity to meditate on the Fool card and see what meaning it has for you.

If you do decide to follow tradition and play some April Fool's pranks, please take care that no one can get hurt (either emotionally or physically). The best jokes are often the simplest ones, like gluing a dollar bill to the sidewalk, or coating some foam balls with chocolate to look like candies. Among group gatherings, award a small prize to the person who comes up with the most ingenious and successful prank.

Sample Invocation:

Lady, Lord, come romp and sing;
With you, the happiness of children bring!
Teach me again how to wish on a star,
Or sneak a tadpole into a jar!

Lady, Lord, come dance and play!
I wish to be a child today;
One with hopes and dreams to catch,
And perhaps a few tricks to hatch!

Other Accents: Dazzling, abundant hues mixed with light-hearted musical accompaniment. A good artist to look into for amusing songs is Weird Al Yankovic, who pokes fun at just about anything!

Alternative Timing: Hilaria (March 25).

Early April

BOAT FESTIVAL (FRANCE)

Magical Themes: Youthful outlooks, luck, wish magic, and movement.

History/Lore: On a sunny day in early April, the children along the streams that feed the Rhine begin launching small boats with candles for masts. Each candle represents the happiness of life's journey. The boats transport good fortune and good wishes to any child who later finds a vessel and brings it ashore.

Decorating Ideas: Any items with a watery feeling, such as blue table cloths, green candles, or fish bowls. Lawn sprinklers and hoses can be set up ornamentally, forming water archways or ministreams around which your activities may be centered.

Garments: If it is warm enough, go with bathing suits. If not, look for nautical raiment like a seaman's cap or yacht gloves.

Ritual Cup: Pure water is probably the best choice. An alternative is cider, which was a favorite beverage for early seafarers because it helped decrease cases of scurvy. Another pleasant accent is a large punch bowl filled with the beverage of your choice, tinted with blue food coloring. On top of this, float small paper or plastic boats, one per attendee. These can be taken home as party favors.

Ritual Foods: In keeping with your riverside theme, consider snack trays overflowing with a diversity of seafood, sauces, crackers, and vegetables. One tasty recipe served hot or cold follows.

Good Fortune Seafood Cakes

1 egg, beaten
1 pound imitation crabmeat
2/3 cup spiced bread crumbs
2 teaspoons Parmesan cheese
1 teaspoon minced garlic
vegetable oil for frying

Directions: Beat your egg until well mixed, then dip good-sized meat pieces (2 inches long) into it. Next, drench the egg-coated crabmeat in bread crumbs that have been blended with the cheese and garlic. Once well coated, turn the pieces into the frying pan and sauté until golden brown. Serve with cocktail or dill sauce, the latter of which encourages kinship. Serves three people.

Incense: Components include clover for fortune, anise for fresh perspectives, and dandelion for wishes.

Activities: This is a terrific holiday for the youngster in everyone. It is a good excuse to go to a natural setting, and provides an excellent chance to spend more time with the children in your life.

Try making a boat of your own so it is filled with personal energy. The easiest way to make one is from old popsicle sticks glued together with water-resilient adhesive. You can add sides to the boat by gluing one stick at the edge and allowing it to dry before adding the next one. A clothespin attached at the seam will keep the sticks in place while drying. Once your boat is finished, paint it, adding any magical symbols you want. Place a small votive candle in the center, and light it when you launch the boat (see figure 3 on page 52). The water gives movement to your magic!

Sample Invocation/Spell: As your ship moves away from you on the current (water can be provided by a hose), add a verbal component to empower your goals. Here is one example, the first two lines of which are recited while you hold the boat in your hands and concentrate on your intentions:

> *Little boat, swim like a fish;*
> *Carry safe, my heart-felt wish.*
> *Toward its goal, I light the way* [light the candle];
> *Begin this magic here, today* [launch the boat].

Other Accents Structuring your holiday when the Moon is in Pisces or another water sign is certainly fitting. Pigments to focus on are green-blues, water-blue, and deep blue. Musical accompaniment might be a nature tape with the sounds of waves or waterfalls.

On the altar, place a cauldron of river or spring water (if available). Consider using buttercups and daisies, favorite child-

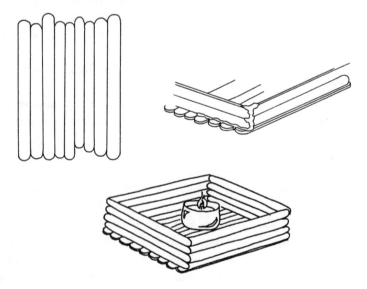

Figure 3. Good luck boat. Top left: the popsicle sticks you glue together to make the base; Top right: using popsicle sticks to make sides for the boat; Bottom: the finished boat.

hood flowers, as decoration. Since this is a holiday structured for the young ones, their toys make good emblems for the four cardinal points. Use a bucket of sand for earth, a pinwheel for air, a toy boat or beach ball for water, and a stuffed dragon for fire.

April 5

FESTIVAL OF KWAN YIN (CHINA, JAPAN)

Magical Themes: Childbirth and care of children; tolerance and mercy; magical arts, especially clairvoyance.

History/Lore: On this day, people make pilgrimages to shrines in order to burn incense to Kwan Yin. Their supplications are meant to insure healthy children and fertility, or to bring compassion and forgiveness into their lives. In these lands, Kwan Yin (Kwannon in Japan) is the ultimate feminine principle and the womb of the world. She is also a goddess who teaches magic, and a source of prophesy.

Decorating Ideas: Eastern import stores frequently carry inexpensive images of Kwan Yin to help adorn the sacred space. Rice or black tea is appropriate to the central altar as an offering.

Garments: Anything with an oriental motif.

Ritual Cup: Grape juice or wine to improve fecundity. For psychic or magical endeavors, use mint tea or a cinnamon liqueur.

Ritual Foods: Dried figs, bananas, grapes, rice, and nuts for fertility. Olives for harmony between people. Sushi, stir-fried mushrooms, and fortune cookies for insight.

Incense: Lotus, Kwan Yin's sacred flower.

Activities: Cast your circle using chopsticks or a Katana instead of your athame or wand. Find ways to include children in your ritual. Have a special blessing for the youths of your group which includes anointing them with lotus oil, and present a gift of rice, although they may not want it.

Sample Invocation:

Goddess of kindness, your blessings we invite;
Keep each of these children within your sight;
Grant them health and joy beyond compare;
Keep them ever in your care.

Other Accents: Any images of children or lions, both of which are protected by Kwan Yin. Music that features bamboo flutes or other Eastern instruments.

April 8

BIRTHDAY OF BUDDHA (CHINA, JAPAN, THAILAND)

Magical Themes: Contemplation and thoughtfulness; positive actions and motivations; peace and freedom; kindness to animals.

History/Lore: In the East, the prevalent belief is that April 8 is not only the Buddha's birthday, but also the date of his enlightenment and passage into Nirvana. Buddha set out on a pilgrimage to discover the path of serenity and liberty. This later became known as the Eight-Fold Path (right and proper convictions, intentions, speech, action, livelihood, effort, mindfulness, and concentration).

Throughout Japan, Buddhist priests perform a special ceremony marking this occasion. Worshippers gather in the temple and pour a ladle of sweet tea over an image of Buddha, then quaff the tea in devotion. Children, bedecked in flowers, gather outside in the streets to dance in Buddha's honor.

Thailand commemorates this day in a slightly different manner. Those who can, purchase a captive animal (birds and fish are popular) and set it free out of respect for Buddha's teachings.

Decorating Ideas: Flowers in abundance, especially chrysanthemums, which are emblems of long life and creativity in Japan. Add any statues or posters of Buddha you can find.

Garments: Simple robes are fine here, or any piece of clothing with an oriental pattern to the fabric.

Ritual Cup: Without question, tea; specifically an oriental blend would be nice. Other options include sake or plum wine, both of which are popular in Eastern lands.

Ritual Foods: It is thought that Buddha obtained his insight while sitting beneath a fig tree, so any dishes you can prepare with this fruit will augment your efforts. Here is one dessert recipe. The bread in this dish accents the magical energy for insight, foundations, and continued sustenance:

Insight Fig Pudding

1/4 pound of crusty bread
3/4 cup milk
1/2 cup heavy cream
1/8 cup butter
1/4 cup brown sugar
dash of cinnamon and ginger (optional)
2 eggs
2 ounces of figs, diced
1/2 teaspoon vanilla extract
2 tablespoons white sugar

Directions: Preheat your oven to 350 degrees. Take a small bread dish (8 x 4 x 2 inches) and grease it thoroughly. Cut your bread into 1 inch pieces then toss with figs and any chosen spices (cinnamon and ginger). Place evenly in your baking dish. Next, warm the milk, cream, and butter until well blended, slowly mixing in the brown sugar, eggs, and vanilla. Pour this over your bread mixture. Sprinkle the top evenly with white sugar, then place the baking dish in a larger pan filled 1 inch deep with hot water. Bake in the oven for 35-45 minutes until a test cut comes out clean. Serves 4-5 people.

Incense: Buddha was not a person focused on elaborate trappings, so I suggest a simple sandalwood incense for augmented awareness.

Activities: Whether working alone or in a group, this is an excellent day to arrange for quiet, meditative time to ponder your beliefs and how your actions can positively reflect that faith. At a circle, a single bowl of tea might be passed among participants as a sign of unity. For those celebrating alone, leave a bowl of tea on your altar to welcome Buddhic energy into your sacred space.

The tradition of Thailand is a rather lovely one which has several applications. Besides performing magic to bring betterment to the animal world, many zoos and aquariums have sponsorship programs where you can "adopt" a creature by helping with its upkeep. My only caution is to thoroughly investigate the way the funds are spent before you make any contributions.[2]

Sample Invocation/Spell:

> *Guardians of the four winds, help me find the way*
> *To speak, to act, in accord with my Path;*
> *Help me begin today*
> *With convictions that are guided*
> *By intentions which are pure;*
> *Let the spirit of enlightenment*
> *In my heart now stir.*

Other Accents: Generally keep the tenor of this celebration on the simple side. Bring any items you need into the sacred space to help focus your meditations. Perhaps use oriental-style incense burners or paper lanterns as part of the decorating theme.

---

2. If you would like to sponsor a dolphin, write to the following address for information: Dolphin Research Center, Box 2875, Marathon Shores, FL 33052. Telephone: 305-289-0002.

April Full Moon

TEMPLE OFFERING (BALI)

Magical Themes: Veneration and thankfulness to the Divine; honoring the gods and goddesses of your tradition.

History/Lore: As the Moon rises out of the sea, offerings are prepared by women and children alike. Tropical fruits such as banana, pomegranate, and pineapple accompany small sweets and hundreds of flowers for the procession to the temple. This offering usually takes the final shape of pineapples which are borne on the heads of the village women into the sanctuary. Here, the priest blesses both the offering and the women. As they depart, they are joined by the children of the village, who have made flower rosettes to leave behind with their prayers to the gods.

Decorating Ideas: Hibiscus flowers are favored, but really any lush, sweet-smelling petals are apt. Follow the Polynesian theme with fresh, whole pineapples and coconuts on the altar which can be enjoyed after your ritual. Make paper palm tree leaves to mark the perimeter of your circle.

Garments: Saffron robes, worn toga-style, are traditional. A simple pattern to make such a robe begins by taking a piece of *reversible* fabric which, when folded in half lengthwise, reaches from your shoulders to the floor with about one foot extra. Sew this up one side about 3/4 of the way so it resembles a tube. One foot from the top of the piece, sew a thin line of elastic all the way around, affixing the two ends together with a pin or other ornament. This leaves a perfect hole to put one arm through, while the other is left bare (see figure 4, page 58). You can also add trim to the overhanging edge of fabric.

Ritual Cup: Juices or wines with a tropical flair. One easy recipe for ritual punch is to take a quart of apple wine and add one can of undiluted, frozen tropical juice concentrate (your choice). Blend these in a bowl with ice, 1 quart of ginger ale, pineapple chunks, papaya, and a garnish of coconut flakes. Serve cold.

Ritual Foods: Think in terms of a Polynesian luau: pineapple-glazed ham, tropical fruit salad, saffron-scented rice, fish canapes served on large, flat seashells, etc. Lay these foods out on a picnic table beneath a Full Moon; you can use tiki torches to light the area.

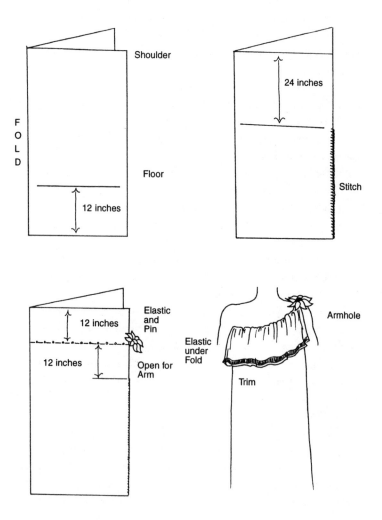

Figure 4. Traditional toga-style robe.

Incense: A nice combination is achieved by blending dried flower petals and powdered fruit rinds (or aromatic wood scented with essential oils). This creates a refreshing blend which is not overly heady and maintains your tropical ambiance.

Activities: Welcome your guests with a lei of silk flowers that they can keep to adorn their own altars. Fresh flowers are lovely, but they won't last long. Silk blossoms are easily fashioned into a ring by twisting the stems together, each flower being placed just below the first. Afterward, the stems should be wrapped in green craft tape for durability. Add some leaves to improve the visual effect.

Have each person present bring a small token offering to place on the altar for their favorite Divine visage. These gifts should be items easily biodegradable or safely eaten by animals so that they can be released to the winds to carry their prayers and blessings.

Finally, the children of your group can make tissue flowers (similar to those done for weddings) to bring into the sacred space. To prepare these, lay about ten colored tissues on top of each other (flatten all creases). Cut this pile in half for smaller flowers, or leave whole for larger ones. Tie the entire pile tightly in the middle. Let the children pull up the layers of the tissues on each side so they form lightly crinkled petals (see figure 5 on page 60). Use one color, or layer in various colors for different effects.

Sample Invocation/Spell: This is one you will have to write, since the form it takes will change drastically according to the god/goddesses you are honoring and their attributes. (Refer to Part I, page 18, for hints on creating your own spell or invocation.)

Other Accents: This is definitely a festival which begins with the first sign of the Moon juxtaposed against the night horizon. Colors should be bright and festive (Hawaiian shirts for example). Background music might be calypso, the sounds of drums and waves, or other songs with a tropical flavor.

A fun addition to this celebration is to create a mime-type hula dance where stories about your tradition's gods and god-

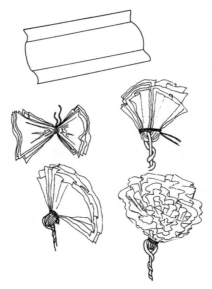

Figure 5. Tissue paper flower. Begin with pieces of tissue paper; tie the pile as shown; fold the tissue and tie again to make a knot as shown here; then pull the tissue paper gently, to make a lovely flower.

desses are recounted by and for those in attendance. Think of it as an elaborate game of charades, where music and the theatrical flair are added for effect.

Lastly, if possible, try to hold your celebration near a lake, waterfall, beach, or other large body of water.

April 18

RAMA'S DAY (INDIA)

Magical Themes: Chivalry, courtesy, and virtue; reincarnation.

History/Lore: Rama was the seventh incarnation of Vishnu, the Vedic sun god. The incarnations of Vishnu tell the story of the evolution and growth of the soul. In each of Vishnu's lives, his wife was the goddess of beauty and luck. The Hindus regard Rama as a paragon of gallantry and honor. To celebrate the date of his birth, they often retell stories from a favored epic poem, the *Ramayana*.

Decorating Ideas: Any embellishments which can represent a change of state (such as eggs in one bowl and chicken in another); blue and purple accents for a contemplative atmosphere.

Garments: Sari or toga-style robes.

Ritual Cup: Flexible.

Ritual Foods: Bread or rolls with poppy seeds, which are favored by Vishnu.

Incense: Ambergris, if available. If not, try jasmine and musk. Please try to find synthetic ambergris or musk if possible, as these are taken from animals.

Activities: If you can find a copy of the Bhagavad Gita, scan it for some meaningful readings to use at your gathering. Otherwise, recite some favorite verses with appropriate magical themes.

One of the magical tools associated with Vishnu is a mirror. In keeping with this, each member of your circle should bring a small mirror to bless for self-discernment. Around the edge, or upon the handle, affix some copper wire with a bit of your hair, then charge the mirror with the incantation below. Once prepared, use the mirror as a scrying surface that can be used to reveal (symbolically) your motivation or intent in magic. For example, dark clouds might materialize if you are being manipulative; while bright, white wisps might appear if you are working with the proper attitude.

Sample Incantation:

Rama, from the heavens bestow
Verity; in this mirror show,
Reflect to me my motives true;
Help me attain a prized virtue.

April 22

ST. GEORGE'S EVE (ENGLAND, RUSSIA, HUNGARY)

Magical Themes: Victory in the face of tremendous odds; protection against negative magic and spiritual forces; solar rituals/spells.

History/Lore: The story of St. George, while apocryphal, has remained a strong influence in certain countries. As the tale goes, St. George rescued the king's daughter by conquering a ruthless dragon and then leading the beast into town. He is also considered the patron saint of horses and a personification of the Sun (which chased the blackness of evil from the land).

Decorating Ideas: A medieval motif would be fun, with banners, dragon portraits, candlelight, simple tablewares (wooden bowls, pewter plates), etc. Adorn the altar with all the athames and wands of those present to charge the tools. These equate nicely to swords.

Garments: A simply made item which reflects the spirit of the Middle Ages is a T-tunic. Tunics are not gender specific and do not require expensive fabric to create. Old sheets work fine!

Begin with approximately 2 1/2-3 yards of fabric (45 inches wide) for the average-size person. Fold the fabric in half from top to bottom and lay out flat. Next, lay a button-down, long-sleeved shirt of yours in the center of the fabric to use as a pattern. Cut, leaving about 2 inches on each side for sewing space and general comfort (see figure 6, page 63).

Next, cut a hole for your head, centered on the fold. Try this on a few times to make sure it is comfortable, remembering that you will be sewing this edge under. Turn the fabric right side out and put on any trim you like, 1 inch in from the neckline and the edge of the sleeves. Turn the fabric so the right sides are together and hem the bottom edge. Sew the main seam, from wrist downward, stopping about 3 inches from the bottom (see figure 6). This part is left open for more mobility, but both edges will have to be turned under to prevent unraveling. The tunic is

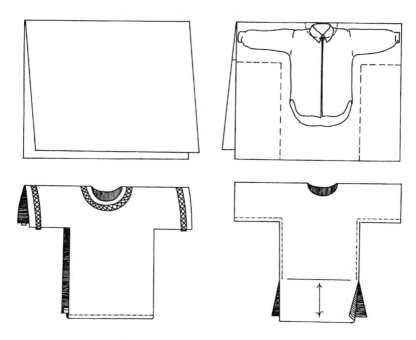

Figure 6. Medieval-style T-tunic. Top left: uncut fabric folded over; Top right: lay a shirt on the fabric so you can see where you want to cut away for the head and where you want to cut the fabric for arms and body; Bottom left: adding the trim; Bottom right: where to sew the seams, leaving the bottom of the tunic open.

now basically finished except to add a belt and any jewelry you might like (see figure 7, page 64).

Ritual Cup: Mead, a honey-based wine, was a favorite medieval beverage. To make nonalcoholic mead, mix 1 quart of apple cider over a low flame with about 1/4 cup honey (taste frequently for sweetness). Once you have a pleasant flavor, add some cinnamon sticks, sliced ginger root, and a few cloves. This produces a lightly spiced beverage which is protective and healthful in nature.

Ritual Foods: Since the weather is turning warmer, you may want to have an ox or pig roast in proper medieval style.

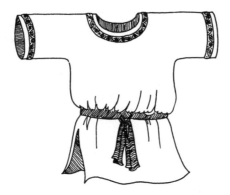

Figure 7. Finished T-tunic.

One possible side dish to prepare is a sculpted, garlic-spiced rice (garlic is a protective herb often used for banishing), thickened with cream soup. To this base, add red or green food coloring and carve the rice on a serving platter to resemble a dragon. That way, as you serve the dish, you can also quite literally slay any negativity which may be hindering your life.

Incense: Roses seem particularly associated with St. George, so this is the best scent to choose. Also consider any herbs or spices equated with solar energy, including angelica, cinnamon, ginseng, marigold, and rosemary.

Activities: For the children of your party, make a large paper dragon and a number of small cardboard swords or spears. They can then play a blindfolded game of slay-the-dragon, much like pin-the-tail-on-the-donkey. To add a magical flair, have each child declare what it is they are trying to change in themselves before taking their turn. This will lend energy to their goal while still maintaining the feeling of a game.

It was traditional to decorate the doors and windows of the home, or of any housing for animals, with rose briars and an abundance of flowers for safety. The belief was that the magic of evil sorcerers would get tangled in the thorns neatly hidden beneath the flowers. Also, women of this region liked to bathe in fragrant waters, as a princess might, to encourage the saint's protection of them. Similarly, the ringing of blessed bells during your observances is said to scare off vampires and evil influences.

Last, but not least, a wonderful activity for young and old alike is the making of magical shields which can be hung in the home or employed during the ritual for protection. For children, cardboard cutouts will do for a base, to which scrap fabric, feathers, beads, buttons, glitter, and a little glue can be added. Let the children design their own emblematic pattern for safety.

For adults, I suggest a more sturdy background so that the shield can be a long-lasting magical tool. Plywood, leather, and papier-mâché are all good choices for a foundation. Exactly how you decorate the shield is really up to you (see figure 8). Suggestions include painting or woodburning magical sigils, rubbing protective oils into the surface (myrrh, lemon, rose, etc.), and gluing stones like carnelian or chrysolite to the surface. Make sure to visualize white light pouring from your hands into the finished shield so that it is literally saturated with protective power.

Sample Invocation:

Powers of the Sun, we call and charge you,
Remove any shadows which haunt our lives;
Keep us ever safe and whole, lighting our way
From out of the darkness, into the day.

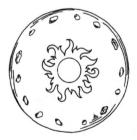 

Figure 8. Ceremonial shields. Left is a round shield; right is a kite shield.

Alternative Timing: In Belgium, the Sunday following St. George's Day is celebrated with another feast in his honor where the horses, livestock, and pets are ritually blessed.

Other Accents: The color of the day is decisively gold or yellow, to honor the solar aspect. There are several tapes and CD's available from groups like the King's Singers, with medieval madrigals, etc., to accent your overall atmosphere.[3]

May

May 1

MAY DAY, BELTANE (ENGLAND)

Magical Themes: Beauty, fertility, and good fortune; protection of animals; balance of yin-yang energy; joy.

History/Lore: The most lavish of all Spring holidays, Beltane may take its name from the god Belenus who presided over the herds. May Day owes its roots mostly to Rome, where a special flower festival known as Floralia was observed. In Greece, athletic games were held on this day, in which the winners were crowned with laurel leaves.

The tradition of going a-maying comes from Tudor England, where young people went into the woods at dawn. Their ingathering of fresh flowers and branches would subsequently be hung over all the doors and windows in town. Meanwhile, the men went hunting for an appropriate Maypole to be the central attraction during the festivities. In many rural areas in England, the subsequent processional of greenery into the village is like a parade, honoring Robin and Marian (archetypes of the youthful god and goddess). This particular tradition

---

3. *Madrigal History Tour*, Moss Music Group, The King Singers. New York, 1984.

Figure 9. Marigold wreath.

may also have some import for crowning May Queens, who are always young girls, honoring the maiden aspect, like Spring itself.

May Day is steeped in interesting bits of superstition which are liberally intermingled with traditions from each celebrating culture. In Europe, bathing in May Day dew will insure your beauty, and taking the first draught from a wealthy neighbor's well allows you to "steal" their prosperity. In Germany, young lovers secretly plant trees before the windows of those desired, believing this helps their feelings to grow as strong and sure as the tree itself. In Bavaria, trees are placed in front of newlyweds' homes to insure the longevity of their relationship.

Decorating Ideas: A favorite Irish decoration is a hoop of rowan and marigolds with silver and gold balls suspended in the center to represent the Sun and Moon. Something similar can be achieved by obtaining a craft base (straw, wire, etc.) already formed in a circle. To this, attach a bed of fresh leaves all around with marigolds interspersed. The balls can be spray painted appropriate colors, and the decoration kept for future May celebrations (see figure 9).

Two other lovely decorations for the altar are daisy and leaf chains. To make a daisy chain, find flowers with the longest possible stems. Make a loose knot in the stem just below the flower and slide the stem of another daisy through it, tightening slightly.

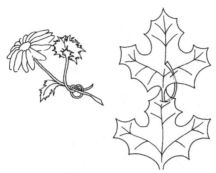

Figure 10. Daisy and leaf chains.

Continue this with each added flower, making the sequence long enough to encompass the perimeter of the altar (see figure 10).

Leaf chains are made in a slightly different manner, by taking the stem of the first leaf and pushing it through the top point of the next, then back up through the bottom of the original leaf. Again, try to find sturdy stems that have enough length so your chains won't fall apart easily. Or, if time permits, add a dab of glue to secure them in place (see figure 10).

Garments: Comfortable, washable, and durable are the key words for this holiday. Since you will be spending time outside in the woods and dancing around the Maypole, make sure nothing you wear can be tripped over.

Ritual Cup: Woodruff wine is a favorite May beverage, or any drink with a flower or two as garnish.

Ritual Foods: Ultimately, May Day is a feast of flowers for the eye, so why not make it one for the stomach as well? Many flowers are edible with flavors akin to herbs and vegetables.[4]

Incense: Stay with your petal theme, using aromas like lily of the valley and other wildflowers.

Activities: Garden parties, picnics, barbecues, hikes in the woods, and other outdoor gatherings are perfect for May 1. An old Irish tradition says that if you pour milk on your threshold in the morning it will bring luck to your home. In Russia, another

---

4. Ideas for floral beverages and foods can be found in my book, *Kitchen Witch's Cookbook*, and *A Witch's Brew* (both published by Llewellyn, 1994 and 1995 respectively).

custom is to leave offerings of eggs (a fertility symbol) and pies for the trees.

But what would May Day be without a Maypole? The best bet for these today is to get a solid piece of wood from a lumber yard and secure it in the earth. The streamers of the Maypole are hung from a central point at the top. There should be an even number of streamers each brightly colored, 3 inches wide, and about 4 yards longer than the pole itself.

A circle is formed around the pole, boy-girl-boy-girl, each of whom picks up one strand. The boys/men turn in a direction opposite to that of the girls/women, and a happy dance begins. As each boy encounters the next girl, he moves slightly outward so that his strand weaves over hers. On the next pass, he moves inward so the strand weaves under. This continues until the dancers can go no further. Traditionally, at this point, the young man takes the hand of the girl he now faces and they spend the day merrymaking together.

My favorite May Day activity is that of making woven baskets, overflowing with flowers, sweets and poems, which are left anonymously at homes to bring joy to the finder. The basket is of simple design, woven out of construction paper. Cut strips out of 8 1/2 by 11 inch sheets of paper, some short and some long, so you get a variegated effect. Then tightly twist the bottom of the resulting woven sheet so that it forms a cone for filling (see figure 11).

Finally, in the evening, when the Beltane fires are lit, bring a pet (or a picture of one) to bless in the smoke of the flames.

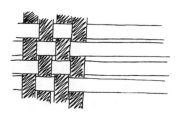

Figure 11. Woven May Day baskets.

Figure 12. May Day goddess image. To make this image, you will need a dowel, buttons for the eyes and nose, leaves to make a hat, and leaves and flower petals to make her dress. Use your imagination!

Scottish farmers did this with their sheep, passing each one through the purgative smoke to keep them healthy. If the fire scares the animals, a smudge stick or bit of incense can be substituted (see figure 16, page 100).

Sample Invocation/Spell: Try reciting this little poem while dancing around the maypole:

> *Each tress I claim for joy and wealth;*
> *Each step I take will bring me health!*
> *While through these strands I weave and duck,*
> *I draw to myself a bit of luck.*

Other Accents: Bright pastels in a variety of hues, alongside yellow and red to honor the Sun, are appropriate. A goddess image can be made by taking a large flower with a solid stem, turning it upside down, and removing a few leaves. Place a piece of doweling through the center and affix a head of herb-stuffed cloth to the top with string. The overturned flower petals and underleaves become the dress for the goddess (see figure 12).

May 3

BONA DEA (ROME)

Magical Themes: Women's mysteries; purification and blessing; wish magic.

History/Lore: Bona Dea is the Goddess of the Earth and bountiful blessings. In Rome, this was strictly a woman's holiday. No men were allowed at the festival, which lasted all night and was full of revelry.

Decorating Ideas: This is a fire festival, so think in terms of bright oranges and red; lots of candles, torches, and images of the Goddess; any white flowers.

Garments: I suspect this ritual was often done "au naturel" to celebrate the body. However, if that is not possible for you, go with something very light (like chiffon). Your garments should be shamelessly feminine and easy to move in.

Ritual Cup: Coconut milk, cow's milk, or any other beverage which venerates the Goddess.

Ritual Foods: Any round fruits like apples or melons. Since this festival has lots of dancing and jumping, keep your edibles light. After the festivities, have a coconut-cream pie ready which naturally takes on the appearance of a full Moon.

Incense: Any lunar herbs, especially broom and rose.

Activities: The traditional activity is fire-pit jumping for good fortune and cleansing. If open fires are not allowed, use the coals of an hibachi or other small, contained fire. As you pass over the flames, make a simple wish and it will come true.

If you are celebrating in a remote spot, have everyone make ornaments for their body to rejoice in its beauty and life-giving power. One idea along these lines is undergarments decorated with feathers, beads, paint, etc.

Sample Invocation:

Bona Dea, Good Goddess, Sacred Lady,
Join us in our dance this night.
We rejoice in our womanhood.

For bodies which bear life and sustain our young,
For being made in your image,
We reclaim the power of our sexuality
And celebrate our unity.

Other Accents: The Goddess is connected with the lunar sphere, so night celebrations are most fitting. Try silver coverings and candles for the altar. Leave your magical bowls and cups in the sacred space to be blessed with harmonic energy.

Alternative Timing: December 3 or any Wednesday, both of which are associated with rites of Bona Dea.

May 5

FEAST OF BANNERS AND KITES (JAPAN)

Magical Themes: Vitality, persistence, freedom, lifted burdens, and the god aspect.

History/Lore: As part of a favorite sport in Japan, the sky is literally turned into a sea of kites and pennants on this day. Most kites are made by hand from rice paper and bamboo. With these, hundreds of fish streamers adorn homes to celebrate the attributes of strength and might.

Decorating Ideas: The major themes in the kites and windsocks seem to be those of dragons (ancient mysteries and wisdom) and the carp (perseverance and strength). One source for fish motifs is the children's card game go-fish, which is already cut into a generic shape which symbolizes the carp. Punch holes in the mouth or tail portion of each card and hang them from strings with bells to make serviceable windchimes.

Garments: Any fabric or item with oriental patterns, such as kimonos, obi belts, or chopstick hairpieces. To make a short kimono, traditionally known as the kosode, follow this pattern. Begin with $2^{1}/_{2}$ yards of 60 inch wide fabric, folded in half. Cut

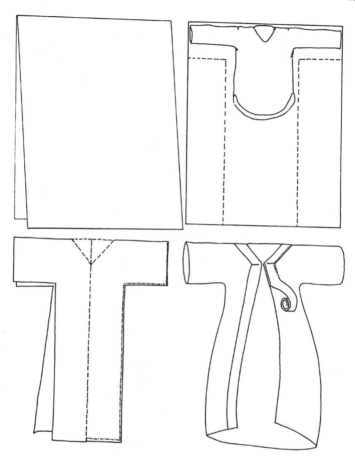

Figure 13. Traditional kosode. Top left: folded fabric; Top right: lay a shirt over the folded fabric to measure for size; Bottom left: cut the front and neck; Bottom right: add decorative trim.

the sleeves, making them as wide as you like. The width of the body of the kosode should be about 4 inches wider than a button-down shirt which fits you comfortably (see figure 13).

Once this basic structure is ready, in the center of what will become the front, cut upward from the hem to the neckline. Cut out a triangle, with a base approximately 4 inches wide, at the neck (wider if you have a large neck and shoulder measurement). At this point, you can sew up the sides. The sleeves, unless too long to be comfortable, will not need a hem since they are cut on the selvage—the prefinished edge of the fabric (see figure 13, page 73).

To give your kosode a decorative appearance, take a long scrap of fabric which is at least 5 inches wide and 45 inches long. From each edge, turn inward 1 inch of the fabric, then iron the entire piece down the middle, so that the rough edges are on the inside. This should be fitted over the unfinished front edge of your kosode and sewn down to create a smooth-textured neckline (see figure 13). Make sure to choose fabrics that suit your magical intentions.

Ritual Cup: Sake or plum wine. For children, a plum juice can be prepared by peeling 12 large, ripe fruits and simmering them in 1 quart of water for 1 hour. Strain and chill. This juice can be used as a base for glazes or sauces, and is magically associated with love and intrigue.

Ritual Foods: A menu consisting of egg rolls, fried rice, and tofu lightly sautéed in soy sauce, cut in the shape of kites or fish.

Incense: Sandalwood is a favorite scent from the East, excellent for cleansing and increased energy.

Activities: Kite flying, what else?! If you can make your own kite with magical emblems symbolizing your goals, all the better. Having a kite take flight at the first sign of dawn, then released, is a way to spiritually disengage from a problem or mark the beginning of a new effort.

An alternative activity is performing the rite of passage for young men on this day, or any other rituals which celebrate the masculine face of the Divine.

Sample Invocation/Spell:

FOR EASING WORRIES:

From the ground to the sky,
Lift my cares, by and by;
With the winds now transformed,
My spirit, reborn.

FOR THE GOD ASPECT:

Brother Wind, Father Sun,
Here and now the spell's begun.
Lord of Dance and of the Flames,
Strength and courage I duly claim.

Alternative Timing: Kite Festival (March 5, Japan and China).

Other Accents: Kitaro's tape or CD *KojiKi* has a wonderful Eastern flavor to it;[5] any music featuring a bamboo flute. Colors should be bright and merry, and those adorning the kite should be suited to your magical intentions. Reds and golds favor the god aspect.

Early — Mid May

RAIN CEREMONIES (GUATEMALA)

Magical Themes: Weather magic and divination

History/Lore: Performed over a five-day period by local priests, the exact date of this observance/ritual is determined through divination. Once started, the gods (both pagan and Christian) are implored for aid. Prayers are offered at the village church. Then over the next four days, the prominent men of the village climb mountain paths to pray at shrines before returning to their homes. On the last day, everyone gathers again at the village church with as many icons as possible, hoping that their prayers have been accepted and that rain will soon follow.

Decorating Ideas: Any god/goddess images. Depending on the type of weather magic you are doing, different types of

---

5. Warner Brothers Records, *KojiKi*, Kitaro. California, 1990.

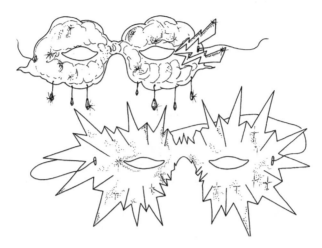

Figure 14. Ceremonial weather masks. A) Rain Mask: basic components are cardboard, cotton, silver glitter, blue paint, glue, and an elastic band; B) Sun Mask: basic components are gold-tone paint, cardboard, gold/yellow glitter, red/orange paint, glue, and an elastic band.

containers should adorn the altar. For dryness, try sand; for sunshine, have a brazier; for rain, cups or shells of water; and for snow, ice would have positive sympathy.

Garments: Wear a garment whose color represents the type of weather you are invoking. You can also make a weather mask which depicts this weather. The use of masks as part of ritual clothing was common to the ancients. They believed that mimicking the weather they desired would help to bring it about. Figure 14 shows two simple examples of masks which can be made at home and worn during your festivities.

Ritual Cup: Use fruit or spice beverages that correspond alchemically to your metaphysical intentions. For example, Sun magic can be accompanied by hot, spicy drinks to which a little red or yellow food coloring has been added for effect.

Ritual Foods: As with your ritual cup, maintain the theme of the weather in the presentation of food items. Mashed potatoes with a little blue food coloring can be shaped like clouds, and round squashes can be cut and served in the figure of a blazing Sun. Snowflakes can be prepared by cutting patterns into taco shells which are then deep fried and either salted or sugared as a side dish.

Incense: Think in terms of natural items which respond strongly to the weather at hand. Sunflowers and morning glories are components for Sun magic, while leaves or dried grass are more fitting for rain.

Activities: Depending on your goals, you may want to have a special weather dance, moving clockwise to draw in a weather pattern. While moving through your dance, add small embellishments which will give power and direction to your intentions. For solar magic, have each person add spices or kindling to a fire cauldron or bonfire as they pass a certain point. For rain magic, rattles, rice, rain sticks and the sprinkling of water are methods commonly used throughout the world. Crushed ice cubes can serve as snow.

Sample Invocation/Spell: To alleviate a long spell of rain, the old children's rhyme, *"Rain, rain go away"* can be quite serviceable as a magical chant. While you recite it, move in a counterclockwise manner, carrying a torch or brazier filled with burning embers to "chase" the water back into the sky. Another version of this, which I have seen work, is to use a fan or feather to symbolically blow the clouds away.

Alternative Timing: There are many holidays which use weather predictions through omens and signs as part of their traditional configuration, including Groundhog Day and the first day of Spring.

Other Accents: Match your colors, music, and lighting to the type of weather magic you are performing: red, yellow, or gold for the Sun or dryness; blue or green for rain; and white-blues for snow. If you are using this date to perform weather divinations instead, I suggest yellow, which is strongly associated with oracular energy.

May 16

Brendan's Voyage (Ireland)

Magical Themes: Hospitality, providence and adventure; possibly summerland rituals.

History/Lore: This holiday commemorates the great medieval legend of St. Brendan who, in the sixth century, traveled in search of the Garden of Eden. The journey lasted forty days and nights plus seven years, and was filled with unique adventures, including landing on the back of a great fish. At one point, Brendan is said to have found the fairest of all islands, but was forbidden to come ashore. It was not until his death that he was allowed to cross into that region and live in paradise.

Several medieval maps were based on this story, marking "Brendan's Islands." Various hearty souls tried to retrace his route, including the Portuguese, who established the Azores during their quest. It is said that Christopher Columbus was inspired by this tale.

Decorating Ideas: Seafaring themes—a boat wheel to represent the circle, sextons for the four directions, and old sails made into dining flies, altar cloths, camping walls, or personal magical banners, etc.

Garments: Puffy-sleeved shirts (swashbuckler style), pants, and boots; or try a sporting goods store for sailing accessories.

Ritual Cup: Tropical juices or wines. Also, since champagne is used to christen ships, a champagne punch might be a nice touch.

Ritual Foods: A seafood extravaganza! Begin with light appetizers like crab-stuffed peapods and celery stalks. Here is a recipe for the filling (feeds about 6 people):

Hospitality Seafood Appetizer

Blend together:

> 2 cups finely diced crab or imitation crabmeat
> 2 tablespoons mayonnaise or creamy ranch dressing
> 1/4 teaspoon garlic powder

1/4 teaspoon minced onion
dash Worcestershire sauce (optional)
dash salt and pepper (optional)
paprika (sprinkled for garnish)

Stuff above mixture into:
18 four inch pieces of celery
18 large stir-fried peapods, opened

After this dish, move to a seafood salad or bisque along with a filet of fish. For dessert, how about a fish-shaped gelatin mould?

Incense: Kelp, when rinsed, properly dried and finely powdered, makes a good incense base, to which you can add other herbs as desired. Alternatively, willow wood and bark has an affinity with water.

Activities: Mini-regatta races! Here, each person makes their own miniature sailing ship (according to whatever rules you set up), then launches the ship in competition. If you are not near a body of water, any children's pool will usually work if there is a good breeze. If not, carefully set up some electric fans! In either scenario, focus your mind intently on those things you have always wanted to do (perhaps portraying them on your sails). Let the launching of your ship signal the application of magical energy to that goal.

Sample Invocation/Spell: Gather some seawater (or water with salt added) in a small container. Beneath a waxing to Full Moon, walk in a sunward circle sprinkling the water and saying:

Providence, reach me;
Kindness, teach me;
Adventures, be mine,
Come the next Full Moon's shine.

Anoint yourself with a little of the leftover water. Keep the rest where, each time you see it, you will be reminded to repeat the incantation to empower the magic further.

Other Accents: Any music with the sound of waves. Altar decorations that include seashells, starfish, driftwood, holy stones, sand, and other gifts of the sea.

May 18

FEAST OF PAN (GREECE)

Magical Themes: The god aspect; men's mysteries; the connection of humankind with nature; the "wild" within.

History/Lore: Pan is the Greek god of nature, especially the woodlands. He is a playful deity, who loves good wine and celebratory songs. The Greeks, never ones to overlook a good opportunity for lighthearted parties, commemorate Pan on this day, and the male aspect of the universe itself.

Decorating Ideas: Bring orchids and thistles into the sacred space along with some fallen branches, leaves, and other forest items. Make the circle look as natural as possible.

Garments: Fake furs, horns, and other tokens which will help you connect with the untamed nature of your own animal-self.

Ritual Cup: Wine! The most popular by far in Greece was simple (but sublime) grape wine aged to perfection. Here is one recipe that I have found very pleasant:

Feast of Pan Grape Wine

1 gallon water
1 12-oz. frozen grape juice
1 12-oz. frozen white grape juice
3 pounds honey or sugar
1/2 package active yeast

Directions: Begin by warming the juices with the water. Add the honey or sugar slowly, until it is completely dissolved. Cool the liquid to lukewarm. Meanwhile, suspend your yeast in 1/4 cup warm water. Mix this with the cooled juice. Cover loosely and let sit over night. Pour into bottles with *loose* corks. These will pop out periodically over the next few weeks of fermenting. Once this has slowed, cork the bottles tightly and allow to age for 6-8 months before using. Test periodically for sweetness. If too tart, return to the stove and add just enough sugar to please you.

Bring the mixture to a boil, then bottle in an airtight container. Store in a dark area until used.

Ritual Foods: Any recipes which incorporate masculine herbs and edibles. Ideas include banana-cream pie with almond garnish, glazed carrots with cashews, dandelion salad, cucumbers with dill sauce, onion and garlic-stuffed mushrooms, and rice with shallots.

Incense: Musk, mullein, pansy, patchouly or poplar— musk because it is the natural marking scent of animals; the others because they are strongly associated with Saturn.

Activities: If there is any way to have a ritual in the woods, by all means do so. Use the trees as your circle perimeter. Invite Pan to join your dances. Imitate animals as you move, leaping and exploring your own inner sense of wildness. Honor the patron gods of your tradition and consider a meditation which focuses on and empowers your masculine aspects.

Sample Invocation:

Lord of the Dance, Lord of the Vine,
Join in our rite; let the Sun shine!
Playful are we; rejoicing to see
The god within all men,
So mote it be!

Alternative Timing: Holidays which honor the Sun.

Other Accents: Daylight hours, especially noon, when the Sun is in its glory. Natural color schemes with highlights of gold and yellow. Tasteful phallic depictions and god images.

May 19 — 28

KALLYNTARIA AND PLYNTERIA (GREECE)

Magical Themes: Cleansing and purification, specifically for magical tools and icons.

History/Lore: This was the Greek version of our spring cleaning spurts. During this entire week, the Greek people would wash all the sacred images of their gods/goddesses in nearby lakes and streams. Afterward, the effigies were adorned with jewels before their trip back home (or to their appropriate temple).

Decorating Ideas: None. This is not a time to make a mess. In fact, any lingering decorations from other celebrations should be carefully taken down, polished, and put away for the coming year.

Garments: You're going to get dirty, so wear old, comfortable clothing.

Ritual Cup: Lemonade. You will want something refreshing, and the juice of the lemon is already aligned with purification. This way, your body will be cleansed along with your sacred space!

Ritual Foods: Continue the theme with foods known for their purgative qualities. Onion soup, garlic-basted chicken, stuffed hot peppers, or chili are all good choices.

Incense: Cinnamon, clove, frankincense, myrrh, pine, or sandalwood.

Activities: Take out all your magical tools and god/goddess images. To cleanse and purify them, either move them through the smoke of burning incense or asperge them. For the latter, a combination of mineral water with lemon juice, powdered clove and a hint of pine oil works well. This process will help remove any residual energy your tools may have picked up while lying around the house.

Sample Tool Blessing:

Be purified and blessed,
Of negativity be free.
God/goddess charge this implement
With magic energy.
Let it help me in my art,
A focus, filled with might;
Let it vibrate with my heart
Working ever toward the light.

Alternative Timing: Any Spring day. On or just after the Autumn Equinox (for biannual cleaning).

Other Accents: All of your household cleaning appliances can become magical implements today. Vacuum cleaners, dust rags, feather dusters, wash pails, mops, and sponges might be blessed along with your other magical tools so that each time you clean, special energy is imparted to your home.

May 29

ROYAL OAK DAY (ENGLAND)

Magical Themes: Protection, safety, overcoming, honoring the mighty oak, and tree magic.

History/Lore: In 1651, young King Charles II took haven in an oak tree when being pursued by Oliver Cromwell. This led to his escape into France. Charles was finally restored to the throne in 1660. Each year since, on his birthday (May 29), his triumph is celebrated with flowers and oak branches being strewn throughout the city of London. Charles himself planted acorns on this day, in memory of his fortunate experience. As an interesting side note, the oak tree was sacred to the Druids and is a long-standing pagan symbol of protection.

Decorating Ideas: A favorite decoration in English homes is oak boughs hung over doorways, windows, etc. These are sometimes garnished with fresh flowers. For a more magical appeal, bind the flowers and leaves with red thread to protect your home from evil.

Garments: The regalia of the 1600's was very elaborate, and is rather difficult to recreate at home. Instead, I suggest wearing something nice for your observance, and making circlets of oak leaves for each member to wear.

Ritual Cup: For protection, use any of the following teas: raspberry, blackberry, ginseng, or wintergreen. For tree magic, I suggest using the juice of any fruit born from a bough.

Ritual Foods: If performing magic for safety, make a thick beef and barley soup, adding a bit of basil, dill, and onion. To honor the oak tree, make foods which can be sculpted to take on the appearance of trees or acorns. Two ideas along these lines are a nutty cake with green foliage made from frosting, or sheaves of stuffed celery with the leaves left on.

Incense: Dried oak wood or leaves to which rose geranium petals, violet, and clover are added for safety.

Activities: Besides making your decorations from fallen oak branches, I suggest acorn gathering or planting. When gathered, acorns can be used in a wide variety of craft items, lending their energy to protect the home from lightning. If carried as an amulet, acorns ward off sickness. Sow acorns around the perimeter of your sacred space or home to create a sanctuary. They can also be used to surround gardens to keep the plants healthy.

Sample Invocation:

Great Spirit of the Woods,
I call and greet you!
Gathered now beneath your branches,
We celebrate nature and the safety you grant.

Come and bless this Circle
With comforting shade and the protection of your boughs.
We welcome and honor you,
Lord of the Oak.

Alternative Timing: Arbor Day; New Year of the Trees (January 23, Israel).

Other Accents The mighty oak is sacred to Jupiter, Thor, Zeus, Rhea, and Hecate, so any one of these Divine figures could be called upon to bless your magic.

June

The Month of June (all days)

FESTIVAL OF THE SUN (INCAN)

Magical Themes: Element of fire; solar attributes; honoring the dead; divine tributes.

History/Lore: While this holiday spills over into Summer a bit, it begins in Spring. Around 1000 A.D., on each day of the month of Inti Raimi, the Incan people dressed the mummies of former emperors in their best robes. The mummies were then brought into the court of the Sun Temple, facing the worshippers. Pure white llamas were bedecked in scarlet with gold harnesses and offered to the solar gods; then food was shared among all in attendance. Afterward, all the people would dance and sing until the Sun slipped into sleep past the horizon.

Decorating Ideas: Vibrant reds and golds all around to honor the Sun; anything which gives off light; depictions of the Sun, or solar deities.

Garments: Your best robes. In this setting you are the Priest/Priestess, representing the Divine. Adorn your robes with any gold jewelry, complementing them with headpieces. The head has long been regarded as the seat of God.

Ritual Cup: Hot, fiery liquids. Try cinnamon or ginger liqueurs. Alternatively, warm some orange tea to which these herbs are added in healthy portions.

Ritual Foods: Continue your solar theme with golden-colored foods. Serve bright, round squashes, sliced carrots, pineapple sections, and anything prepared on the barbecue.

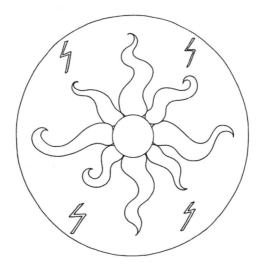

Figure 15. Solar mandala made of colored sand.

Incense: Crush together 3 bay leaves with some dried carnation petals, 1/4 cup of pine or cedar shavings, and a dash of clove. If possible, burn this incense on an open fire.

Activities: Make offerings of tea, rice, frankincense and saffron to your favorite solar god/goddess. Build a bonfire and dance around it sunward to bring renewed energy and vigor into your life. If you are near a beach, use colored sand to create a solar mandala like the one shown in figure 15. Also consider having guided meditations which focus on the element of fire. Use some flame source to help, looking closely for the salamander spirit.

Sample Invocation:

Lord of the Dance, Lord of the Fire,
Lord of the Sun, rise ever higher.
Flames leap for joy; joy come to me,
Spark now my magic, as the embers burn free.

Alternative Timing: Beltane; many summer festivals; birthday of the Sun (September 20).

Other Accents: Use large sunflowers to mark the perimeter of your magic circle. A cauldron of fire can be set up as that part of the central altar where any illness or negativity can be burned away. Possibly place your altar facing southward, toward the region of fire.

June 4

ROSALIA (ANCIENT GREECE)

Magical Themes: Love; sexual passion; feminine maturity; honoring Aphrodite or other love goddeses.

History/Lore: The rose is the most beloved of all flowers on Earth, owing its origins to Arabia along with the prayer rosary, its namesake. Depending on the color of the blossom, different meanings are intoned. Red, of course, is romantic love, while pink is young infatuation, and yellow the hue of friendship. The white rose is indicative of peace or death, depending on the culture.

In Greece, this date was observed in many ways. Primarily, worshippers sprinkled hundreds of rose petals in the temples of Aphrodite, while burning rose incense for good fortune. Women also washed their skin with rose water, insuring their continued beauty.

Decorating Ideas: An abundance of rose bushes, bouquets, and petals should fill the sacred space. If these are not available, try to find paintings or other floral depictions to substitute.

A particularly lovely accent is a rose-covered trellis. This can take quite a few flowers to accomplish, so for a less costly option, use paper flowers in deep, rose hues. Affix them to an archway or other fixture near the sacred space, dotted with a little rose oil. Be careful with the amount of scent you use here; you don't want to attract bees.

Garments: Anything flowery or crimson in color. Make yourself a headpiece from silk roses, and don any jewelry with a petaled motif.

Ritual Cup: Rose punch or wine. For the first, steep 6 cups of well-packed rose petals in 4 cups of warm (not hot) water. Let them sit until the water is heady with their scent. Strain into a punch bowl. To this, add 4 cups of sodawater and ice cubes with flowers frozen within. Float fresh roses on top along with sliced oranges.

Ritual Foods: Roses are edible, and high in vitamin C. Try some well-washed petals as a salad garnish. Alternatively, make some candied roses by dipping single petals into sugar boiled to the hard-crack stage. Let these dry on a greased cookie sheet. They can then be eaten as is, or used to decorate cakes and other dishes.

Incense: Rose or other scents sacred to Aphrodite, including sandalwood, myrtle, and clover.

Activities: This is a perfect day to make yourself some prayer beads consecrated to bringing love and joy into your life. Begin with about 3 cups of fresh rose petals. Place these in 1 cup of water with 1 tablespoon orris root. Cook over a very low flame until the mixture takes on a sticky, paste-like texture. Cool until you can handle the paste.

Next, form balls out of the rose mixture. The size is really up to you, but about 1/2 inch diameter works well for stringing. Let these dry a little more (about 1 hour), then press a needle through the center of each to form a neat hole. At the same time, dab the beads with some rose-scented oil to enhance their fragrance. The beads must now dry completely (about 1 week in a nonhumid area). If you happen to have some artistic ability, you can etch petals into them at this time, as they will be very hard.

String the beads at comfortable intervals onto a nice chain or ribbon. As you secure them in place, visualize romantic red light filling each. Call on Aphrodite to bless your efforts. Remove one bead and place it in rich soil any time love needs to grow generously in your life.

Sample Invocation:

Aphrodite, Goddess of Love and Passion,
Bend down your ear to hear
The cry of one who desires to love and be loved;
Pour out your power and aid my quest;
Let my true love now be blessed.

Alternative Timing: Two other festivals for Aphrodite, April 23 and June 24; May Day, St. Valentine's Day and St. George's Day.

Other Accents: Other items associated with this goddess include copper, turquoise, doves, and swans.

June 13

FEAST OF EPONA (CELTIC)

Magical Themes: Movement; fertility; the warrior spirit; messages.

History/Lore: Epona was a goddess generally depicted as riding a horse or a goose through the sky. The latter is attributable to her image as a Mother figure and provider, sometimes carrying corn. Her fertility aspect is vividly displayed by her possessing four breasts and holding a goblet.

During the Roman occupation, the cavalry adopted Epona as a patron goddess. The story of her transporting priests to other realms probably helped with this interest, along with her strong association with the horse, an important military element in the legions.

Decorating Ideas: Place horseshoes, open end up (to catch blessings) over the entrance to your sacred space. Try using a riding crop as a wand, a horse blanket as the cover for the altar, hay bales at each quarter to mark the circle; and leave some dried grain as an offering to the goddess.

Garments: The first thing that comes to my mind is cowboy apparel. Horses were very important to the American western heritage, so this costuming should help with your overall focus.

Ritual Cup: Any grain-based beverage like beer is a good choice. Please note that there are nonalcoholic beers available in the supermarkets for those who prefer not to imbibe.

Ritual Foods: Again, consider cereal-type foods. A corn chowder served with fresh wheat bread and oatmeal cookies for dessert is one option. Here is a recipe for chowder to honor Epona.

Feast of Epona Chowder

1 cup barley
1 cup lentils
6 cups water
1 16-oz. can creamed corn
salt and pepper to taste
2 stalks celery, chopped
2 carrots, diced
1 medium onion, diced
2 medium potatoes, cubed

Directions: Begin by boiling the barley and lentils in water for 30 minutes. Now add all other ingredients, stirring regularly. Cook for 1 hour over a medium-low flame until vegetables are tender. For a richer soup, use 2 cans of creamed corn, substituting 2 cups cream for 2 cups water.

Incense: Things that remind you of an open meadow; clover, sweet grass, daisy petals, etc.

Activities: Whether you're working alone or in a group, this meditation/visualization is often very revealing. Begin by getting comfortable and making sure you will not be disturbed. Visualize yourself in a beautiful meadow on the edge of a forest. A sense of peace and quiet falls over you. Now, call out to the spirit of the horse. Ask it to come to you.

When the horse arrives in your vision, request permission to mount so that the creature may carry you to a place of learning. If permission is granted, climb on and see where the horse takes you. The destination will likely be symbolic. Finally, thank the horse for its gift and let it move away. Slowly return to a normal level of awareness.

An alternative activity is a game of horseshoes. Your target represents a goal in your life. Tossing the horseshoe motivates energy. A ringer brings success!

Sample Invocation:

Epona, Lady who rides the sky,
Send your steed to my side;
Let me learn of strength and honor;
Let courage be my guide.

Other Accents: Birds and dogs are also honored by Epona. If you have either, welcome them in your sacred space.

June 17

THE CLEANSING LILY (JAPAN)

Magical Themes: Purification; protection from evil; stopping rain; white lily, purity, and beauty.

History/Lore: This is an ancient Shinto festival designed to dispel early Summer downpours that can lead to flooding. At dawn, lily stalks are gathered at a local mountain. Seven women wearing white robes carry these to the nearest Shinto shrine or temple for a blessing. The flowers stay in the temple overnight, then a priest places them on the altar. As the priest recites prayers, seven maidens dance with flowers held to the sky. Finally, the celebrants walk through the town's streets waving tiger lilies. This invokes moisture-free air.

Lilies are popular among other religious traditions, too. In Christianity, the white blossoms are a symbol of Christ. In China, families use lily buds when anointing their hearth to honor the kitchen god. Finally, Muslim people drink a lily beverage called *nufu* when toasting Allah and the health of friends.

Decorating Ideas: If you can't find tiger lilies, try lily of the valley as an alternative.

Garments: Anything white in color.

Ritual Cup: I would suggest milk, which is simple in nature. If it is a hot day, quaff a coconut milk shake for purification.

Ritual Foods: Lily buds are high in protein and taste a bit like chestnuts when cooked in batter. They are effective for many culinary efforts, especially when diced and lightly fried as an accent to pork, poultry, and mild fishes. For a delightful desert, the following recipe has its origins in the East.

Maiden Cakes

Directions: Take a basic cake mix and add 1/4 cup of lily honey, and 2 cups of the following (in any proportion): dates, candied ginger, oranges, plums, nuts, apricots, and cherries. Bake according to the directions on the cake mix, or for 35 minutes at 350 degrees. This cake has seven ingredients to represent the seven temple maidens noted above.

The lily honey in this recipe is made by steeping 1 cup of lilies in 4 cups of honey for 1 week. Strain and serve with fresh, hot bread during or after your rite.

Incense: A favorite combination of scents originally published in Pliny's *Naturall Historie* is lily with calamus, cinnamon, saffron, and myrrh.[6] Any combination of these is acceptable.

Activities: Have members of your group gather as many lily buds as they can to bring with them. String these together to hang in a window, or the eastern quarter of the circle. To stop a storm, remove one and toss it to the winds. To purify the sacred space, let the petals dry and add them to your incense.

---

6   Pliny's *Natural Historie*, ten volumes (Cambridge, MA: Loeb Classical Library) was first published in the 15th century. This well-known work forms the basis for many modern studies.

Another activity is making essence of lily. To begin, place the buds in alcohol in the proportion of 1/4 cup petals to 1 cup alcohol. Infuse this for seven days, strain, and repeat this procedure seven times. The final product can be used in cooking, perfumery or anointing.

Sample Invocation:

Round the circle, 'tis where we go;
Follow where the lily blows,
North and east, south and west,
The Watchtowers, we each behest.

Round the circle, sunward dance;
Follow where the lilies prance,
Toward God and Goddess, throughout the night;
Let our magic now take flight!

Other Accents: The number seven is important to this holiday. Use this figure in any way you can to enhance the magic further.

The Summer Calendar

ummer's theme is one of energy, abundance, leisure, and vitality. The Earth is now in full bloom. Fruits begin to appear on the trees, vegetables are filling out the garden, and the smell of fresh-cut grass is on each wind. Children can be found merrily playing outdoors, glad for bare feet and warm sunshine. Meanwhile, I tend my barbecue and enjoy the company that the warmer months have brought to our home.

Happiness is truly Summer's motif. Honor it with bright, vibrant colors that remind you of life itself: red, orange, and yellow for the solar disk, and lush greens for the home and circle. In addition, every color imaginable is evidenced in the floral array, so savor that abundance.

The sacred space should be accented with all types of petals, potted plants, sunflowers, morning glories, any green foliage, and emblems of fire. Scents for the season include hot, exciting herbs such as cinnamon, clove, frankincense, peppermint, rosemary and woodruff. Possible Divine entities to bless your efforts include:

Ptah — Egyptian god of creativity;
Bridget — Irish goddess of health and inventiveness;
Acat — Mayan god of fruitfulness;
Freya — Teutonic goddess of productivity;
Bona Dea — Roman goddess of fertility and the Earth;
Tien Kuan — Chinese god of joy and well-being;
Amaterasu — Japanese goddess of the Sun and happiness;
Apollo — Greek and Roman god of health;
Venus — Roman goddess of love;

Cupid — Roman god of romance;

Jambhala — Buddhist god of prosperity;

Mars — Roman god of power and strength;

Suwa — Arabic goddess of courage and energy;

Amun Ra — Egyptian god of the Sun;

Dyaus — Hindu solar deity;

Li — Chinese goddess of the Sun;

Sul — British goddess of the Sun;

Helios — Greek god of the Sun;

Mercury — Roman god of movement, communication;

Kunado — Japanese god of roads and travel;

Vijaya — Hindu goddess of success;

Gwalo — Nigerian rain god;

Hadad — Babylonian storm god;

Mama Quilla — Incan goddess of rain;

Sarama — Japanese goddess of wind ;

Saranya — Hindu goddess of the clouds;

Vulcan — Roman god of fire and the forge;

Hemera — Greek goddess of the day;

Stones associated with Summer include July's ruby, which insures luck in relationships, keeps nightmares away, and brings joy to the wearer. August's stone is the sardonyx for fidelity and excellent marriages. September's stone is the sapphire for fairness, equity, and sincerity.

Spiritual efforts enhanced by summer timing consist of spells, rituals, and celebrations centering around relaxation, improved health, fruitfulness, increasing energy, prosperity, and anything pertaining to the element of fire.

General Summer Celebrations

The celebrations of Summer focus on veneration of solar deities; marriage and coming of age; industry, trade, and crafts; tending crops; and feasting and fun. Summer, as a time of warmth and plenty, brings people together to share the bounty and enjoy the gentler aspects of nature and its cycles. Following are some of the festivals common to a number of cultures in Summer.

HANDFASTINGS AND WEDDINGS

The entire month of June is the Roman month of marriage. In A.D. 100, marriages were observed by the woman wearing her hair up, and donning a special wedding dress and an orange veil. At the end of the ceremony, the couple's hands were bound to symbolize their union. A joyful procession followed, winding through the streets to the husband's home. Here, the door was anointed with oil (protection) and adorned with wreaths of wool (warmth and security). The bride's hair was then loosened by her husband, who carried her across the threshold in a kind of ritual abduction. Both actions marked the transition from child to wife for all to witness.

The Greek version of this observance had the mother-in-law waiting with a torch to safely guide the couple over the threshold. She then placed the couple before the hearth, showering them with nuts and sweets for prosperity and fertility.

Today, many couples still choose this month to declare their love with friends and family. It is a lovely tradition which moves into the modern liturgy with no difficulty whatsoever. Mark your chosen space with an abundance of white flowers to honor the goddess and to bring joy to the couple. Use the Roman symbolism of united hearts and hands by creating a garland of elder, magnolia, and roses. This is wrapped around the couple's wrists for love and fidelity.

For a special treat, prepare honey-glazed almonds to share sweet love and happiness with all the guests. Start with 1 cup of honey and a pinch of ginger (passion) in a sauce pan. Bring to a full rolling boil, then add 1 cup of almonds. Let these get coated completely, then pour onto a small, greased cookie sheet to cool and harden. Wrap with decorative lace mesh to represent the "tying of knots."

Finally, instead of rice, sprinkle the couple with husked nuts (sunflower seeds are a good choice) to insure that they will never want. These should be left where they fall to share with the birds nearby.

TRADE FAIRS

During the Middle Ages, good weather brought financial benefits along with the sunshine. Merchants could travel again, and farmers and craftsmen could easily get their goods to market. Trade fairs were one outgrowth of this increased mobility.

These were arranged on differing dates in large towns and villages to show goods, enjoy performers, and haggle for wares. Everything from fine furs to glass products could be found. This particular celebration offered the secondary benefit of permitting everyone to stock up for the fall and winter months.

In a modern setting, the trade fair can be recreated with only minor variations. Best arranged to coincide with a festival, the fair can attract artisans and performers ready to offer merchandise and services. Then, everyone at the festival will be able to restock their spiritual paraphernalia and enjoy the talent your community offers. The only caution here is to check your region for laws regarding sales tax, licenses, and permits which may be necessary to hold special events.

MOP FAIRS

These took place in rural western Europe. They were akin to trade fairs but, instead of goods, were created to find hired help for one year. People needing employment came to the fairs hoping to find a suitable position with fixed wages plus board and lodging. Each wore tokens of their talent or trade and received offers from prospective employers. Some areas followed this observance with a Runaway Fair about a month later. This gave unhappy servants a chance to look for another job!

Considering the difficult employment atmosphere people face today, a job fair has merit. In this case, various businesses in the New Age community can advertise any openings they have or are aware of. This can be accomplished through journals to reach a larger number of people. Similarly, those seeking employment can write blurbs about their experience, desired position(s), etc., and circulate that data back to interested parties. This way, both employer and employee can be working among likeminded people, without any moral conflicts!

ALASKAN WHALE DANCE

In early Summer, the fishermen of Alaskan villages donned whale masks for this celebration. They then danced from door-to-door throughout their town, sharing precious whale meat with the residents. This action was meant to appease the whale spirits and thank them for their sustenance. It was also performed to insure abundance for the next year.

For your purposes, this festival exhibits two important features. First is the symbolism of the whale itself. Equated with the breath of life, the womb (note the story of Jonah), and deep esoteric mysteries, the whale spirit can be called upon for aid in your metaphysical studies. Try a visualization where you swim with the whale into the deepest ocean to retrieve the treasures of learning. When you break the surface for air, bring those lessons with you, inhaling them to develop in your heart.

Second, this festival pays homage to a creature which provided food. Therefore, sometime during your summer celebration schedule, consider setting aside one day to thank the spirits of livestock or poultry (unless you're a vegetarian). This would be an excellent time to refrain from eating meat. Emblematically, abstaining is a sacrificial act allowing one creature to live another day.

NEW GUINEA YAM FESTIVAL

In certain regions of New Guinea, the yam is regarded as having a soul. To honor this spirit, and give thanks for the local staple, tribal groups slip on yam masks and dance in tribute to the yam harvest.

Magically, yams are equated with Venus, the element of water, the emotion of love, and providence. If you hold your own yam (or other tuber) festival, keep these themes in mind. In addition, celebrate any edibles unique to your region or which help provide income to local residents. Prepare various blessed dishes in thanksgiving to the natural world, adding a prayer for the Earth's continued bounty.

FIRE FESTIVALS

Summer is the season of fire. Humankind greeted its warmth and light with festivals to give strength to the Sun. What more appropriate way to do so than with myriad fire-based observances?

Taking place throughout the summer months, festival fires burned throughout the countryside, sending their flames toward the sky. As they burned, rituals were (and are) held in veneration of solar deities. Often, these rites were combined with magic for protection, trusting that the light would banish any evil.

Fire festivals are pagan in origin and need little, if any, alteration to function in modern circles. The element of fire is the central character for this celebration. A cauldron of coals, a barbecue grill, a bonfire, or candles can help portray this theme, as can covering the altar with a golden-yellow cloth and decorating the sacred space with red and yellow flowers.

A gratifying project for any fire festival is to make a special smudge stick with summer flowers and herbs. A few weeks

Figure 16. Flower and herb smudge stick constructed of long cuttings of mint, basil, rosemary, lavender, and sage tied with cotton thread.

before your observance, gather long cuttings of mint, basil, rosemary, lavender, and sage. Rinse them so they are free of dirt, then hang them upside down to dry. Be sure not to bundle too many together or they will mold.

Then, just before your celebration, intermingle the herbs and tie them securely as shown below. Use a cotton thread for best results (see figure 16, page 100). You can now burn this to mark the edge of your sanctuary, bless the participants, and as a cleansing incense to purify your magical efforts. These smudge sticks have tremendous longevity. When you are done with yours, just douse it with water and hang it up to dry for reuse.

THE CIRCUS

Almost every country in Europe had a traveling circus with acrobats, dancers, and performing animals. Announced by a parade filled with drums, elephants and fantastic costumes, a circus was always greeted happily by any town. It meant improved revenue and a rare opportunity for diversion.

The circus began in Rome and had a distinctly Pagan flavor. The Circensian Games were devised to bring eligible women into Rome for the warriors. Originally, the festival honored the triad of Jupiter, Juno, and Minerva with foot competitions, boxing, wrestling, and horse races. Later, nautical events, games, and feasting were added to the festivities, which slowly developed into the circus as we know it.

Something along these lines can be fun for a large group, with each family or individual creating a game or event to participate in. If possible, the activities should be symbolic to your ritual. One possibility is a game of "keep-it-up," using a festive yellow ball (the Sun) which is moved clockwise around the circle. When someone drops the ball, they sit down. The last person standing can become the honorary priest/priestess for the day.

In keeping with the Roman flavor, honor Juno by using empty coconut shells as your ritual cups. For Minerva, decorate the area with tiger lilies and geraniums. Finally, for Jupiter, burn cedar and saffron as your incense.

GOOD DAY

In England's Epping Forest, a young man named Daniel Day came upon a giant oak. This was a favorite spot for Gypsies to take shelter during storms. For Daniel, however, it was just a picturesque spot to eat beans with friends. He so enjoyed these outings that it became an annual event, slowly drawing more and more people to eat beneath the bowers.

Eventually, it became more like a carnival than a picnic, with entertainers and puppet shows. As people arrived, they greeted each other by saying, "Good Day" in honor of the founder of the feast! This tradition continued until the unfortunate Mr. Day was fatally injured by one of the oak's branches falling on him. In true good humor, Daniel had the wood made into his coffin before he died.

I like this holiday for many reasons. First, there is an inescapable charm about picnics. That, combined with Mr. Day's pleasant disposition, makes me wonder if we don't need more holidays celebrating the simple joys of life. Gather some friends together and go for an outing. Bring tasty food, including beans for luck! Remember to greet everyone you see with a smile and good wishes to improve their fortune.

Finally, consider some Gypsy magic to round out your day. Make a rye and pimento bread, and bring your favorite type of melon to snack on. Both of these foods will ensure love in your life.

SUMMER'S END

Usually taking place on a weekend in early September, this is a slightly different type of fire festival. This time the embers are lit to ward off the coming chill of Autumn. Magic for good health and mild weather are appropriate. An attitude of thankfulness fills the air now, for the warmth that was and will be once more.

Similar in form and function to the Autumnal Equinox observances, a Summer's End festival is a time to put your house in order (spiritually and physically). This is a period of abundance balanced with wisdom. Consider making a special Sun

Figure 17. Sun wheel made of rowan branches, red thread, vervain, and rue.

wheel using rowan branches, red thread, vervain, and rue. Together these will keep negativity away, protect you from evil influences, and bring health to all the occupants of your home throughout the Winter.

To prepare, soak long, thin rowan branches in water overnight during a Waning Moon (for banishing). Fashion these into a circle with an equidistant cross in the center representing the four major points of the magical calendar. Bind the ends securely with red thread (the color of life). Let the branches dry until the following Full Moon. Then decorate the circle with vervain, rue, and golden ribbons for sunbeams (see figure 17).

June

June 21

SUMMER SOLSTICE

Magical Themes: The fire element; luck, health, wishes, and love; harvesting magical plants.

History/Lore: In England, the Druids gathered on this day for sunrise ceremonies marking the solstice. Sometimes called Midsummer, the day marks the point at which the Earth has moved halfway around the Sun in her annual journey. Days will now begin to get shorter and the weather grows cooler.

Folklore claims that this is an excellent night to try to conceive a child, perform love magic, or divine for insight as to future relationships. To protect your home, place thistles around the doors so the powers of darkness cannot enter. Finally, take care where you walk tonight, for fairies are afoot! To see them, rub fern seed on your eyelids, and to protect yourself, keep rue in your pocket.

Decorating Ideas: Buttercup, clover, and roses sprinkled on the altar in a whimsical array. Scandinavian homes were decorated with birch leaves and boughs. Germans adorned fig trees with flower garlands and crimson or gold egg shells.

Garments: Lively and lighthearted accoutrements. Make yourself a crown of dried flowers that can be used during ritual. For an inexpensive base, purchase a circlet comb and wire silk or dried flowers into the solid end.

Ritual Cup: Dew or rain water collected on this night has special powers for prophetic visions, especially pertaining to love.

Ritual Foods: For good fortune, have a cabbage salad as part of the postritual feast. For health, include a pot of steamy chicken soup with a little hot pepper to honor the Sun.

Incense: Fennel, birch, St. John's Wort, and lily were the traditional scents in English homes on this day, and were sometimes fastened to the threshold. Alternatives are marjoram and basil for love, or thyme to appease the wee folk.

Activities: Follow the Italian tradition of exchanging a pot of basil and cucumbers with your sweetheart. If the basil grows thick, your love will be filled with joy. To see if your relationship is going to blossom, pin a piece of St. John's Wort to the wall of your bedroom. If it droops, the signs are negative, but if it flourishes through the night, the omen is positive. To dream of your lover, weave a chaplet using nine different flowers and place it under your pillow.

To carry away any sickness or ill-fortune, remove your floral garland (made earlier) and light it aflame. Roll it down a hill into running water so that negativity is carried away. For safety reasons, make sure the hill is dirt or stone covered.

Finally, Midsummer is the most potent time to harvest your magical herbs. Use a special knife for this purpose (perhaps your athame), taking care to thank the Earth for its gifts. Dry seeds and flowers in open netting hung from the ceiling. Leafy herbs, like mint, can be bundled together upside down to dry effectively. Take care to rinse all your plants *before* drying, as it will be difficult to remove dirt later.

Sample Invocation:

FOR HARVESTING HERBS

I thank Gaia for her treasures:
Grown by the Sun,
Nurtured by rain,
Sustained by the Earth,
Freed by the winds.

This plant is the Circle —
Gathered in with loving hands
To bless my magic.

FOR LUCK AND HEALTH

The Sun dances,
*   the wind prances*
Within my soul,
*   to make me whole.*
The Earth flowers
*   The rain showers*
With magic, free,
*   grant fortuity!*

Other Accents: Midsummer is the perfect time for rituals held at dawn or noon to venerate the solar aspect. Keep your accent colors bright. Play tempestuous music, full of rhythm and energy.

Late June

BAWMING THE THORN (APPLETON, ENGLAND)

Magical Themes: Tree magic.

History/Lore: Each year, children of this town decorate a huge hawthorn tree in the center of town using flags, ribbons, and flowers. Once it is fully adorned, they gather and dance beneath its boughs. It is believed this observance dates back to early forms of pagan tree worship.

Decorating Ideas: If the ceremony is held outdoors, definitely trim as many trees as you can near the sacred space. For this, I suggest bundles of nuts and dried fruits for animals to enjoy, along with ribbons, balloons, bows, etc. The only caution is to be certain you gather all the balloons after your celebration. They are harmful to birds and other creatures.

Garments: Make yourself a tree costume to honor these great natural oxygen-makers. A simple technique is to wrap your lower body in brown fabric, securing it under your arms with a pin. This gives the appearance of a trunk. Then either place waxed leaves in your hair, or use a temporary green dye for foliage.

Ritual Cup: Juice, punch, or wine prepared from any fruit-bearing tree.

Ritual Foods: Again, I would suggest looking to tree-grown fruit for ideas. A main dish of peach-glazed pork with orange-flavored carrots on the side, and a fruit salad consisting of apples, pears, tangerines, cherries, etc. is one good option. Use different types of leaves as garnishes.

Incense: Any heady-smelling wood, like cedar or sandalwood.

Activities: A wonderful project, which also creates a permanent decoration, is a dried flower tree. For this you will need to gather a large flower pot (6-8 inch diameter), a 1½-2 foot long branch (straight enough to be the trunk of your tree), some plaster of Paris, a foam ball (4 inch diameter), a circle of foam which fits into the flower pot, dried moss, and a selection of dried or silk flowers.

Figure 18. Dried flower tree. Left: sectional view of tree branch placement in flower pot; Center: dried moss and flowers arranged in pot; Right: foam ball placed on nail at top of branch.

Figure 19. Finished dried flower tree.

Begin by setting the branch into the flower pot using the plaster. Place the largest end down so it has a natural trunklike appearance. This will need to dry completely before you continue.

Next, cover the top of the flower pot with two half-circles of the foam. This is hidden by dried moss and other small flowers. Now attach the foam ball onto the top of the stick. Be careful that it does not split. If the branch is too thick, place a nail into it and press the ball onto that instead (see figure 18, page 107).

Begin to cover the ball with smaller flowers first. Sea lavender is a favorite that helps hide the base completely. Add leaves next, with flowers coming last. If desired, a ribbon can be tied neatly just beneath your tree's foliage as a final touch, as shown in figure 19.

Please note that this holiday traditionally centered around the children of Appleton, so get your young ones as involved as possible. Let them make their own miniature trees, using sticks secured in the earth and scrap materials. They can play a ribbon-tying game as part of decorating.

For this, have precut ribbons and a stop watch ready. Tell the children to think of one wish to repeat each time they tie a ribbon. The person to tie the most bows in three minutes gets a prize, and the best chance to have their wish come true!

Sample Invocation:

Great, ancient bowers
Reveal, now, your powers:
Let my will be strong as your trunk,
My Path sure as your roots,
My Soul, growing like your leaves toward the light.

Great woodland spirit
As beneath thee I sit,
Teach me, I pray;
Help me find a new way.

Alternative Timing: Arbor Day, Earth Day, New Year of the Trees (January 23, Palestine).

Other Accents: Every shade of green. Find a tape or CD of woodland sounds, especially if you're celebrating in an urban area. Depictions of creatures which perch in trees can become central to the elemental points of your circle (butterfly for air, squirrel for earth, etc.).

July

July 3

FESTIVAL OF CERRIDWEN (CELTIC)

Magical Themes: Rewards of hard labors; ingenuity and fortuity; prosperity and fertility.

History/Lore: Cerridwen is the Celtic goddess of grain, the Moon, and abundance. She tends the cauldron called Amen which holds a sacred beverage, bestowing creativity and knowledge on those that partake of it. Her symbol is the pig, an important source of food to early peoples.

Decorating Ideas: Bowls of grain (or grain-type cereal) for the altar; a large cauldron central to the sacred space filled with your chosen ritual beverage; depictions of the Moon.

Garments: Take a fresh ear of corn and carefully slice off the kernels. Using a needle and thread, string these together, leaving space between them for proper drying. Once completely dried, move them together and measure out a length to wear as a necklace at your celebration.

Ritual Cup: Beer, as a grain-based beverage, is one option. Another is warm barley water, which is very healthful. This is prepared by using a light beef or pork stock to which the barley is added and cooked. To use this as a remedy, the beverage is strained before serving.

Ritual Foods: It's Summer, so why not boil up corn on the cob and have a pork roast? Baste the pork with a mixture of lemon juice, butter, and mint to accent the lunar nature of Cerridwen. Or, make a marigold mustard to add fiery, inventive power to your efforts. This is prepared by finely chopping 2 dessertspoons full of marigold flowers and mixing them with 8 oz. of hearty mustard. Store in an airtight container.

Incense: Sunflower and iris petals for wisdom; yellow flowers or herbs for creativity.

Activities: Activities for this festival should center around your cauldron. Fill it with water and float whole, fresh peaches on top. Bob for the peaches to bite a bit of sagacity. Later, ladle out your ritual beverage to each participant asking, "What is your need?" The recipient should respond with something to the effect of, "I desire creativity or wisdom in _____ [fill in appropriately]." The priest/priestess then says, "Then drink your fill."

Sample Invocation:

Stir this beverage, round and round,
Earth and air and fire bound.

Cerridwen, your cauldron sure,
Create in us a magic pure;

Stir the cauldron to the right
Help our magic take to flight.

Cerridwen, where these drops flow
Creative insight now bestow!

Other Accents: If any members of your group wish to have their personal cauldrons blessed (and/or incense burners, cups, etc.) this is a perfect opportunity. Their presence in the sacred space will promote sympathetic energy with Cerridwen.

Midsummer Waxing Moon

FESTIVAL OF THE TOOTH (CEYLON)

Magical Themes: Prayer and blessing; honoring spiritual teachers; inner peace.

History/Lore: In the fifth century A.D., a 2^1/2 inch eye-tooth belonging to Buddha was brought to Kandy, Ceylon. It is mounted on a gold lotus leaf and enclosed within seven jeweled caskets. Once a year, the relic is taken through the streets. This continues over the next ten days with processions, dancing, prayer, and feasting in tribute to Buddha, who taught the path to Nirvana.

Decorating Ideas: Gold fringe and tassels adorn the elephants who carry the tooth, so this feature might be transferred to your altar cloth. To make temporary tassels, take 10 inch strands of yellow and gold yarn or cord. Cut enough to fill your grip about half full. Fold them in half; then, about 2 inches from the top end, secure them with some ribbon. You can use a silk lotus flower as an accent. The tassel can now be stitched loosely onto the corner of your altar cloth, and removed later using a seam ripper or scissors.

Garments: The traditional robe of the Buddhist priest for this rite is saffron-colored.

Ritual Cup: Use a gold-tone cup if possible. This is what the priests use to gather river water in Ceylon. The liquid later becomes the holy water for the temple.

Ritual Foods: Flexible. However, you can maintain congruity by using gilded leaves to garnish your dishes. This can be accomplished with whole, dry bay leaves, painted various hues of gold and dried on a cooling rack. Magically, this accents energy for success, inner resolve, and purification. The leaves are reusable.

Incense: Burning coconut shell is traditional.

Activities: Meditate to encourage inner harmony and self-reconciliation. Thank those who have taught you important spiritual lessons by taking them to dinner or bestowing a thoughtful gift.

The children of your group can make a serviceable prayer wheel by taking a pinwheel and marking it with words, symbols, or runes that depict their requests. They blow on the toy to release their prayers. The air will carry those wishes to the gods.

Sample Invocation:

As the Moon grows full, and fills the night
Grant to me an inner sight.
Discernment come! With magic bind;
Bring to me peace of mind.
To my heart, let kindness flow;
To my mind, wisdom show;
Through my soul, a healing glow,
As the Moon grows full.

Alternative Timing: Birthday of Buddha.

Other Accents: In Ceylon, most of this observance takes place during evening hours. Elephant images and lotus flowers are also fitting.

July 10

PANATHENAEA (GREECE)

Magical Themes: Making magical regalia; creative arts, specifically needlework, sculpting and flute playing; wisdom.

History/Lore: Held in Athens to celebrate their patron goddess, Panathenaea is a six-day celebration. On the final day, Athena is presented with a new robe. This is shown all over the city in a paradelike manner, followed by musicians and people carrying offerings to the temple. After the gifts are presented, the robe is draped over Athena's image and the heralds announce her pleasure in the raiment.

Decorating Ideas: A shield and spear upon the altar to honor Athena's chosen tools; depictions of an owl; oak and olive leaves to outline the perimeter of the circle.

Garments: Any jewelry with ruby, turquoise, or onyx is associated with this goddess. Also wear your finest magical regalia.

Ritual Cup: Wine was adored by the Greeks. It was used in this festival as a seemly offering to the Goddess and a beverage for her worshippers. The most common types were grape wine and honey mead.

To make some mead to enhance resourcefulness and personal judgment, begin with one liter of apple wine. Warm it in a nonaluminum pan, adding a handful of mint leaves and a pinch of sage. Let this sit for 30 minutes. Strain and add about 1/4 cup of honey. Serve hot or cold.

Ritual Foods: A full-flavored Greek feast! Have stuffed grape leaves with souvlaki, spinach pies, herbed potatoes, and some baklava for dessert.

Ritual Souvlaki

Marinate overnight in the refrigerator
> 1/4 pound of beef per person.
> Use your favorite tenderizing sauce.

Grill the meat until it is light brown — "done" all the way through.

Serve on a bed of lettuce, tomato, and onion, sprinkling a goodly portion of feta cheese over the top. Spice with Italian dressing and garnish with a side of pita bread.

Athena's Spinach Pie

For the spinach pie, take about 2 cups of cooked spinach and drain it completely.

Mix this with 1 cup diced tomatoes and 1/2 cup finely chopped onions.

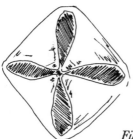

Figure 20. Athena's Spinach Pie.

Spice with a hint of basil, oregano, garlic, and olive oil.

Stuff inside prepared bread dough, rolled flat and folded over (see figure 20).

Bake for about 18 minutes at 350 degrees, or until the bread turns golden brown.

Open to add feta cheese and sliced tomatoes, if desired.

Incense: Musk and geranium.

Activities: Have a sewing competition for magical robes. The winner can become the priest/priestess for the day, helping to coordinate all planned activities. The children of your group can make small costumes for their stuffed animals or dolls as a separate contest. Here, several prizes reflective of the occasion should be on hand.

A project most everyone can participate in is making a blessed pincushion for future sewing projects. For this, each individual will need a 10 inch circle of close-knit, lacy fabric, another 9 1/2 inch circle of cotton fabric, a small stuffed animal (symbolic of your goals) and 1 cup of potpourri with an inspiring scent. Lay out the circle of lace and stitch the cotton circle in the center of it. Next, pour your potpourri out so that it fills the inner circle. In the middle, place your chosen animal, then gather the edges around it carefully. The base of the animal should be totally surrounded with the potpourri and fabric. Tie this with a ribbon, adding extra lace or decorations to hide loose edges (see figure 21 on page 116). Anoint periodically with essential oil to refresh its aroma.

Figure 21. Blessed pincushion.

Sample Spell: Repeat this as you make your pincushion:

Stitch and sew, stitch and weave,
In this magic, I believe.
Within each knot, power tied;
Until it's needed, there abide.

Alternative Timing: Mass for the Broken Needles (February 8, Japan).

Other Accents: Athena is credited with creating the flute, so any music that features this instrument would be a nice accent. Also consider a patchwork cloth for the altar and other pieces of needle craft to brighten the sacred space.

July 12

Good Luck Day

Magical Themes: Serendipity!

History/Lore: According to an old legend, Gabriel revealed this day to be particularly fortuitous. Any attempts to regain health, plant gardens, find a new home, or travel abroad will be met with unusually good luck. In addition, should a child be born on this day, or a new job started, both will be very successful.

Decorating Ideas: Green is the color of good fortune, so use accents of it throughout your home and circle. Further, some hints of orange are appropriate to honor Fortuna, Lady Luck!

Garments: If you have a "lucky" shirt, hat, coat, or other garment, find a way to wear it on this day. Also, remember to carry your good luck charms.

Ritual Cup: Whip 2 cups of coconut milk with 1 banana and a hint of nutmeg for a truly fortuitous beverage. Serve in bright green glasses, if possible.

Ritual Foods: Black-eyed peas and cabbage are in symmetry with good fortune. Prepare a dark green salad for luck with finances, peas spiced with dill for fated prospects in love, and a green-apple pie for health.

Incense: Heather and violet, or allspice and orange.

Activities: Repeat any of the activities enjoyed in your youth to bring luck. Pick up a found penny, carry a rabbit's foot, toss salt over your shoulder, get out of the "right" side of bed, keep an old key in your pocket, or pick an ash leaf!

For your home, make a lucky amulet using an old, polished horseshoe as a base. Use a hot glue gun or florist's wire, add dried ferns, heather, roses, violets, and small cinnamon sticks to bring good fortune. Hang the shoe open end up to "catch" luck, or open end down to shower everyone who enters with auspicious energy.

Sample Invocation/Spell: Repeat this incantation in three sets of three. A good luck penny (one with your birth date on it) should be used as a prop for this spell:

> *See a penny, pick it up,*
> *All the day I'll have good luck.*
> *Keep that penny at my side*
> *So the fates are satisfied.*
> *This charm recited three by three —*
> *Magic serendipity!*

Also this Date: Lobster Festival in Nova Scotia. This honors King Neptune and the Maid of the Sea (a god and goddess type) in thankfulness for good fortune and filled nets.

Alternative Dates: Good Luck Day (January 2, Macedonia); St. Patrick's Day.

July 19

FESTIVAL OF ISIS (EGYPT AND ROME)

Magical Themes: The feminine aspect; fertility; protection of children and mothers; magical knowledge and power; healing.

History/Lore: The most complete goddess known to history, Isis was worshipped for at least 3000 years. When she and Osiris ruled Egypt, they helped create the foundation of true civilization. In essence, Isis embodied the land of Egypt as a faithful wife, compassionate healer, and mother figure.

Isis was venerated by a Roman cult, which observed this festival in accordance with the Nile's annual flood cycle until A.D. 4. Because the Nile is rich with minerals, it was associated with Isis' fertility and blessing. The symbolism of the life-giving element, similar to a woman's menstrual cycle, should not be overlooked in this holiday.

Decorating Ideas: Clover leaves, willow boughs, ivy, and water plants are all seemly for the magical space.

Garments: Jewelry with amethyst, beryl, sapphire, or aquamarine. Egyptian-style robes made from linen. The Egyptian priest's wrap was similar to a knee-length skirt, secured at the side. Women went barebreasted with a tubular dress covering the rest of their length down to the ankle. Most of these garments were white. Bare feet were common.

Ritual Cup: Beer or wine. Generally, Egyptians preferred the former, but Isis is credited with inventing wine.

Ritual Foods: Egyptians were fond of lavish feasts. In the height of their prosperity, a festival meal consisted of garlic with sour cream, goat cheese, dates, and pomegranates for appetizers. A main dish of game foul, roast pig, lamb, or salmon followed. For dessert, honey cakes.

Incense: Myrrh and cedar.

Activities: One activity which took place during this festival was an attempt to receive dreams and visions. In a ceremony usually presided over by the king or priest, the individual seeker went into seclusion in Isis' temple and slept. Sometimes they would do so for a set number of nights, waiting for Divine insight. Most frequently, the hope was to discover a cure for some malady.

To do this yourself, you will want to cast a complete, formal magic circle with a comfortable place to sleep in the center. Burn angelica, mugwort, jasmine, or rose as an incense to inspire visionary dreams. Petition your desired god/goddess with your specific needs, then meditate until you fall asleep. Be sure to make notes of any dreams upon waking so you can interpret them later.

Sample Invocation:

Great Lady of the Nile,
I extend a welcome from my sacred space.
Pray, come and join me here.
I have entered your temple with the desire to learn.
Plant me here, in your fertile soil.

Fruitful Mother, Healer of our Ills,
As I sleep in your protective arms,
Bring to me dreams of things unknown;
Of health, of the future, of my soul.
Let me awake, renewed and whole.

Alternative Timing: In North Africa, it is believed that Isis was born on August 15. This date is commemorated with a boat blessing and the lighting of candles to celebrate her mother aspect.

Other Accents: For music, consider favored Egyptian instruments, including the harp, lyre, tambourine, small drums, or the sistrum, which was sacred to Isis.

July 25

TENJIN FESTIVAL (SHINTO — JAPAN)

Magical Themes: Health and healing.

History/Lore: To purge themselves of summer sicknesses, the people of Osaka, Japan follow a ritual dating back to A.D. 949. They each bring a human-shaped piece of paper into the city shrine. This is rubbed on their bodies, then taken to the Dojima River and dropped in the water. The belief is that all disease is shed with the discarded paper.

Decorating Ideas: Sets of paper dolls created by the members of your gathering. These can be hung around the perimeter of the circle or the altar.

Garments: Any, but you might want to wear a color which, to you, represents health.

Ritual Cup: Some type of nutritive broth. Two good choices are teas of sumac and comfrey, or apple and mint.

Ritual Foods: The ultimate favorite food for getting well — old-fashioned chicken soup! Also any type of apple dish to keep the doctor away.

Incense: I suggest a base of oak wood shavings to which seven of the following are added for wholeness: thyme, tansy, nutmeg, marjoram, juniper, geranium, mint, pine, rose, lemon balm, or cinnamon.

Activities: The basic tradition performed in Japan is pretty adaptable. If you don't have a moving water source nearby, have a large cauldron filled with water central to your circle. Each person should rub the paper dolls over their body in the area of need, then dunk them in the cauldron. This water can be taken later for proper disposal by the priest/priestess.

Also have each member bring a gathering of seven long cinnamon sticks, some ribbon, dried or silk carnations, and ivy. These are laid on the altar and blessed for well-being. The cinnamon is then tied into the ribbon (the knot will hold your magic) and decorated with ivy leaves and carnations to inspire health. This token is kept by all participants to bring vitality into their homes.

Sample Chant: As the dolls are dropped into the water, have everyone chant:

Washed away, Washed away,
Sickness is gone;
Health shall stay.

This chant will start off softly, but probably rise naturally as the final images are cleansed. As the cauldron is removed, it quiets again to a whisper; then silence.

Other Accents: Depending on your point of view, this ceremony can be held at sunrise or sunset: sunrise to bring renewed health and energy, or sunset to banish sickness.

Late July

HOPI KACHINA DANCES (NATIVE AMERICAN)

Magical Themes: Calling spirit guides, guardian spirits, and other helpful aid from the netherworlds.

History/Lore: Every year, the Hopi hold special rituals which commemorate the Kachina. These are supernatural beings which help insure the tribe's survival. When the dances are performed by young men of pure hearts, the Kachina will send rain and healing to the whole community. They will also possess certain tribal members for the duration of this observance.

While the actual ceremonies begin in February, they culminate in July in a final dance called Niman to mark the end of the Kachina's visit. Beginning at sunrise and ending at sunset, this dance is an elaborate farewell and show of gratitude. Once completed, the Kachinas return again to the spirit realm until the following year.

Decorating Ideas: Go with a Native American theme. Use dream catchers, natural rattles, woven rugs, and desert hues to fill the circle.

Garments: Use imitative magic by dressing as the natural spirit you hope to contact. Simple masks made from cardboard can help with this.

Ritual Cup: For increased psychic awareness, make a cinnamon-peppermint tea.

Ritual Foods: It might be best to fast for the hours before this ritual and have light snacks afterwards. This meal can consist of raw vegetables for grounding, fresh berries, and juice.

Incense: A mixture of bay, thyme, and lemongrass.

Activities: Since the Kachina are providers, dances for rain and good harvests are very fitting. In the case of the latter, dance around your own garden or window boxes to bless the soil. Rain dances should be accompanied by a ritualistic pouring out of water, shaking of rattles or rain sticks, or drumming to maintain sympathetic energy.

Another good activity to perform individually is a meditation to obtain messages from spirit guides. The most successful way to do this is through visualization while in a trance-like state. Once you are calm and centered, see yourself somewhere where you feel safe and totally at peace. Repeat the invocation below to open the door for guidance, then wait. Try not to have any expectations regarding what your guide may look like or say. Remember that animals and plants can be our teachers too! Make notes of your experience later.

Sample Invocation: Five is the number of psychic insight, so repeat this verbal component five times:

> *Spirit guides and Masters all,*
> *Those that would show me grace,*

Tis' to you I come and call,
While working magic in this place.

Spirit guides and Masters hear,
The prayers of one who would learn;
Remove from me outmoded fears,
Peace and wisdom born in turn.

Spirit guides and Masters meet
Your servant in this humble place.
Your lessons, timeless, with thanks I greet;
Come, join me in this sacred space.

Alternative Timing: Any date which celebrates a specific spiritual teacher.

Other Accents: I suggest performing this celebration at night using soft candlelight. This atmosphere is more conducive to reaching the intuitive nature, being aligned with the Moon.

August

August 1

LAMMAS (CELTIC)

Magical Themes: The harvest; gifts of the land; the wheel of life; skill.

History/Lore: In Old English, this holiday's name literally means *"Loaf Mass."* It is dedicated to agriculture, specifically the first harvest of grains for baking bread. The initial loaves made from this harvest were always saved as an offering for the altar. Even after the advent of Christianity, first sheaves of corn could be found over church doorways in honor of the Corn Maiden, the goddess of providence.

Decorating Ideas: Baskets of corn, grains, crabapples, hay bales, pitchforks, acorns for elemental points or altar accents (save them from the previous Autumn).

Garments: In Scotland, farmers make wreaths of corn to wear on their heads to venerate the harvest god. For your purposes, a garland of corn husks might be easier. Braid several lengths together as you would your own hair, then secure into a circular form, adding an acorn or small gourd as embellishment.

Ritual Cup: Apple cider or any fruit juice which comes from the first local harvest in your region.

Ritual Foods: A wonderful type of cake is a modest cornbread made with freshly picked raspberries. Here is a recipe:

Lammas Raspberry Cornbread

1 1/2 cups cornmeal
1/2 cup flour
1/4 cup vegetable oil
1 1/2 cups buttermilk
1 teaspoon vanilla
2 tablespoons butter
1 cup berries
2 teaspoon sugar
1 teaspoons salt
1/2 teaspoon baking powder
2 eggs
1 teaspoon ginger (optional)
2 tablespoons honey

Directions: Preheat your oven to 425 degrees and grease an 8" x 8" x 2" pan. Blend all your ingredients, except butter, honey, and berries, beating thoroughly for 1 minute. By hand, fold in the berries until evenly distributed. Pour into cooking dish and bake for 20 minutes. Meanwhile, melt the butter and honey together.

Use this mixture to baste the top of the bread during the final 5 minutes of baking. Serve hot or cold. Serves 6 people.

Incense: Apple or berry.

Activities: An early version of this holiday is associated with Lugh, a god of mastery, especially in the arts. If there is anything in which you wish to improve your proficiency, call on Lugh in your magic.

This is a fine day to attend a country fair, or plan a harvest picnic with others of a like mind. A fun game of Pagan origins to include in your outing is divination by sickle throwing. Have the children of your group take some cardboard and cut out the shape of a traditional sickle. Wrap the blade end with aluminum foil so it looks like an edge.

Now, think of a question. Spin around three times and toss the blade in the air while reciting the incantation below. The way it lands indicates your answer. If the open part of the sickle is facing you, that means opportunity is coming your way; if it points away from you, that means the path is not cleared yet. If the point of the sickle is toward the left, it is a sign of difficulties; if toward the right, smooth transitions. If the handle drops at your feet, it portends a time of work which will be rewarded, like the harvest!

Sample Incantation:

Blade of Silver, shining bright,
Reveal my answer with your flight.
Blade of Silver, guide me well;
With your fall, my fortune tell.

Also this Date: Many rituals with similar themes are held on or around this date, notably Native American corn festivals which rejoice in the Earth's bounty.

Other Accents: Any instrument played principally by using your hands is suitable to venerate Lugh.

August 1-3

DAYS OF THE DRYADS (MACEDONIA)

Magical Themes: Affinity with the spirits of the woods and water.

History/Lore: Dryads are linked directly to specific flowers, trees, or other natural objects, like rivers. The Macedonians considered these spiritual entities to be demi-gods, and as such deserving of appropriate veneration. Consequently, throughout this observance, no cleaning was to be done, nor any vine severed. Anyone wishing to wash had to carry iron to safeguard themselves from the *Drymiais'* (Dryads') anger. Similarly, anyone who disobeyed the taboo against disrupting water sources or greenery was certain to provoke mischief.

Decorating Ideas: In keeping with the reverence for nature, silk or dried flowers are the best choice. If you do want fresh flowers, pick them the day before, keeping them cool and watered until your observance.

Garments: Any items with depictions of natural settings and creatures.

Ritual Cup: Any liquid laced with a touch of honey. This sweetener is enjoyed by fairy folk.

Ritual Foods: Victorian women sometimes made sweet cakes for the fey. A good recipe for these cakes, which you can also enjoy, follows:

Fig Cakes

12 oz. dried figs (insight)
3/4 teaspoon dried thyme
3/4 cup flour
1/4 teaspoon clove
3 eggs
3/4 cup sugar or honey
1/2 cup chopped nuts
3/4 teaspoon baking powder
1/4 teaspoon nutmeg
2 teaspoons rum flavoring

Directions: Chop your figs finely, then mix them with the sugar or honey until well coated. Blend this with the thyme and nuts, followed by your other dry ingredients. Next, lightly beat the eggs with the rum flavoring. Mix this with the dry ingredients until they are moistened. A little cream may be added for smoother texture. Finally, bake this in an 8 x 8 inch greased pan at 325 degrees for 30 minutes. Leave to cool for about 10 minutes before turning out to cut. Drizzle with honey or sugar frosting. Yield: 32 half-inch bars.

Incense: A mixture of oak, ash, and thorn leaves, wood, or bark. These three trees are the sacred fairy triad of Britain.

Activities: Once your cakes are made, keep some for after the ritual and place the rest in the area where you want to attract devic energies. This acts as an offering and salutation. In addition, carry a four-leaf clover to detect the presence of Dryads or other natural spirits.

The children of your group (or home) will delight in this holiday. It affords the perfect opportunity to scamper through the woods (or local park) in search of fairy rings and paths. Have them make a map of these for "sighting" parties in the future!

Sample Invocation: You will need a small strand of sweet-sounding bells for this invocation. If you are not outdoors in a wooded setting, you should also obtain some pine needles and flower petals. Sprinkle these around the circle at the appropriate parts of the invocation.

> *Spirits of nature, from the Earth now shine;*
> *Show yourself to us, here 'midst the pines;*
> *Sing and dance for the day, or an hour;*
> *Let us be merry, here 'midst the flowers.*

> *Teach us of Earth, of the dew drops you cast;*
> *Tell us your history, your place in our past.*
> *Come all ye Dryads, to our circle come round;*
> *Appear to us here when the little bells sound.*

Alternative Timing: May Day, Lammas, Samhain; any traditionally active periods for the fairy folk.

Other Accents: Try marking the perimeter of your circle with straw, a favorite fairy hiding spot.

August 9

FEAST OF THE MILKY WAY (CHINA)

Magical Themes: Enduring love; arts of weaving and spinning.

History/Lore: As the story goes, the Sun God's daughter fell in love with an unassuming herdsmen one day while weaving. Unfortunately, her love led to languid repose after she was married and her needlecraft was neglected. The Sun God grew angry at this and banished the herdsman to the other side of the Milky Way. This man gets to see his love only once a year, thanks to magpies who build a bridge for him with their wings.

Decorating Ideas: Images of magpies and celestial objects. The Chinese decorate their sacred areas with rice, melons, and embroidery samples which also serve as offerings.

Garments: Any ornamentally embroidered item.

Ritual Cup: Rice wine.

Ritual Foods: Since rice is one of the things tossed at newly united couples to insure happiness, children, etc., a rice casserole spiced with traditional love herbs is fitting.

Love Rice Casserol

Directions: For 4, ¹/2-cup servings, prepare 1 cup of long-grain rice in 2 cups of boiling water. Add 1 teaspoon of thyme, rosemary, and marjoram to the water, along with a sprig of saffron. When this is fully cooked, toss the rice with freshly diced tomato, a little lemon juice, and salt and pepper to taste.

Incense: Jasmine and rose for romance. For the artistic side of this holiday, I suggest yellow lunar flowers such as gardenia and jasmine.

Activities: Making miniature scenes from flower pieces, rice, and almonds is traditional. For your purposes, arrange the

Figure 22. Almond and rice rune of partnership.

base items into a magically harmonious form, such as the rune of partnership. In this example, there are two almonds at the center of the rune to represent the individuals. Radiating from these, lines of rice are glued and decorated with little leaves and petals to look as if they were sprouting (see figure 22). The finished emblem inspires growing love.

Sample Prayer: Fill in the blanks according to the goals of your efforts on this occasion:

> *Lady and Lord of the Night Sky,*
> *Heed my prayer.*
> *Grant to me (*love/inspiration*)*
> *   on this night which remembers you.*
> *I put my (*hopes/skill*) before the altar of the Milky Way*
> *To be showered with the blessings of Stars and*
> *The (*romance/imagination*) of moonlight.*

Alternative Timing: Panathenaea, St. Valentine's Day, Mass for the Broken Needles.

Other Accents: Possibly a shepherd's crook, which is used as a wand or athame for directing your magical energy.

August 11

PERSEID METEOR SHOWER

Magical Themes: Heroic energy; astrological studies; wishes.

History/Lore: On or around this date, up to sixty meteors an hour are visible in a clear sky, centered in the constellation of Perseus. Since this phenomenon began around A.D 800, people have gathered to watch it. For a while, it seems as if the sky is alive with fire.

Somehow, this seems very appropriate to the constellation of Perseus, his personal "fire" being the focus of Greek legends. Perseus defeated the Medusa, constructed the Atlas Mountains, and delivered Andromeda from a sea monster. These heroic accomplishments entitled him to be honored as a constellation.

Decorating Ideas: Use aluminum foil or cardboard, paint, and glitter to make constellations to place on the walls. These will sparkle in candlelight.

Garments: Have a little fun. Use black garments to which you have added metallic or glow-in-the-dark paint. The patterns applied should look like moons and stars. This way, when the lights are off, the only thing visible will be moving celestial objects, dancing with you!

Ritual Cup: An astrologically representative beverage with twelve ingredients (one for each sign of the zodiac). One example is blending 2 cups apple juice with a drop of almond extract, $1/2$ mango diced, cantaloupe pieces, a dash of nutmeg and allspice, a bottle of fruity wine, and an equal portion of champagne over a bed of ice. This is served in glasses garnished with fresh mint leaves.

Ritual Foods: Round out your celestial array with foods symbolic of the Moon, Sun, and planets. To this end, try cucumbers in sour cream and dill sauce as an appetizer. Follow with a hearty barley and cheese soup flavored with chives and sage. For dessert, serve a healthy portion of fresh tangerines and grapefruit.

Incense: For strength, use pennyroyal, bay, and carnation. For wishes, blend violet with dried dandelion petals and a hint of sage.

Activities: Stand outside and count the number of meteors you see. As you do, focus your mind on a question. At the end of the shower, look up your final count on a list of numerological correspondences for its meaning.

Sample Invocation:

Perseus, Lord of great deeds,
Help me in my quest;
Renew in me the strength to face tribulation
With a brave soul and courageous spirit.

As we waltz beneath your heavenly array,
Dance with us, weaving hopeful starlight
Into our hearts.

Other Accents: An after-ritual costume party might be enjoyable. Come as your favorite constellation!

August 13

FESTIVAL OF DIANA AND HECATE (ROME)

Magical Themes: Prayer and thankfulness; the cycle of life; women's mysteries.

History/Lore: In Roman mythology, Diana is the youthful Goddess and Hecate is the Crone. In this way, this festival honors the full circle of creation from birth, to death and rebirth.

In Christian times this celebration became the Assumption of Mary. Its earlier version, however, was a day for Roman women to venture to the temples of Diana or Hecate. There, prayers were recited for abundant crops for the coming season, and the women also thanked the goddesses for answering their supplications of the previous year.

Decorating Ideas: For Diana, cover the altar with apples, moonstone, almonds, mugwort, and hazel leaves or branches. For Hecate, add garlic buds, poppies, and moonwart.

Garments: Something silver to commemorate both goddesses' lunar aspect.

Ritual Cup: I suggest a cream liqueur: the milk to symbolize the more youthful goddess, and the alcohol for the mature woman.

Ritual Foods: Lunar edibles, including buttered cauliflower and broccoli florets, a white-cheese mushroom soufflé, potatoes, poppy seed rolls, and watermelon with vanilla yogurt.

Incense: Jasmine and ginseng for Diana; myrrh and musk for Hecate.

Activities: A holiday best celebrated on, or near, crossroads (old meeting young, life vs. death). This is a festival for the night. Both goddesses have strong lunar and underworld associations, giving you occasion to consider your own dark-self.

Ultimately this holiday also celebrates the feminine aspect within each of us. Meditations and musings on what "yin" means to you are appropriate, as are exercises to integrate positive feminine characteristics into your life.

An excellent date to choose for a coming-of-age ritual or croning rite for a woman. Also a good time to extend extra support and appreciation toward the women notable in your life.

Sample Invocation:

Daughters of the Moon,
I call as one of your own.
Let me bask in your splendor
As we reclaim the night.

Help me appreciate the Goddess within
And manifest Her without;
Help me confront my shadows
With the Moon as my guide.

Daughters of the Moon
I am your child.
Wrap me once more in your gentle arms,
There to nurture and grow.

Alternative Timing: October 31 is a good day to remember Hecate, the patroness of witches! August 17 is one date on which a festival for Diana was held wholly in her honor.

Other Accents: Any emblems associated with these divine figures: bows, arrows, and the bear for Diana; the night owl, willow trees, torches, and dogs for Hecate.

August 18

EISTEDDFOD (DRUIDIC — WALES)

Magical Themes: Bardic skill; initiation; rune work.

History/Lore: This tradition was so important that it was announced a year and a day in advance. First came a parade of bards wearing blue and green robes, representing potential officials and bardic candidates respectively. The full Druids wore simple white robes that symbolized virtue.

Following the processional to the standing stones, prayers were said to open the festivities. Those wishing recognition as bards presented all manner of music and stories for those in attendance. Prizes were given to those worthy, including the coveted award of the bardic title. Anyone accepted as a bard then read from a book of runes, and received a blue knotted belt in recognition of their new station. After this event, the bard was always honored and welcomed in Welsh homes and taverns.

Decorating Ideas: Outside or in, bring some good-sized stones to mark your circle. If you wish, paint them with emblems appropriate to the element they represent. If possible, add a sprig of dried mistletoe, the most sacred of all druidical plants, to your altar.

Garments: Those among you who follow druidical ideals should don white. Any desirous of following a bardic magical tradition (one which remembers history in story and song) should wear green. Anyone wishing to move into a stronger leadership role in their group or community should wear blue.

Ritual Cup: Since this celebration is commemorated with a great deal of speaking and singing, a lemon-honey tea is advisable to soothe the throat.

Ritual Foods: How about a well-loved Welsh dish, rarebit, for creative versatility. Folklore tells us that dishes like this were made by peasants as a substitute for real rabbit, which was too costly for them. Here is a recipe:

Druidic Welsh Rarebit

12 oz. cooked broccoli (hot)
5 slices toast
3 1/2 tablespoons butter
3 1/2 tablespoons flour
1/2 teaspoon salt
1/4 teaspoon pepper
1/2 teaspoon Worcestershire sauce
1 cup milk or cream
3/4 cup cooking wine
1 1/2 cups diced cheese

Directions: Using a sauce pan over a low flame, melt your butter. To this slowly add the spices, Worcestershire sauce, and flour, stirring until smooth. Next, beat in the milk, slowly bringing the entire mixture to a boil. Gradually add cheese and wine until the sauce is creamy. Lay bundles of broccoli over each piece of toast and serve with sauce. Serves 2-3 people.

For a unique touch, cut out aluminum foil in the shapes of beneficial runes and place them on your bread before toasting in the oven. This will leave the mark of magic on the toast to be internalized as you eat.

Incense: Scents which invigorate or inspire you.

Activities: These will vary greatly, depending on your intentions. In a group setting, individuals who would like to begin more bardically-centered services to the whole should come prepared to perform. Everyone in attendance can vote to determine who will take the position of bard among you.

This position can be served for a term, such as a year, or be a permanent honor. In either case, the magical bard should be marked with a blue knotted ribbon, even as the ancients were. Women can use this as an ornament for their hair, and men can wear it as a favor, hung from a belt.

Sample Spell: Gather three long strands of white, blue, and green yarn or ribbon. Also take one more of any color to represent yourself. Repeat this verbal formula seven times, while carefully covering the strand of self with your magical goals (the other ribbons). Keep this token with you as a portable amulet for creativity.

Together I bind,
Round and round, wind
Blue to water the seed,
Green to make it grow,
White, the light within,
The magic now begins!

Alternative Timing: Festival of the Minstrels (August 16, England).

Other Accents: Leave your favorite musical instrument on the altar to be blessed during your festivities.

August 21

SACRIFICE TO HERCULES (ROME)

Magical Themes: Business; honoring the god aspect; strength, mostly physical in nature; control of anger.

History/Lore: Ancient Romans made offerings to the god Hercules on this day. Also known as Herakles to the Greeks, he became the patron god of businessmen. The proper tithe at this time of year was one-tenth of a merchant's annual profit. In addition, a huge banquet would be held in Hercules' honor, any leftovers of which were released to the Tiber River.

According to legend, the twelve labors of Hercules were a sentence imposed on him by the Delphic Oracle to atone for a fit of anger, basically putting Hercules' strength and energy to more positive uses.

Decorating Ideas: Logos and business cards from your office or personal company positioned around the room or altar; amethyst to control the disorderly self; figs and dates for physical strength.

Garments: A Roman toga or your normal business attire.

Ritual Cup: There is a beverage known as Roman Punch, which was enjoyed tremendously in England around 1800. While it had little to do with Rome, its ingredients are masculine and thus useful to this festival.

To prepare, mix 1 quart of orange juice with 13 tablespoons of orange liqueur (the number of forbearance and conviction). Pour this over ice with 2 quarts of champagne. Garnish with pineapple chunks, tangerine bits, and marigolds (for the solar aspect).

Ritual Foods: Raw vegetables were a favorite food in Rome, both as dessert and appetizers. In choosing your vegetables, select ones that have a natural masculine association (cucumbers) or which can be cut accordingly (celery). Carrot sticks, long scallions, broccoli florets with stems, and thinly sliced green peppers are some other choices.

Incense: Musk and other rich, sensual aromas for the god aspect; bay leaves and black tea for vigor or lemon balm mixed with ginger for success.

Activities: Focus positive energy toward your profession on this day. Put a symbol of your job in the center of the circle and have everyone extend their hands toward that point. Visualization and chanting can follow, according to your goals.

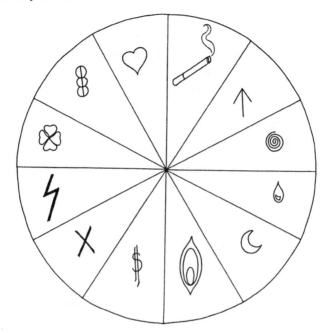

Figure 23. Personal symbol calendar. The symbols are examples of the kinds of things you may want to overcome or achieve for each of the twelve months: January—quit smoking; February—improve conviction; March—spirituality; April—cleansing self; May—improve psychic abilities; June—fertile efforts; July—improve money; August—improve relationships; September—self-joy; October—peace with self; November—healing; December—love self.

Keep this token at your office or job site to maintain and release power where it's intended.

If there is anyone among you who has been ill, make them the center of your circle. Chant their name, using positive affirmations which are mirrored by the entire group. An example would be, "Sandy is healthy," or "Sandy is strong." Continue until your chant naturally quiets to a whisper.

Finally, in the spirit of Hercules' twelve labors, make yourself a special calendar. Begin with a circle of cloth made from twelve colors, one for each month of the year. On every section, paint or sew a symbol of one thing you want to overcome or achieve that month (see figure 23, page 137). Put this in your personal magical space. Each time you see the calendar, it acts as a reminder to perform spells and rituals pertaining to the theme of the month you are in. Bless and empower this tool using the incantation below, repeated once for each month, as you apply your emblems to the surface.

Sample Incantation:

Twelve labors have I set,
Twelve goals to follow through.
I will not cease until they're met;
My magic will stay true.

In _____ (month) it's _____ (goal) I seek.
By this mark, the spell's complete.

Alternative Timing: Feast of Kites and Banners (May 5, Japan).

Other Accents: In wrestling with the bull-headed snake, Hercules tore off one of its horns, which became the cornucopia. This emblem would be a terrific highlight for your altar. After your ritual, take it to work as a periapt for fruitfulness.

August 26

BIRTH OF KRISHNA (INDIA)

Magical Themes: Immortality of the soul; victory over seemingly impossible circumstances.

History/Lore: This day celebrates the rebirth of Vishnu as the child Krishna. It is said that Vishnu reenters the world whenever it needs guidance. Hindus go to midnight observances where images of the baby Krishna are heralded with the word "victory" to welcome the god among them. Of all Vishnu's incarnations, Krishna was the most engaging, kindly and sometimes mischievous.

Decorating Ideas: Items associated with Vishnu include topaz, the color yellow, bay, laurel, and vines.

Garments: The sari. This is comprised of a long piece of cloth, often ornamental, which is wrapped around the upper body. The loose end is brought over one shoulder and secured in place by a pin.

Ritual Cup: A beverage savored in this region of the world is dark, rich coffee spiced with cardamom. If the weather is hot, serve this over ice.

Ritual Foods: In India, a predominantly Hindu nation, a favorite dinner might consist of flat bread called *nan*, with a spiced chicken roasted over straw. For our purposes, a barbecue will suffice. The additional benefit in using the following recipe is that most of the herbs are magically associated with victory and success:

Victory Chicken

2 pounds boneless chicken
2 cups plain yogurt
3 tablespoons dark orange bergamot tea
3 tablespoons crushed garlic
1 teaspoon powdered ginger
1/2 teaspoon cinnamon
1/2 teaspoon cardamom
1/2 teaspoon pepper (any)
2 bay leaves, crushed
4 tablespoons butter

Directions: Prick the chicken on all sides with a fork. Marinate the meat at room temperature, in a covered container, using the yogurt, tea, and garlic. Leave this to soak for 4 hours. Meanwhile, melt the butter with all remaining herbs. This will be used as a sauce. About 30 minutes before dinner time, prepare your grill, waiting until the coals are white. Cook the chicken once on each side before beginning to baste with the butter. Turn and baste frequently until the chicken is done throughout. Serves 4-5 people.

Alternatives: A nice addition to the barbecue sauce is 4 tablespoons of honey and 1 tablespoon fresh lemon juice.

Incense: Any yellow solar herbs such as sunflower, chamomile, and chrysanthemum.

Activities: A notable day to contemplate memorial services, especially those commemorating spiritual teachers. Also perform rituals, spells and charms to bring success into your life. One good exercise is to recite positive affirmations throughout the day, each time you encounter a set of stairs going upward. With every step, claim your victory. With the descent, relinquish negative habits and thoughts.

You can also make yourself a victory amulet by combining any four of the following in a small, blue pouch that can be carried about: agate, hematite, tulip petals, grass, oats, or blackberry leaves. Augment this by using the spell given below.

Sample Spell: Repeat this six times, a number associated with Krishna:

> *Success and Victory, here I claim*
> *My life will never be the same.*
> *From this day forward, with power Divine*
> *Success and Victory will be mine.*

Alternative Timing: All Souls' Day, Samhain, Day of the Dead, Royal Oak Day, St. George's Eve.

August 29

WINEGROWERS' FÊTE (FRANCE)

Magical Themes: Honoring Pales, Ceres, Bacchus; making ritual wine; the energies of satyrs and fauns.

History/Lore: In the 16th century, a guild formed among the winegrowers of Vevey, France. Each year, until 1889, they held a special festival, attended by thousands of people, that had many similarities to the Cerealia in Roman times. Louis XV costumes were donned. Next came a parade guided by a depiction of Pales, the goddess of flocks, wearing a robe of blue. She was followed by white oxen, children dressed as shepherds, and yodelers. Next to come was Ceres in a flowing red gown, accompanied by harvesters and bakers. All around this, fauns and satyrs danced merrily, wearing appropriate garb. Afterward, everyone retired to a night of feasting and drinking in the company of friends and local leaders.

Decorating Ideas: Corn for Ceres (or any cereal item); a shepherd's crook, or pieces of wool for Pales; wine, grapes, or ivy for Bacchus.

Garments: If you're good at costuming, anything from the Louis XV era is one choice. Otherwise, dress yourself as a faun or satyr.

Ritual Cup: French wine, of course. Grape juice for children.

Ritual Foods: Since Pales is the goddess of flocks, lamb is an excellent option. One recipe from France calls for thinly sliced lamb, marinated with scallions, garlic, lemon juice, tarragon, marjoram, wine and olive oil. These slices are then stuffed with a chicken and mushroom filling, broiled, and basted, for the enjoyment of all.

Incense: Finely chopped corn husks as a base to commemorate Ceres. To this, dried raisins and bits of wool thread are added for Bacchus and Pales.

Activities: One of the most enjoyable ways to celebrate this holiday is by throwing a wine-making party. Everyone who wants to participate should bring a gallon jug with a cork or screw top, 1 12-oz. can frozen fruit juice, 1 pound fresh or frozen fruit, 3 pounds sugar, 1 package active yeast, 1 tea bag, 1/2 inch fresh ginger root, and 1 orange or lemon (whichever matches your other ingredients best).

The juice (undiluted) goes into a nonaluminum pot with 3/4 gallon water, the sugar, and fruit which has been peeled, cored, and cleaned. Bring all to a low rolling boil. Add the ginger root, tea bag, and citrus, continuing to boil for 15 minutes.

Figure 24. Magical candleholder.

Cool to lukewarm and strain. Next, add 1/2 package of the yeast which has been suspended in warm (not hot!) water for at least 15 minutes. Stir once and cover the pan with a heavy towel for 24 hours. Strain the entire mixture into your gallon jug and cork *loosely.* After about 10 weeks, you will be able to secure the top more tightly as fermentation slows. Enjoy this at next year's Winegrowers' Fête.

Another activity especially pleasurable for children is making ornate candleholders from old wine bottles. These, once completed, will not be limited in use to just this observance. In addition, using up bottles and scrap craft items will help in your efforts to recycle!

Begin with the bottle as a base. From here, many effects can be created including:

• gluing a fabric remnant around the base. Lace this up one side and paint with magical insignias (see figure 24);

• gluing seashells over the entire bottle. This is a nice piece for the western quarter of your circle;

• dripping candle wax of different colors over the outside edges of the bottle. Use in the southern quarter of your circle;

• covering the bottle with lace, to which feathers are added, for the eastern quarter of the circle.

Sample Invocation:

Ceres, Pales, Bacchus, Come!
Gather your cups and lift them high
To catch the blessings from the sky.

Then take a knife to cut the vine.
Today we shall celebrate the making of wine!

Ceres, Pales, Bacchus, Attend!
We thank thee for all the abundance you send.
Founders of our feast, join us we pray;
We honor your presence, here today.

Alternative Timing: Palilia (April 15, Ancient Rome); Choes Festival; Vinalia (November 11, Ancient Greece); the Bacchic rites.

Other Accents: Bedeck the perimeter of your room or circle with real or plastic bunches of grapes and Indian corn decoratively laid out over pieces of wool cloth. Use candles secured in old wine bottles to light the altar.

September

Early September

APACHE SUNRISE CEREMONY (NATIVE AMERICAN)

Magical Themes: Coming-of-age for women; transformation.

History/Lore: This is a four-day ritual in which a young woman becomes an adult member of the tribe. This rite is believed to insure her longevity and blesses the other participants.

Before dawn on the morning of the ceremony, the girl will come to a predesignated area with a decorated cane which she will always keep as an emblem of long life. She also wears a disk of abalone on her forehead. When the first rays of the Sun touch the shell, it is believed the "changing woman" enters her, thus making her an adult. A series of prayers, songs, dances, and stories follow. These serve as education on the transition from birth to her new role.

Decorating Ideas: Depending on where you are holding this ritual, a black curtain can be set up behind which the girl can wait. This way, no matter what time of day it is, she will still move from darkness into light. Also any symbols which have strong associations with positive change, such as the butterfly, are appropriate.

Garments: Buckskin blouse and skirt are traditional, with feathers placed on the shoulder and in the hair. These items are to bring the girl light-footedness while dancing. They are also regarded as protective amulets, usually being made from eagle down.

Ritual Cup: Blend together 1 cup of frozen raspberries, 1 cup of frozen strawberries, and 2 cups of orange juice. Magically, this is for friendship, happiness, luck, health and meditation.

Ritual Foods: It would be best to fast for one to three days before this ritual to cleanse the body of all impurities. If this is impossible for medical reasons, consider a ritual bath instead.

After the rite, a light meal should be prepared with some of the girl's favorite foods to enjoy.

Incense: At the end of this ceremony, the girl is often showered with pollen to bless her. Thus, any flower with the pollen intact can act as a foundation for incense to grace the entire group!

Activities: The actual activities that take place on an occasion like this need to be very personalized. In all cases, however, something should be done during the ritual which marks the transition you are making. To illustrate, if trying to change a bad habit like smoking, crush the cigarettes beneath your feet. Afterwards, lock the pieces away in a box, throwing away the key to terminate that part of your life.

If using this date for a coming-of-age, a change in hair style, clothing, and location in the circle are all suitable. In this instance, an item the girl can make for herself is the longevity stick, following the Apache tradition. To prepare, the girl should choose a wood known for its strength and longevity: redwood and oak are two options. The wood should be soaked to release the bark, then sanded thoroughly. Finally, anoint the staff with oils of lavender, lemon, and sage to insure long life. Once completed, this is a personalized tool to use like a wand (or walking stick) as the child takes on her adult role in your gathering.

Sample Prayer: For the candidate to recite:

Old Ones,
Those that existed before all else,
I stand before you as a child —
One who has grown and learned much
At the feet of her elders,
Take me under your wing.

I come to you today, no longer a youth,
But as one who must walk a new path.
Give me strength and wisdom for this role,
That I might serve the greatest good
Throughout my womanhood.

Alternative Timing: Bona Dea (May 3).
Other Accents: Pictures of the girl at various stages of her youth placed around the room. Surprise guests from the youth's past to share this moment with her.

September 9 (approximate)

CHRYSANTHEMUM DAY (CHINA AND JAPAN)

Magical Themes: Long life; renewed vigor; fealty.
History/Lore: On the ninth day of the ninth Moon, chrysanthemum wine is enjoyed in China to insure longevity. In a land where age equals wisdom, this is indeed an important

Figure 25. Scented vinegar jar.

event. The Japanese also observe this festival with ambitious flower shows. Originally, this was the date when all feudal lords met with the Shogun as a show of fealty. As a side note, the chrysanthemum has been cultivated in Japan for over 2000 years. It was honored as the central emblem on the Japanese flag: a chrysanthemum with sixteen petals gathered around a central disk. In both China and Japan, this flower is grown for its loveliness and used in cooking.

Decorating Ideas: A plethora of chrysanthemum buds. Leaves from the plant can be used to cover small tables, or placed in a bowl on the altar. Roots bound together make a good token of the earth element.

Garments: Any items with a petaled motif.

Ritual Cup: A simple chrysanthemum wine can be made by warming a quart of white wine over a low flame. To this add 2 teaspoons of sugar. Pour the mixture over 16 fully opened chrysanthemum buds, leaving to soak until they become slightly translucent. Strain and serve cold.

Ritual Foods:

Long Life Salad

Directions: A healthy salad is prepared by mixing 1 pound of salad shrimp with 3 diced, cooked potatoes, 3 sliced hard-boiled eggs, and 4 large, chopped chrysanthemums (washed). Toss and garnish with sweet french dressing and a hint of lemon juice. Serves 3-4 people as a side dish.

Incense: If you can't obtain dried chrysanthemum, try lavender for long life.

Activities: During your observances on this day, leave a container of freshly picked chrysanthemum heads on your altar. After the festivities, place them in a decorative container which has a secure lid. Pour warm cider vinegar over top of the buds, securing the lid and adding a little ribbon (see figure 25, page 146). Give this as a gift to someone who has been ill. It makes a lovely scented vinegar, good for marinating pork or as a salad dressing for health.

A game children can play is divining their future with chrysanthemum petals. Pick petals in a wide assortment of colors and place them in a bowl, well mixed. Then, have each child close their eyes and pick a petal. The color of the petal indicates what the child's life will be like (make your interpretations very positive). Here is a sampling of ideas along those lines:

red—a life of excitement and adventure;
yellow—a life with many friends and full of creativity;
white—a peaceful life, perhaps a home in the country.
purple—riches and stature;
two petals stuck together—a happy marriage.

Sample Spell: Take a bowl full of chrysanthemum petals and sprinkle them around yourself while reciting this incantation nine times:

Petals scattered to the winds,
So this magic may begin:
Once for luck, twice for health,
Thrice for joy, four for wealth,

Five for trust, six for peace,
Seven that faith may never cease,

Eight that love will soon be mine,
Nine — long life, within me shine!

September 13

ALL SOULS' DAY (EGYPT)

Magical Themes: Honoring Nepthys; remembering the dead; summerland rituals.

History/Lore: On this day in Egypt, the fires of the temple were lit in honor of Nepthys (Nebthet), the protective goddess of the dead. Sometimes she is also associated with the edge of the desert (an in-between place) which can be fertile or dry, depending on the Nile.

Decorating Ideas: Oak and nettle, silver, and iron are all associated with Nepthys. Also, the hieroglyph of her name has the sign for a basket, so fill a few with aloe plants for the altar.

Garments: If remembering those who have passed over, their favorite outfit is a nice touch.

Ritual Cup: To promote emotional healing, use a base of papaya and passionfruit juice, sprinkled with a garnish of coconut.

Ritual Foods: The Egyptians were fond of roast pig. The Norse also regarded the sow as a magical creature which symbolizes eternal life. So, in this setting, pork in some form is doubly fitting.

Incense: Myrrh and tobacco for Nepthys; for Summerland rites, a base of cypress wood (if possible), to which lavender and violet are added to bring serenity to the heart.

Activities: I hesitate to specifically outline activities for memorials and summerland rituals because of their highly emotional and personal nature. First to consider is the individual being remembered and what they would appreciate. Include their favorite magical music, invocations, dances etc., as a way of sharing your sacred space with that memory. Bring something personal of theirs into the circle and invite their spirit to join you.

While some folks find it unnerving to see happy people at a memorial or funeral, I think the element of joy is important to the healing process. At times like this, it is good to remind yourself that death is a beginning, and a new opportunity for the soul to grow and learn. With time, the understandable sadness you feel should be replaced with happiness for your loved one(s) in their new existence.

The Egyptians remembered their ancestors. They made food offerings for visiting family spirits. This was based on the idea that providing spirits with token offerings in the afterlife kept them from haunting their descendants In your setting, this translates into a special meal prepared for your family or coven, with edibles which the people you are commemorating enjoyed.

Sample Invocation:

Nepthys, Guardian of the Land of the Dead
Release the soul known as _____
To join us this day,
For we honor his/her memory.

Let _____ *come to us to dance once more,*
Among those that love him/her.
Let us have fellowship of spirit
And rejoice in our common bonds.

We open the door and our Sacred Space
To you _____.
Be welcome among us.

Alternative Timing: Samhain; Day of the Dead (November 2, Mexico); Festival of Hungry Ghosts (August 16, China)

Other Accents: Pictures of your loved ones can improve the connection with the spirit world. Invite people with solid channeling abilities to join you if possible. They might be able to share a message from the deceased.

Use of a Ouija board is appropriate, with proper cautions. To make a simple version of your own, cut 3 x 5 cards into thirds and write the entire alphabet on them (one letter per piece). Lay these out with a little tape on a table along with two other squares that say "yes" and "no." Use a glass or light ashtray as your "pointer," touching it only with your finger tips. Concentrate on the individual to whom you wish to speak, and

Figure 26. Homemade divination board made of 3 x 5 cards and a glass.

try to test the response you get with a very personal question. If you are uncertain, dismiss the spirit *immediately* to avoid any intrusion into your space by an unwanted entity.

September 15

BIRTHDAY OF THE MOON (CHINA)

Magical Themes: Awakening the lunar aspects (intuition, fertility, creativity); prosperity.

History/Lore: In many eastern lands, the Moon represents the supreme feminine aspect (or yin) of the universe. This holiday comes from an ancient story about the emperor Ming Wong, and his dedicated priest. The two were walking together in the garden one night when Ming Wong asked of what the Moon was made. Instead of trying to explain, the priest transported the emperor to the Moon by magic. Ming Wong was so overjoyed by this experience that, as he returned to Earth, he played his flute while showering people with gold. When members of the royal house inquired the next morning about the beautiful music and showering of gold, Ming Wong claimed that the miracle transpired because it was actually the Moon's birthday.

Decorating Ideas: Lanterns or candles burning all night (in fire-safe containers); white oriental paper lanterns to represent the Full Moon's façade.

Garments: Silver or white robes to represent the Moon.

Ritual Cup: Grapefruit juice for sharp awareness; also egg nog for the lunar aspect.

Ritual Foods: The favorites, by far, in China are candies and Moon-shaped cakes. One easy way to prepare the latter is to use crescent rolls as a base. The center of the rolls can be stuffed before baking with lunar fillings such as broccoli, mushroom, cauliflower, butter and herb sauce, blueberries in natural syrup, or lemon cream

Incense: In China, one incense is made from cassia wood, whose seeds bring immortality. Sandalwood, lotus, and jasmine are other options, all having an "Eastern" flavor and lunar associations.

Activities: Traditionally, fruits of the harvest are taken to rooftops to bask in moonlight. This brings well-being and blessings to all those who partake of the foods later. If you don't have a roof, use any surface that faces the Moon, like a picnic table. Lay out any nonperishables that you plan to prepare for a meal later that night.

An activity in which the children of China participate is watching for falling sky flowers. In effect, this is meteor gazing, and according to Chinese beliefs, seeing one portended fertility for young women and wealth for young men.

Another game you could set up for the littlest members of your group is a coin hunt. This can be done in a pile of hay or sand to which a healthy helping of nickels and dimes has been added (silver, for the Moon). For the most positive and balanced outcome, participating children should be very close to the same age. When a signal is sounded, they all jump in and hunt for their prosperity. Later, they can take the coins to a store and purchase one of their wishes!

Sample Invocation:

Lady Luna, with silver guise,
Ever shining, ever wise,
Grant me through your Moon beams, bright
Creativity, productivity, and fresh insight.

Lady Luna fill this glen
So our magic can begin.
Dance the skies till morning's light;
Hold us safe, through all the night.

Other Accents: Flute music, in memory of the emperor who founded this holiday; a birthday cake for the Moon, complete with white frosting and silver garnishes.

September 17

ELEUSINIA (GREECE)

Magical Themes: Honoring Demeter; connection to nature; fertility.

History/Lore: Local legend claims that Demeter taught the Eleusinians how to grow crops because of their kindness to Persephone. During this festival, which has many secret rites, Demeter (nature) is honored for her lessons. The activities for this celebration can actually continue into October. Demeter is the Greek goddess of flourishing lands.

Decorating Ideas: Cat's-eye stones, sunflowers, and any silver items; bowls or baskets of barley.

Garments: Personal choice.

Ritual Cup: A berry juice or wine. Because berry bushes produce so many fruits, they make an excellent tribute to this goddess. Alternatively, try sunflower coffee. Dry the seeds, then roast them to a light brown in the oven. Once cooled, grind them to an appropriate consistency for your percolator. Measure as you would regular coffee.

Ritual Foods: Beef and barley soup with berry pies. Any harvest items, such as corn and squash. Sunflowers are also edible, tasting somewhat like artichokes. Boil the buds, adding a little pepper and butter for a side dish.

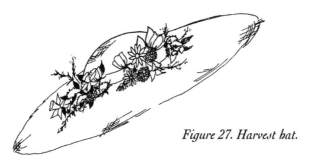

Figure 27. Harvest hat.

Incense: Myrrh and musk.

Activities: Make yourself a harvest hat! Begin with a woven corn hat like those worn by farmers on hot days. Gather silk flowers which are representative of the elements such as:

> **earth**—fern, honesty, magnolia, primrose, tulip;
> **air**—broom, clover, dandelion, goldenrod, lavender, mint leaves, pine;
> **fire**—bay leaves, carnation, holly, marigold, snapdragons, woodruff;
> **water**—crocus, daffodil, daisy, gardenia, Irish moss, morning glory, tansy.

Place these on your hat in the appropriate quarters, securing them in place with glue or florist's wire. Add a bit of ribbon for an accent and wear during your ritual or at any summer outing (see figure 27)!

Sample Prayer:

Demeter, Mother of the Earth,
Let the abundance we see around us
Also blossom in our hearts.
Teach us the lessons your land reveals,
Of planting, growing, harvesting,
And of the fallow time, when all is being cleansed.
We would to live in harmony with nature;
Pray, be our guide.

Alternative   Timing: Lesser   Eleusinian   Mysteries (February 1-3).

Other Accents: Any paintings or drawings of farms whose crops have grown full and plentiful.

The Autumn Calendar

utumn's theme is one of bounty resulting from hard labor and positive efforts. The Earth is sharing its wealth, but this prosperity is not without some overshadowing portents. The frosty months are just around the corner, giving Autumn a cool air and a more conservative demeanor.

Traditionally, Autumn is the time when housewives can and preserve foods to stock their shelves for Winter. The curtains around the home are changed to heavier, darker tones. Warmer clothing is subsequently unpacked, and set out for the children. Hats and coats are donned to deter the sniffles caused by chilly morning air enroute to school. Spiritually, this equates to husbanding your health and resources so that neither gets overextended. It also means a renewed focus on your cognitive mind, including religious studies.

Autumn's colors are those of the harvest itself. Burnt oranges, deep reds, and brilliant yellows are everywhere. Summer still shows its strength with hints of green throughout the foliage. Winter is not without some representation too, nipping the edges of leaves with bits of brown.

The sacred space for Autumn is full and bountiful. Waxed leaves, huge pumpkins, squash, apples, and other foods abundant to this season are perfectly suitable. Scents for the season include many from your own kitchen, such as cinnamon, basil, apple, and sage. Divine entities to bless your efforts include:

Istat Ix — Mayan goddess of insight;
Gwion — Welsh god of learning;

Althea—Greek goddess of abundance;
Dionysus—Greek god of the vine and fertility;
Freya—Teutonic goddess of fruitfulness;
Sati—Egyptian goddess of productivity;
Apollo—Roman god of health;
Kedesh—Syrian goddess of well-being;
Bannik—Slavonic god of the home;
Penates—Roman gods of the hearth;
Pax—Roman goddess of peace and harmony;
Jambhala—Buddhist god of plenty;
Vasudhara—Hindu goddess of prosperity;
Thor—Scandinavian god of protection;
Hadad—Babylonian god of storms;
Mari—Basque goddess of weather;
Saranya—Hindu goddess of clouds.

Gemstones associated with Autumn are: opal in October, which brings victory and success; topaz in November, providing the ability to move without a trace (topaz is also a stone which deepens friendships and love, and protects against fire); and, turquoise for December to prevent the wearer from experiencing any harm should they fall.

Spiritual efforts enhanced by Autumn timing include spells, rituals, and celebrations centering around completing unfinished tasks, preparedness, frugality, practicality, abundance, and study.

GENERAL AUTUMN CELEBRATIONS

Autumn is a time of gathering—a time to conserve resources and make provision against the coming Winter. It is also a time for giving thanks for the fruits and pleasures of Summer. In general, autumn observances center on harvest festivals, feasts honoring specific crops and their associated deities, religious pilgrimage, weather divinations, celebrations of thanksgiving, and rituals reflecting the approach of the Winter Solstice, with its shortening of day and lengthening of night. Here are some interesting examples of autumn rites:

Harvest Festivals

Having some origins in the Bacchic rites, which celebrated the collection of grapes for wine, harvest festivals are a tribute to the Earth's abundance. Throughout these gatherings, thankful appreciation to Gaia is shown through offerings of first fruit, libations, and song.

In rural areas, farmhands came together to cut the last stalk of corn. This was done so all parties would be equally responsible for the death of the "corn spirit." Another similar custom is found in Lithuania, where people dance with the last sheaf of corn reaped. In this case, the corn is dressed as an old woman (a type of the crone) and waltzed around for good luck. If you like this idea, make your own corn crone by using a whole ear of corn as your base. Let it dry so that it takes on a wrinkled appearance before decorating.

Figure 28. Corn crone. Left: a ball of fabric is attached to the top of the corn cob with string. Right: completed corn crone.

The end with the stalk becomes the crone's head by affixing to it a ball of fabric with a length of string. Drape the body
with a bit of scrap cloth for a dress. Another fabric remnant is
cut to form an apron (see figure 28, page 157). If using this doll
for a group observance, pass her around the circle clockwise as
you dance for good fortune, or counterclockwise to mark the
shortening days.

Harvest celebrations indicate one more step toward maturity on the ever-turning Wheel. The frost (or rains) appear as
gentle reminders to us that Winter is not far behind. The hunting season now begins. Hold a special ritual to protect animals
that may become injured accidentally during these months. If
you, yourself, hunt for food, give thanks to the creature and the
Earth for its providence.

For the children of your group, hold a corn-husking game
before your feast. Here, the first child to discover an ear of corn
with red in it gets to claim a prize. Traditionally, it was being
King or Queen of the night's festivities, or claiming a kiss from
someone admired.

This is an excellent time of the year to begin drying and
canning foods as your forefathers did. Label them with the
moonsign of preparation and any affiliated magical significance.
This way, your spiritual efforts get preserved for year-round
blessings! If you do not have time for this, restock your canned
goods to symbolically refill the well of self before the fallow season.

REMEMBERING THE DEAD

Ancient peoples associated this season with death and the underworld, since darkness was becoming more predominant.
Consequently, the partition between worlds became thin, allowing spirits to sneak through! Because of this, bits of food were
left on tables, window ledges, and at grave sites to appease any
wandering souls.

One example of this custom comes from China. On the first
day of the tenth month, the Chinese hold a Festival of Death.
Here, ancestors are offered clothing and money through ritual

fires. Based on the belief that spirits need protection from Winter's cold, the participants burn these tokens to send them to the netherworld! In Mexico, November 1 is set aside for rituals similar in theme. Individuals dress in costumes and have family picnics at a cemetery to share with loved ones. The tone of this event is lighthearted, with all manner of skeleton and skull edibles as garnishes.

Both these examples are fairly fitting to the Pagan/Wiccan views on death. Since we regard this passage as a beginning or transition, continuing to share time with those who have passed over seems appropriate. It also affords healing and a sense of closure to those relationships.

Exactly how such rites are observed is fairly personal, but cues can be gathered from the examples given. Make some of the deceased's favorite foods to enjoy, leaving some behind as a "gift." Make sure these are consumable by wild animals.

Bring a picture of the loved one(s) into the sacred space. Share good memories of them with those that have gathered. Have each recollect some cherished memory about each ancestor or friend. Incorporate as much of the positive aspects of their life's story as possible. When done regularly, this ritual becomes a kind of oral history to be passed on from generation to generation.

One item interesting to produce at these memorials is a memory quilt. For this project, everyone attending brings one piece of scrap cloth which represents the person they are honoring. Just like the sewing bees of old, everyone sits around in a circle, adding their stitches to the whole piece. As they do so, conversation centers around happy memories of those who have passed over.

It may take many gatherings over the years to finish this. Once completed, it makes a beautiful cover for the altar, filled with all the best recollections of those we have loved woven into it.

FOOD FESTIVALS

Reminiscent of, or an actual part of, harvest festivals, food celebrations center around a specific edible. Exactly what foodstuffs are featured depend on the culture, the region, and the local folklore. In Haiti, for example, yams are honored when the crop is ready for harvest. Bowls of this vegetable are offered to all recently deceased progenitors. They are also placed before the household gods. After these rites, the dinner meal centers around yams, including a yam-and-fish stew.

Two other Autumn food festivals occur in Sweden and Scotland. The first, known as the "Dividing of the Cheese," occurs in September. This holiday is observed by Swedish herdsmen who have aged their cheeses in cooperative cellars for a year. When the cellars are opened, the entire day is spent sampling and sharing. Magically, this theme emphasizes giving to those in need and the concept of perfect trust.

Later in September, Carrot Sunday was remembered in Old Scotland. Carrots were gathered, tied into bunches, and taken to churches overnight to have spells incanted over them. Anyone gathering a forked carrot was very fortunate, as it was a good omen. The next day, the carrots were taken back home for blessing the residents and for regular consumption! On a spiritual level, this equates to rituals and spells for improved luck and positive prophecy.

No matter the edibles, or their emblematic associations, food festivals are best celebrated by eating and having old-fashioned fun. In early America, they were accompanied by barn dances and spelling bees. For these, the loft of a farm was decorated with garlands of fruit and vegetables as a reminder of the harvest.

Games involving foods were also provided so children weren't left out of the merrymaking. These included potato-peeling contests, apple eating, and pumpkin hops. In the first two cases, there is plenty of room for magical variations. With potato peeling, use the remnant peels as you would an ink blot or tea leaves, interpreting the meaning from their shape.

Alternatively, as was done with apples, toss a peel over your shoulder and see what letter of the alphabet it appears to represent. Someone with a name starting with that letter will become important in your life's work. Potatoes are emblematic of foundations, being a root crop.

For apple eating, the object of the game is to see who can eat an apple the fastest. Afterward, the children count the number of seeds in the center. Make up some entertaining, positive associations to go with that count. For example, two seeds would portend good friendships, three is a sign of someone with perseverance in life, four is for success in business, etc.

THE PILGRIMAGE TO AND FROM MECCA

Every Muslim must make at least one pilgrimage to Mecca in their lifetime to visit Mohammed's place of birth. This journey, known as the *Hajj*, must begin on the seventh day of the month of *Dhu'l* (this varies on the American calendar). Before arrival at the sacred city, the pilgrims must bathe, pray, and slip on ritual garments. They then proceed to a temple, believed to have been built by Abraham, and walk around it seven times. Afterward, a visit to the Mosque is made to drink from the sacred well. And with this, their journey has only just begun!

Next, they climb the hills of Safa seven times reciting prayers. On the eighth day, all pilgrims gather in the desert to worship from noon to sunset, and gather seventy pebbles from the sand. These represent the evils of the world, and are thrown at pillars as a means of purification.

When the travelers finally returns home, sometime in early November, they are greeted in the streets of Cairo with cries of, "Blessings on the Prophet. Oh God, favor him!" Their horses are adorned with ostrich plumes, bells and seashells —the signs of a pilgrim. They are welcomed home with a feast, where gifts are presented to their family. Presents include water from the sacred well, palm leaves, combs, shawls, and dust from Mohammed's tomb. Until the next set of pilgrims sets out, each person who has traveled is given the honors befitting such a quest.

The Mecca pilgrimage is a reminder of our own reclusive times; periods in our life when we must leave what is "safe" and "comfortable" to discover true spirituality. Autumn, being a time of drastic change, is the perfect season to consider such a retreat for yourself or your group.

For some individuals, the spiritual pilgrimage can be leaving home for the first time. For others, it equates to a vacation alone, a few days of meditation and study, participation in a workshop, or a change in life style. Whatever approach you choose, allow yourself time to integrate the lessons learned over the last year, and acknowledge yourself as a child of the Universe.

DIVINATIONS

Combined with many holidays throughout this season, especially Halloween, are all manner of divination techniques. For example, the Inuit of North America hold an elaborate tug-of-war between "Summer" and "Winter" on November 3. Only individuals born in those seasons may participate as part of the tug. The outcome forecasts the weather to come. Should Summer win, the weather will be mild. If Winter overcomes, then the climate will be harsh.

St. Matthew's Day (September 21) is also filled with portents for weather and love. If it is fair, the clear skies will last four more weeks. In Germany, girls make straw and pine wreaths on this day. These are piled together, and one is chosen randomly in the dark. A green wreath portends happiness and health; the straw wreath warns of sadness or illness.

The number of types of divinations used throughout this season almost boggles the mind. Nuts or stones are placed on fires to see how love interests will fare. If they spark and pop, things are bound to be argumentative! In rural areas, roosters are given five piles of grain to choose from to foretell the general mood for the family's year. Each mound is named in advance, the first nibbled at giving the forecast. Finally, twisted apple stems or whole peels are used to discover the name of one's future love.

Any or all of these methods are entertaining to try at points during the Autumn cycle. Consider making your own tarot deck or rune set from natural items.[7] Find a hazel twig to "water

---

7. See my *Victorian Flower Oracle* (St. Paul, MN: Llewellyn Publications, 1994) for instructions to make these.

witch" with. Learn a new type of divination skill, all the while enjoying the richness of your magical heritage!

YOM KIPPUR

The most sacred of Jewish observances, this is the Day of Atonement (early October). The devout spend the entire day in fasting and prayer, seeking pardon. This forgiveness is not only for oneself, but for any of the Hebrew faith and Israeli nation who have erred. An old allegory illustrates to children the importance of this date. An angel was commanded to go to Earth and gather the most precious thing he/she could find. In the end, the item held dearest to god was the tear of a truly repentant individual.

While most magical traditions do not talk about "sin," we all have faults which could be tackled during this observance. Extend the hand of peace to family members or friends from whom you have been estranged. Most importantly, make peace with yourself. A cleansing bath is one ritual to follow during this holiday. Fill a tub, adding pine and lemon for purification. Then sit in the soothing water to meditate on ways to heal your heart and the schisms in your life.

SUKKOTH (MID OCTOBER)

This is a Jewish harvest festival, also known as the Feast of the Ingathering. It dates back to the time when many of the Jewish tribes were farmers who slept in their fields to protect them from thieves. There, they would set up the Sukkah, a humble booth made of leaves and branches.

This celebration lasts nine days, during which the family commemorates the early farming years with meals in a Sukkah-style enclosure. This is often designed around a porch or garden. Within the home, four plants are set up to be symbolic of the holiday. A palm tree, citron, twigs of myrtle, and willow branches are set out to gently remind the family of ethical lessons: apply the scriptures, do good deeds, and lead a good life. On the final day of celebration, the Jews express joy in the Torah and recite special prayers for rain.

In a magical setting, the theme of this holiday is manifold: honoring history, safety, watchfulness, and respect for sacred writings. Commemorate those individuals who gave foundation and form to your tradition. Perform spells and rituals to improve vigilance. Try writing some new invocations and prayers for your Book of Shadows.

Adopt the Jewish symbols by utilizing their metaphysical associations in an incense. Use dried palm leaves for protection and fertility. Citron will improve health and psychic abilities. Myrtle brings love, and willow wood engenders flexibility.

FEASTS OF LAMPS OR LIGHTS

Designed mostly as symbolic attempts to give strength to the Sun, rituals honoring all light sources have a predominant place in the Autumn calendar. In mid-October, Brazil has a week-long festival of lights which includes a barefoot processional for cleansing away sins. Other analogous celebrations include the Birthday of the Sun (September 20) and the Chinese Sun Salute.

Likewise, the Tibetan Festival of Lights (late November) commemorates the ascension of one of the Lamas founders. The Floating of the Lamps in Thailand (mid-October) is a symbol of awakening and spiritual insight. The Feast of the Burning Lamps in Egypt (late November) was observed by all country-men, no matter where they were. In this instance, as many lamps as possible were purchased, lit, and left burning all night.

Figure 29. Symbolic candle.

For your own light festival, there are numerous games and crafts to consider. One possibility is a contest where a yellow beach ball is used to portray the Sun. The longer the solar disk is volleyed off the ground, the more strength you give to its return!

Another option is using this holiday to make candles specifically carved and blessed for your purposes. Throughout the remainder of the year, have family and friends save their wax drippings for remelting and casting. Scent the melted wax with herbal oils that mirror your intended use. Then, pour the wax into a wax milk carton or other well-lubricated container, add a wick, and let cool. To release your candle from the mold, just dip it into boiling water for a few minutes. The finished product can be carved, or wrapped and set aside until you need it (see figure 29, page 164).

THANKSGIVING RITES

Tied in very closely with harvest festivals is the spirit of thankfulness that permeates Autumn celebrations. As the richness of the land is gathered in, we are grateful for our needs being met for another year. This also increases our awareness of those less fortunate, an awareness exhibited beautifully by the Asking Festival of Alaska, described later this chapter.

In the United States, Thanksgiving Day commemorates the Mayflower's passage to America in 1620. One year after their arrival, the Pilgrims celebrated their survival through a feast shared with the Indians, who had taught them to grow corn. Besides eating partridge, venison, fish, and oysters, the participants played games and held races throughout the day. Abraham Lincoln proclaimed this a national holiday in 1863.

One unique "thanksgiving" celebration is the Aloha Festival of Hawaii. This observance lasts for one week and rejoices in the heritage of the Polynesians. It is a time of great feasting and merriment, with special emphasis on gratitude toward Lono, the god of plenty and fertility.

For your own Thanksgiving holiday, follow the suggestions of our ancestors and make a feast with all the trimmings. Bread or stuffing are two integral ingredients, being emblems of providence. The beauty of breads is their adaptability in the magical kitchen. To honor Jupiter, for example, begin with frozen bread dough to which finely chopped, cooked broccoli is added along with sage. As the bread cooks, the smell of the herb rises with your thanks to the god! You could also make apple-almond stuffing in a feast to acknowledge Diana. Here is the recipe (to fill a 15 pound turkey):

Giving Thanks Stuffing

4 tablespoons butter
3 large, sweet apples
1 cup diced almonds
1/4 cup honey
1/8 cup water
allspice and nutmeg to taste
6 cups bread crumbs or croutons

Directions: Melt the butter in a frying pan over a low flame. Meanwhile, peel and finely dice your apples. Put these in the pan to sauté until tender, adding the almonds halfway through. Next, pour the honey and water in the pan along with your seasonings. Stir until everything is well mixed. Pour this over the bread crumbs, adding more melted butter or water for moistening, if needed. Stuff your turkey with the mixture, or bake it in a covered pan at 325 degrees for 45 minutes, stirring twice for even cooking.

September

September 22 (approximate)

AUTUMN EQUINOX

Magical Themes: Balance; the cycle of life, death, and rebirth; caution with resources.

History/Lore: The word *equinox* owes its origins to the Roman goddess *Nox* whose dominion is the night. Consequently the exact meaning of *equinox* is "equal night," a time when light and darkness share the sky equally. From this point forward on the calendar, the daylight hours shrink, which is why Autumn is a season often associated with spirits of the dead.

Many civilizations had different beliefs and practices associated with this date. The Egyptians enacted a special rite called "Staves on the Sun" to help support the solar disk in its journey. While the actual movements of the rite are unknown to us, we do know that celebrants held wooden staves to the sky during the ritual.

Among the Japanese, this is a day to remember one's ancestors, and specifically, members of one's family who have recently passed over. In Buddhist beliefs, heaven lies due west, exactly where the Sun sets on this date. For them, the holiday is called *Higan*, meaning "other shore"—the place where souls abide.

Decorating Ideas: Opposites! Black and white table cloths; one half of the room lighted, the other dark (with candles for starlight).

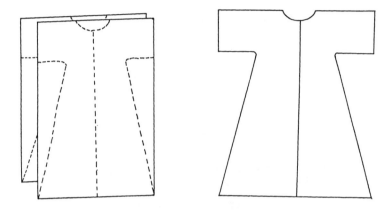

Figure 30. Varicolored ceremonial robe. Left: using a shirt that fits you, cut out your design on a piece of dark fabric and on a piece of light colored fabric. Right: cut each piece down the middle.

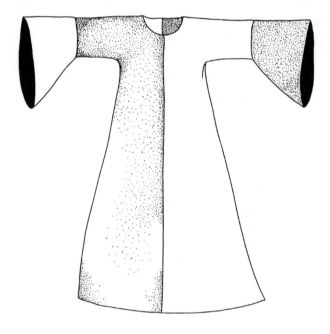

Figure 31. Finished varicolored robe.

Garments: If you enjoy sewing, make a varicolored robe in black and yellow. To ease difficulty of construction, purchase material which is the same on *both* sides. A person who is of average build and around 5'9" tall will need 2 yards of each color. Lay both pieces together on a flat surface. Using a shirt that fits you well, cut out the basic shape of a robe, leaving an extra 2 inches on all sides, and cutting the hem 12 inches from the bottom edge of the fabric. Now, fold this figure in half and cut right down the center of it, from the neck to the hem (see figure 30, page 168). Trade one dark piece for one light piece on each half, then stitch the halves together, using 1/2 inch seams. Sleeves should be the opposite color of the side to which they are attached. These are cut from the 12 inches of fabric you took from the bottom. Hem the edges of the sleeves and robe before doing a final 1/2 inch seam up both sides (see figure 31). Adjust the neckline so it is comfortable, and finish by doubling under the fabric. Add trim as desired.

Ritual Cup: Lemon-limeade. Mix 2 quarts of water with 1/4 cup each of lemon and lime juice. Add sugar to taste. This beverage yields a perfect symmetry between solar and lunar energies, and it is very refreshing!

Ritual Foods: To continue this theme, here's a tasty snack. Fill half a pineapple (Sun) with white grapes (Moon) mixed with cashews, oranges, tangerines (all solar) and raisins. Also, you can substitute a honeydew melon (lunar) filled with fresh grapefruit slices for the pineapple and white grapes.

Incense: Aromatic woods mixed with spices that remind you of Autumn (such as pine).

Activities: The Egyptians ritually lost, then found, an image of a bull during their rites on this day to dramatize the continuing power despite the waning season of the sun god, Osiris. This can be turned into a game of hide-'n-seek for the youths of your group. One child with a stuffed bull becomes the Sun (maybe they can don a yellow hat or shirt). While the others cover their eyes, the "Sun" tries to hide the bull, and him/herself, from the rest of the group. The person to find the child raises the bull high in the sky (moving the Sun back into power), then gets to be the next one to hide it.

Autumn Equinox is regarded as a fire festival. One way to observe it is by employing the element of fire in scrying. For this, assemble a brazier or bonfire with five ingredients, one for each point of the pentagram. Suggestions include rowan wood, cinnamon, lemongrass, dried marigolds, roses, dandelion, ash, oak, and woodruff.

Once the fire is prepared, unfocus your eyes and watch the flames dance. You may notice that an image appears in the center of the flames, just as you sometimes see forms in cloud formations. These images will be representative of your answer. Or the flames may act differently as you focus your attention. If they begin to smolder, it is a negative sign. If they burn steadily, it portends consistency. Bright, active flames indicate change or a positive answer.

Sample Invocation/Prayer:

Light and Darkness, in skies so fair,
With quiet acceptance, duly shared —
The time to sow, the time to reap,
The time of promises, each must keep.

So, as the dusk gives way to dawn
And day gives way to night,
We give our lives to harmony
And balanced inner-sight.

Lady, Lord, see our hearts
Hand in hand, as one
We merry meet and merry part;
The magic is begun.

Also this Timing: Festival of Osiris; Chinese Salute to the Sun.

September 25

DURGA PUJA (INDIA)

Magical Themes: Safety and protection; the mother aspect of the goddess; honoring parents and other adult role models.

History/Lore: This celebration is in remembrance of the goddess Durga, who has ten arms. According to Indian lore, she defeated the thousand-headed king of demons to protect her people. Throughout this festival, children pay their respects to parents, and everyone tries to settle quarrels they have had with friends, in honor of Durga's victory.

Decorating Ideas: Durga's color is yellow. Fill your sacred space with golden items in groups of ten (one for each hand)! Use lemons, yellow squash, and husked corn to help with this.

Garments: Anything of yellow color. White is an alternative, to notify others of your peaceful intentions.

Ritual Cup: Options include any fruit or spice that encourages harmony, including apple, peach, apricot juice, or marjoram tea.

Ritual Foods: Prepare a freshly tossed cucumber, lettuce, and olive salad with saffron rice and any main course. This is to bring renewed peace and accord among those partaking.

Incense: Lavender and violet are two good choices.

Activities: Durga is but one aspect of the goddess Parvati, the wife of Shiva. She is usually shown sitting beside him as a conversation partner. Her attributes include grace, brilliance and companionship. This may be why this holiday is frequently celebrated in India as a family reunion.

If the weather has not turned too harsh or rainy yet, a family gathering is an excellent activity for this day. Get together with old friends, coven members, or classmates. Heal any wounds that were left between you and forge the foundation for improved relationships.

By way of special invitations, make decorative stationary with scented meanings. For this, purchase some notepaper (blank sheets) and gather dried, pressed flowers and leaves. On one corner (usually the lower left or right) try a couple of unique

Figure 32. Special symbol stationery.

arrangements with the plants, maybe using the rune of communication as a pattern to build from. Once you have a design you like, glue the flowers in place with latex adhesive then cover with self-sticking clear film (see figure 32).

Make one of these per person. Put the whole bundle together with some scented potpourri for fourteen days. Choose your scent according to the magical intentions of the gathering. For joy and harmony use lavender; for romantic love, use red rose; and for friendship, use lemon. If you can't find appropriate potpourris, scented oil placed on the underside of the flower arrangement works, as will a spritz of your favorite perfume.

Sample Prayer:

Durga, mighty protectress,
Teach us the ways of harmony.
Help us to reconcile the past, and give hope to the future.

Even as you overcame great evil,
Help us to set aside the pain from old wounds,
Keeping their lessons, but not the anger.
And, once the healing has begun,
Help us to guard peace with each other
As a sacred trust.

Alternative Timing: Any traditional "family" gathering.

Other Accents: Challenge the youths of your group (or home) to come up with their own way to show respect to the elders in their lives or to make peace with each other.

October

October 2

FEAST OF THE GUARDIAN ANGEL (SPAIN)

Magical Themes: Protection, divine blessing and guidance; triumph over evil.

History/Lore: In 1672, Pope Clement X proclaimed this day as a time to give thanks to the angels who have guarded and protected us. In Spain, this feast is commemorated with bonfire blazes on the church porch and music played on the gaita (a kind of bag pipe). Bells announce the commencement of the fiesta, which includes processions, sword dancing, and people dressed in bells and scarves.

After elaborate ceremonies in the church, people return outside to watch a ritual drama. Here, two sides mimic good and evil before the image of an angel. Of course, good always wins!

Decorating Ideas: Bells of all sizes hung on strings around the sacred space and hanging off the edges of the altar. Use colorful scarves to cover the altar itself.

Garments: If you feel inventive, try making a whole robe out of scarves. Secure bells to any end that is not sewn or tied into your construction.

Ritual Cup: Anything garnished or lightly spiced with angelica. This herb was so admired in early history that people believed it was a gift from the angels themselves!

Ritual Foods: Using an angel-shaped cookie cutter, make warm white angels from this recipe (let children frost and decorate):

Angel Cookies

1 1/2 cups butter (soft)
2/3 cup white sugar
3 1/2 cups flour
2/3 teaspoon baking powder
1 1/4 teaspoons vanilla
confectionery sugar (glaze)

Directions: Beat the butter and sugar together to get a creamy consistency. Slowly sift in the flour, sugar, and baking powder, while continuing to stir. Blend in vanilla. Place on a rolling surface dusted with flour, and press to a 1/2 inch thickness. Add more flour to the dough if needed for proper rolling texture. Cut out your angels and bake at 350 degrees for 12-15 minutes until lightly browned. Cool before decorating. Yields about 24 angels.

Incense: Frankincense and myrrh seem strongly associated with "heavenly" realms, so keep with that tenor.

Activities: The children would probably enjoy recreating the tug-of-war. Whichever side wins can become the token guardian angels for your celebration, perhaps by assuming a special role in creating the sacred space.

Within the circle, this is a superb day to commune with your guiding spirits, or to find them, if you have not already. If participating in a group, set aside private time where each individual can go somewhere "alone" to meditate, take notes, etc. Alternatively, one person who is versed in mediumship could open themselves to a message from a collective guide for the entire group.

Sample Invocation:

Guardians of the Spirit World,
Bend down your ears to heed
The appeals of those within this space
For lessons that they need

> *Spirit Guides and Masters, all,*
> *Reveal to us your words;*
> *To our minds and to our hearts,*
> *Let yourselves be heard!*

Alternative Timing: Feast of the Milky Way; any saint's day.

Other Accents: *Chrysalis* by Richard Church is one option for music, as are Gregorian chants and any "airy" New Age sounds.[8]

October 7

KERMESSE (TEUTONIC — GERMANY)

Magical Themes: Reverence toward religious symbols; blessings and revelry.

History/Lore: Kermesse, while originally a pagan festival, blends both Christian and pagan symbolism. Kermesse is a week-long festival, marked by the ritualistic digging up of a sacred symbol. This emblem is mounted on a large pole and brought into town to announce the start of games, feasting, dancing, and song (rather like May Day). One cannot help but wonder if the "digging up" is symbolic of recovering the old gods which were displaced by the church. Some of the activities that follow tend to encourage that conclusion.

For example, one day of the festival is known as Young Men's Day. On that morning, the young men are led by a priest to the church. Each of them wears a mask which represents the ancient gods. Here hymns are played, but not always with rev-

---

8. Robert Church, *Chrysalis*. Llewellyn, 1988.

Figure 33. God and goddess masks.

erence. Afterward, the youths of the area go to nearby homes for beer, cookies, and kummel.

Decorating Ideas: Have each member of your group bring their god/goddess emblems to be blessed at the ritual. These can be placed around the room, or on the altar, to accent the sacred space.

Garments: Masks which portray your personal patron god/goddess are an excellent choice. One simple way to make these is by using an old mythological calendar or book which has large portraits in it. Remove the one you desire and secure it to a piece of sturdy cardboard. Trim around the face you have chosen. Next, place two small holes on one side of the visage and slide a chopstick (or other small stick) through them as a holder (see figure 33).

Ritual Cup: Beer is traditional. Alternatively, mead (honey wine), which was a common beverage for the gods in mythological tales.

Ritual Foods: During the Middle Ages, none but those of noble birth were allowed to hunt in the rich gameland of Germany's Black Forest. This area was likened to the paradise that hunters went to after death. One recipe to come out of this "heavenly" region is given below. Chicken may be substituted for venison, or a heavy portion of freshly cut vegetables for non-meateaters. Serves 4 people:

Sacred Black Forest Stew

> 2 pounds venison, cubed
> 1 cup red cooking wine
> 1/4 cup red vinegar
> 2 tablespoons dried onion
> 1 tablespoon minced garlic
> 1/4 teaspoon thyme and rosemary
> 1/8 cup juniper berries
> 1/2 cup olive oil
> salt and pepper
> 1/4 cup butter
> 2 medium onions, sliced
> 2 stalks celery, chopped
> 2 tablespoons flour
> 1 cup beef broth
> 1/2 teaspoon Worcestershire sauce
> 1/2 cup sour cream

Directions: Marinate the venison in the next eight ingredients for a full day in the refrigerator. Drain. Warm the butter in a large frying pan, add the meat and brown it on all sides. Add the onions and celery, likewise browning them, stirring constantly. Next, add the flour to form a paste, then put in the broth and Worcestershire sauce. Simmer for one hour, checking the meat for tenderness, then add the sour cream. Serve with thick noodles or homemade dumplings.

Special Note: A favorite German dessert to go with this meal is stewed pears. These are particularly fitting if your goddess is Athena. Also, the Chinese believe pears promote longevity!

Incense: Try to choose fragrances associated with your patron god/goddess to set up harmonic energies in the room.

Activities: Younger children can enjoy a game of hide-'n-find while the adults attend to other activities. For this game, have someone in your group ritually conceal a sacred symbol along with a little sweet or prize. This person should be a volunteer who doesn't mind overseeing the children as they search. The child who finds the symbol can hide it for the others to seek out, again adding a little token gift for the "winner." This can continue as long as desired.

For adults, I suggest a ritual cleansing and blessing of the icons they have brought with them. Have some spring water prepared with a little lemon juice to purify the images from any residual energies. Then rededicate them to the god/goddess they represent.

Sample Invocation: Because of the wide variety of god/goddesses which can be embodied in this celebration, this invocation/prayer is rather generic, intended to appeal to the vastness of the Great Spirit:

> *Maiden, Mother, Crone,*
> *Son, Father, Grandfather,*
> *We have gathered before your image(s)*
> *To look upon this guise, and know*
> *It is but a fraction of Your greatness.*
>
> *Purify and bless this likeness*
> *That it may forever be an inspiration*
> *And reminder of our spiritual Path.*
> *Let us not wander from it.*

Alternative Timing: Any day which honors your god/goddess.

Other Accents: Besides the god/goddess images, you can also choose to sanctify any religious jewelry, works of art, books, etc.—anything that, to you, represents and enkindles your faith.

October 12

Holiday of Fortuna Redux (Rome)

Magical Themes: Luck and safety while traveling.

History/Lore: This is a festival to remember the goddess of travelers. It is said that placing chamomile flowers in your suitcase on this day will insure pleasant journeys.

Decorating Ideas: Bumper stickers, T-shirts, old airline tickets and luggage tags, small suitcases, and travel brochures.

Garments: Whatever you plan to wear when you take your next trip.

Ritual Cup: Champagne is one beverage frequently associated with travel, especially by sea. If going by air or car, try coffee, tea, or soda instead (whichever you drink most readily).

Ritual Foods: Most people I know eat "fast" food when they travel on the road, so have your banquet table filled with favorite edibles from the nearest burger stand. Or fill a picnic basket full of foods you sometimes prepare for trips instead.

Incense: Chamomile.

Activities: Make a portable amulet for any trip using mint leaves, a moonstone, a piece of turquoise, and dried chamomile (this is easily obtained in the form of tea). Wrap these in a white cloth, along with a token which can represent you or your family. Strongly visualize protective white light pouring into the bundle as you tie it off with ribbon or string (see figure 34).

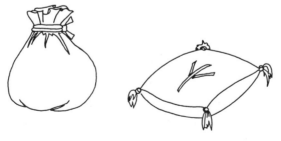

Figure 34. Portable amulet. Left: sachet. Right: pillow.

A slightly larger version, without the stones, is made into a pillow by using two 12" x 12" pieces of sturdy white material. Sew them right sides together, leaving one edge open for stuffing. Turn right side out and stuff with mint and chamomile. Then finish the final edge, while reciting the incantation below to bless your efforts. To decorate the final product, consider adding the rune of protection using fabric paint (see figure 34, page 179).

Sample Incantation:

> *Little bundle tied with white,*
> *Filled with safety, burning bright,*
> *We carry close this magic charm*
> *To keep us guarded from all harm.*

Alternative Timing: Brendan's Voyage (May 16, Ireland).

Other Accents: Prepare your charm in the same hour that you plan to travel in order to increase its effectiveness. Other emblems of safe travel for use in spells and rituals include road maps, old inspection stickers, road signs, and seat belts.

October 19

BETTARA-ICHI (JAPAN)

Magical Themes: Good luck.

History/Lore: Throughout the streets near the Ebishu shrine in Japan, people meander through crowds of merchants. Each of these creative craftspeople has come to sell good luck charms! The most widely purchased trinket is usually a rope within which are knotted gluey pickled radishes. People believe that this object ensnares luck so it cannot escape!

Decorating Ideas: Have each participant bring one homemade good luck charm to adorn your circle.

Garments: Wear something in your "lucky" color (or a lucky shirt, tie, hat, etc.).

Ritual Cup: Drink orange-pineapple juice with a hint of nut-meg. All three ingredients are associated with improving your fate.

Ritual Foods: Black-eyed peas and rice, and any green foods are two options. Alternatively, this recipe from the East can be used. The principal ingredient is cabbage, another luck food:

Good Luck Pork and Cabbage

1 pound lean ground pork
1 teaspoon ginger
1 can minced water chestnuts
1 medium onion or 3 scallions finely chopped
1 egg
salt and pepper
1 medium head cabbage
3 tablespoons cooking oil
1 cup chicken broth
1 tablespoon soy sauce
1 teaspoon garlic powder (optional)
1 1/2 teaspoons cooking sherry
4 teaspoons cornstarch

Directions: Mix the pork with the ginger, chestnuts, scallions, egg, salt, and pepper. Blend thoroughly, as you would a meatloaf. Form the mixture into large meatballs, the number of which should equal your lucky number. Fry these in the cooking oil for about 6 minutes. Remove and drain, retaining the oil.

Next, remove the core of the cabbage and detach the leaves. Fry these for about three minutes or until they become tender. Add the meatballs, along with the chicken broth, soy, garlic powder, and sherry. Simmer in a covered pan for 1-1 1/2 hours. When cooked, remove the cabbage and place the meat-balls decoratively on it. Retain the sauce, adding cornstarch, to use as a gravy on both the cabbage and meat. Serves 4-6 people.

Note: For variety, you can add a little diced orange, nutmeg, or poppy seed to this mixture for serendipity!

Incense: Allspice, holly, heather, oak shavings, rose, straw-berry, or violet.

Activities: Adults can create a scented hot-tea plate which will release fortunate aromas each time it is used. For this you

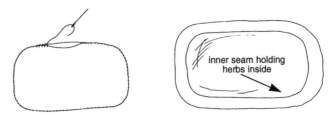

Figure 35. Scented hot-tea plate. Left: sew fabric leaving a three inch opening. Right: finished hot-tea plate with sachet stuffing.

will need one cup of a mixture of either rose petals, violet petals, and heather petals (along with some essential oils for each), or allspice powder, nutmeg powder, and finely grated orange rind. You will also need 4 pieces of 18 x 13 inch fabric, two pieces green, and two of a linen-type material.

Once the material is cut, cut the linen fabric to be 1/4 inch smaller all around than the green fabric. Sew it all the way around, leaving an opening to turn it right side out, and fill it with herbs. Use overstitching to finish the final side (see figure 35). Set this aside for the moment. Next, stitch the right sides of the green fabric together, leaving a 3 inch opening. Turn this right side out and gently place the linen sachet inside, so that the herbs are evenly distributed. Now finish the last edge of the outer fabric and press to even the edges. Finally, about 1/2 inch from the edge of the tea plate, stitch an inner circle. This helps hold the herbs and linen in place. Use this any time you have hot tea. The heat radiating from the pot will release the fragrances of luck.

For children, we can take a hint from the Japanese use of pickled radishes. A less messy approach is to have the children string balls of Styrofoam, using a needle and heavy-duty thread. Each ball should be secured by a knot. Then, using two-sided tape, make a central band of "stickiness" on each ball. Once

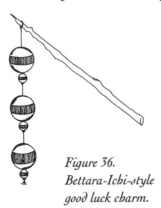

Figure 36. Bettara-Ichi-style good luck charm.

completed, the ropes can be dangled off a stick into a bucket of green construction paper shards (see figure 36, page 182). Each piece of greenery captured portends one incident of good luck for that child in the ensuing year.

Sample Invocation:

Ebisu, Master of Fortune,
Let fortuity reign,
In our homes and our lives,
Negativity, wane.
We beg now a boon —
Good luck, bring again."

Alternative Timing: November 24, Tori-No-Ichi (Japan). This is another festival of good fortune where participants carry decorated bamboo rakes to gather in their luck. The emblems on this rake are all traditional good luck charms.

Other Accents: Using the idea of Tori-No-Ichi, make a special luck-rake for your ritual. Use this like a wand to scribe the circle and direct your magic.

October 25

FEAST OF ST. CRISPIN AND ST. CRISPINIAN (CATHOLIC — FRANCE)

Magical Themes: Care of the needy; escaping difficult situations.

History/Lore: The two brothers, Crispin and Crispinian, are the patron saints of shoemakers. In order to help the needy, they delivered leather to the cobblers' shops by night to make shoes. Eventually, they were arrested for their beliefs, but managed to survive four execution attempts! Later, the Roman Catholic church recognized their kindness with canonization and set aside this date to remember them.

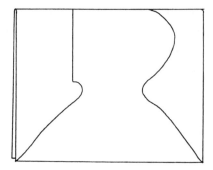

Figure 37. Monk-style hood pattern. Folded fabric is cut at least 20 inches along the bottom, 8-10 inches along the neck line, and twelve inches from top of head to neck.

Decorating Ideas: An old story has it that the first celebration of this holiday so pleased the saints that they lowered a ladder of pea vines from heaven. So, if you have any vines from your garden, or a bowl of fresh peas from the supermarket, keep them handy.

Garments: Monk-styled robes. These are imitated by simply adding a detachable hood to any of your robes and using a rope belt. To make the hood, cut out two pieces of fabric. Stitch up the back seam with right sides together (see figure 37). Turn under the face seam and hem the bottom edge. You can then either leave the front open and adorn with a pin, or sew the opening closed for a full-circle effect (see figure 38).

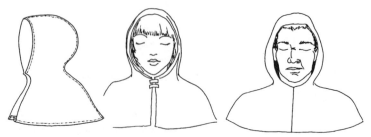

Figure 38. Finished monk-style hoods. Left: turn under seams and hem. Center: hood with pin front closure. Right: hood with front seam sewn closed.

Ritual Cup: In earlier historical settings, beer was regarded as the drink for the "common man." It was also a beverage often prepared by clergy, and so would be suitable to this setting.

Ritual Foods: During the European famine of the 1500's, peas were one item which helped the poor to survive. This may be why the saints were depicted dangling pea vines from heaven. With this in mind, we can look to a French dish which abounds in peas for part of our ritual feast. This recipe serves two people as a side dish.

Ham and Peas from Heaven

1 pound of baby peas
2 slices of honey ham
2 whole cloves
1 small minced onion
1/2 cup beef bouillon
1/4 cup heavy cream
1/2 tablespoon butter
1 teaspoon flour
salt and pepper to taste

Directions: Place the peas (fresh are best) in a sauce pan with the ham, cloves, onion, and beef bouillon. Simmer for about 12 minutes or until the peas are cooked through but not soggy. Remove the ham and peas to blend in the cream, butter, and flour. Stir until you get a smooth consistency. Pour over the ham and peas.

Incense: Rose is the flower predominantly associated with saintly figures; lily is a secondary option.

Activities: In the town where the brothers were buried, there is a procession of shoemakers and a meeting of the cobblers guild. In your setting, this translates into a walk-a-thon, organized to support a charitable cause. Alternatively, buy some good, practical shoes and donate them to a local orphanage or shelter.

This holiday is definitely centered on the "sole" (excuse the pun). During your rituals, take an extra moment to bless your feet (see sample blessing, page 186) which provide daily support and movement.

Make a special powder to place in your shoes to deodorize them, encourage health, and bring beneficent spirits into your life. This is easily prepared by blending together:

Sole Powder

1/2 cup cornstarch
2 tablespoons orris root
1 teaspoon powdered lemon
1/2 cup baking powder
2 tablespoons crushed mint leaves

Alternative or Additional Ingredients: 2-3 drops of pine, bayberry, or cedar oil. Mix and allow to dry before storing in an airtight container. Sprinkle in your shoes as needed!

Sample Blessing:

God/goddess, bless my feet that I might
Walk true to my beliefs,
Stand firm in my convictions,
Move swiftly from darkness,
And steadily toward the Light.

Bless them, that the Path of Beauty
Will always be before me,
Leaving negativity behind.

These are my foundations.
Strengthen them, so I will not stray from my destiny,
But accept this road with grace and understanding.

Alternative Timing: Yule, a holiday in which shoes once played an important role.

Other Accents: If you happen across any old cobbler's tools at a garage sale or junk store, these would make wonderful decorations for the sacred space.

October 27

ALLAN APPLE DAY (CORNWALL, ENGLAND)

Magical Themes: Discovering a life partner.

History/Lore: The unmarried men and women of Cornwall purchase an Allan Apple on this day. At nightfall, the fruit is placed under their pillow until morning. Before dawn, the fruit is eaten without a sound. The participants then go outside, dressed just as they are, to sit beneath a tree. It is believed that the first person to pass them by is their future spouse! Also, if the participants feel no cold while waiting, they will remain warm all Winter (possibly thanks to their new mate)!

Decorating Ideas: Baskets of apples (all kinds); sachets filled with apple potpourri; tree foliage.

Garments: Whatever you are wearing when you get up that morning!

Ritual Cup: Apple juice, cider, or wine.

Ritual Foods: There are many wonderful recipes for everything from fondue to pie made with apples. One rather unique dish dating from 17th-century England is an apple cream. This is basically a cross between gelatin and applesauce! Here's a variation, in which the cream and almonds are added to make the course of love smooth and tender:

Lover's Apple Cream

3 cups applesauce
1 envelope unflavored gelatin
$1/2$ cup sweet sherry
1 cup whipped cream
$1/4$ cup minced almonds
$1/2$ cup apple jack
sugar to taste

Directions: Soak the gelatin in sherry for 5 minutes, then melt it over a low flame. Add the applesauce and remove from the heat.

Once the mixture shows signs of thickening, stir in the whipped cream and almonds. Chill. Meanwhile, place the apple jack in a sauce pan over a low flame. Slowly add sugar until a glaze is formed. When the glaze cools slightly, pour it over the top of each helping of the cream. Garnish with whole almonds or apple slices. Serves 4-6.

Incense: Grind a bit of dried apple wood with dried apple peel. To this, other love herbs may be added, including clove, lemon or orange rind, rose petals, and vanilla.

Activities: To inspire love in your home, or as a gift to give a special someone, make an apple wreath or pomander. For the wreath, you will need to dry 1/8 inch apple slices in a very low oven. Also, purchase a wreath base, glue, and cinnamon sticks (to add a little "spice" to your romance). Fix the apple pieces to the wreath using glue, or alternatively, wire them in place by threading them with thin florists' wire into the base. Add the sticks of cinnamon and a bow for garnishes (see figure 39). Attach a ring of wire at the back for hanging (like a painting).

For the pomander, you will need a large apple and plenty of whole cloves (another love herb). Beginning at the center top of the apple, poke holes using a tooth pick and secure the cloves in place. Cover the apple completely. When finished, roll the apple in a mixture of 1 tablespoon orris root, 1/2 tablespoon cinnamon, and 1/2 tablespoon ginger. Set aside for several weeks until completely dry. The apple will shrink a little. Finally, at the top, use a hat pin to hold a ribbon in place for a hanger. This is a terrific addition to any magical kitchen, releasing the energy of adoration into all your meals.

Figure 39. Apple and cinnamon wreath.

Sample Spell: Apple peels and stems can be used for divination. Also, a spell to bring your true love closer can be performed with an apple. Peel your apple in one long strand and carefully twist out the stem. Dice the two items into small pieces, then, holding the apple in your hand, turn in a clockwise manner twice and begin releasing the apple pieces, saying:

Apple stem and apple peel
All around the spinning wheel,
Travel where my true love lies;
Find the "apple of my eye."

Apples of joy, apples of health,
Apples for wisdom, apples for wealth.
But, most of all, this apple is freed
To bring true love closer to me!

Alternative Timing: Most harvest festivals; holidays honoring Venus, Diana, Zeus, and Apollo, to whom apples are sacred.

Other Accents: Depending on the type of love you are trying to engender, evening hours are best for romantic love magic. Daylight hours are better for playful relationships.

October 31

SAMHAIN, HALLOWEEN (DRUIDIC — ENGLAND)

Magical Themes: Magic, sorcery, supernatural forces, pranks, divination, and fairy folk.

History/Lore: Samhain had its beginnings with the Druids, who honored a god of the dead on this date, as well as celebrating their New Year, the beginning of Winter. The Druids have a history which reaches back to about 2 B.C. They believed that by the morning of November 1, the Sun was safely stored away, like grain, for the Winter. Throughout the night, the souls of those who had died in the previous year were gathered by Samhain to be released from Earthly constraints.

In Scotland, Druids came to a central location and took care of all judicial functions for their order on this day. Questions and crimes were brought before them to be settled. Afterward, ritual fires were lit and observances held.

Samh'in means, literally, "fire of peace." Since the afterlife is a predominant theme for Samhain, it is not surprising that people desired a little extra illumination! Large and small fires dotted the landscape for protection, to welcome the season, or to announce the beginning of a gathering.

Fourteenth-century Italian families made an elaborate feast for the deceased and left it somewhere accessible. Mexicans prepared sweets and special toys, believing the souls of departed children could visit their homes on this day. To help them find their way, firecrackers and yellow marigold petals were placed, leading to the door of the home.

Along with the spirits of the dead, the fairy folk are active at this time of year. Originally, the fey were not depicted as small or fragile, but rather as larger and more beautiful than any human. They were generally regarded by the Celts as the spirits of kings, heroes, and demi-gods, until the Christian church relegated them to a smaller, less grand mode.

The notion of dressing in costume had its origins, at least partially, in Scotland in a custom known as guising. The masks and attire were used in an attempt to scare away malicious spirits. In Ireland, costumed people demanded tribute for the god Muck Olla (possibly a mispronunciation of MacCuill), lighting their way to homes using carved turnips and jack-o-lanterns. These customs traveled to the United States with the immigrants in the nineteenth century and slowly evolved.

It is probable that the Catholic church chose November 1 as All Saints' Day in order to balance what it regarded as the evil influence of spirits (and the people who welcomed them). Since gathering or honoring spirits of the departed was already associated with this time of year, it was a simple transformation.

Decorating Ideas: Hazelnuts for protection; acorns, apples, squash, gourds, brooms, corn stalks, and depictions of traditional "witch animals."

Garments: Costumes are perfectly acceptable.

Ritual Cup: Late October is also the time when the last vestiges of the harvest are gathered in. Late-maturing vegetables and grains are taken to market or preserved. Because of this, a wheat wine is a nice choice for Samhain, in memory of farmers and the Wheat Mother, and to inspire abundance through the Winter. Here is a recipe:

Harvest Wheat Wine

> 1 pound grain wheat (Eastern food
>   marts or health food stores)
> 1 pound raisins
> 1 pound sliced potatoes
> 2 large sweet oranges
> 4 pounds sugar
> $1/2$ inch diced ginger root
> 1 gallon water
> $1/2$ package active yeast

Directions: Place the grain, raisins, and well-washed potatoes in a large crock which has a lid that fits well. Peel the oranges, and clean the peels of as much white as possible. Put the peels in the crock. Set this aside while you warm the water, ginger, and sugar to boiling. Pour this over the ingredients in the crock.

Now, squeeze the oranges into the water, getting as much juice as possible, but carefully keeping out the pith (this will make the wine bitter). Cool to lukewarm and add the yeast, mixed with $1/4$ cup warm water. Cover and let sit in a warm area (70 degrees) for three weeks. Afterward, carefully strain into a gallon jug. This needs to sit for an additional 3 weeks to allow the sediment to settle. Pour off the clarified wine into bottles and age for 1-2 years in a dark, cool area.

Ritual Foods: Pumpkin or apple pie, and a harvest stew which includes things like corn, zucchini, and turnip chunks.

Incense: Either use spicy scents right from your pantry, or protective aromas such as rowan, rue, sage, ginseng, and pennyroyal.

Activities: There is enough folklore and superstition surrounding activities for Hallows celebrations to fill a book by itself! Here are just a few illustrations to consider integrating into your festivities:

• Hang your sleeve in a river running southward and bring it into your bedroom to dream of your future love;

• Wear red to protect yourself from the evil eye, spirits, and undesired fairy folk;

• Leave milk on the windowsill with a white candle to appease wandering souls and the fey;

• Make soulcakes with currants for the departed, as they did in the Middle Ages. These will bring mercy on those who have died. For yourself, whole loaves can be prepared for good luck and protection from early death;

• Country tradition instructed young couples to each place one nut on their hearthfires. If one nut flamed without the other, there would be rejection. If both broke open in the fire, quarrels would ensue. If both burned quietly, the couple would be happily married within the year;

• In Ireland, there is a custom known as "throwing of the shoe." Here, a shoe is tossed over a roof on Hallows' Night. If it lands pointing toward the home, there will be no travel that year. If it lands pointing away from the house, adventure awaits that person in the specified direction. If the shoe lands sole down, good fortune will come around!

Sample Incantation (for Shoe Divination):

I toss this shoe into the air
To see how my future fares —
Will I travel through strange lands?
Will money come into my hands?

Up it goes this Hallows' night
My magic shoe now takes to flight [toss the shoe]
Over the roof top, high in the sky,
To glimpse wherein my future lies.

Alternative Timing: Any festival for the dead.

Other Accents: Go to a nearby park and collect as many acorn tops as you can find. These may be strung together for necklaces or inscribed with runes for divination.

November

November 8

FESTIVAL OF THE KITCHEN GODDESS (JAPAN)

Magical Themes: Hearth and home; domestic tasks; providence.

History/Lore: This day honors Irori Kami, or Daidokoro Kami, the goddess of the hearth and kitchen. She represents the people who daily provide food to our tables (or restaurants).

Decorating Ideas: Rustic kitchen tools, bowls and paraphernalia.

Garments: An apron, pot holders, or chef's hat.

Ritual Cup: The most frequently enjoyed beverage from your kitchen.

Ritual Foods: Depending on your point of view, this is a holiday that either inspires a lush feast or eating out. Personally, I prefer the latter as it means *no dishes*!

Incense: Look through your spice rack for personally pleasing aromas to blend together. Sprinkle them sparingly on self-lighting charcoal.

Activities: Today is a time to honor your kitchen or someone who cooks for you frequently. One way to do this is by making them an appropriate gift: a decorative wooden spoon. Begin by finding a large wooden spoon. Goodwill is a great, inexpensive source for these. On the top of the handle, in back, affix a little piece of thin wire by tying it around the handle, twisting at the back, and adding a dab of sturdy glue. You can hide the wire later using ribbon. Next, take various lengths of dried flowers and arrange them so they appear to grow down toward the serving end. Glue them onto the spoon and to each other until you are happy with the fullness (see figure 40, page 194). For

Figure 40. Decorative wooden spoon.

longevity, spray with a little hairspray or art fixative to protect
the flowers.

Sample Prayer:

God/goddess,
Today we are thankful for providence
And those who give of their time
To put food on our table.
Bless their hands and hearts
With joy, hope, and health,
Now and always.

Alternative Timing: Feast of the Kitchen God (January
20, China).

Other Accents: Asperge your circle with a dishtowel.
Hanging pots and pans can become musical instruments. Make
a large kitchen the center of your ritual, with the stove as an altar
or fire source.

November 9

LOY KRATHONG (THAILAND)

Magical Themes: The element of water; wish magic.

History/Lore: The people of Thailand fashion boats from
lotus and banana leaves on this day. At night, they place a can-

dle in the boats with incense, coins and gardenia petals. The boats are then set adrift on the river and silent wishes are made. If the candle stays lit until the boat is out of sight, the maker's wish will come true.

Decorating Ideas: Watery themes with blues and blue-greens predominate. Use toy boats to mark your quarters, their sails chosen for the elemental color correspondence. Leave a coin of some type in each boat for later in the ritual. Place pennies in the earth boat, dimes in the water boat, gold-toned coins (Canadian Looney) in the fire boat, and perhaps game tokens can be used in the air boat.

Garments: Your choice.

Ritual Cup: In this area of the world, the lotus is regarded as the first flower and the embodiment of purity. It is also symbolic of the past, present, and future flowing together over the water with your wishes. To accentuate this, try an almond-lily tea.

Magic Almond-Lily Tea

1/2 cup ground almonds
1 tablespoon lotus flower
1/2 cup sugar

Directions: Mix together in a sauce pan. Slowly add 3/4 cup of milk, cooking over a low flame for about 15 minutes. Strain and serve hot with whole almonds as a garnish. This is especially effective if your wish pertains to love.

Ritual Foods: A banana split! In keeping with the idea of the holiday, carefully remove the banana from its wrapping and place the peel on a plate. Fill with small scoops of ice cream and garnish as you desire, laying slices of banana alongside the boat you have made from its peel.

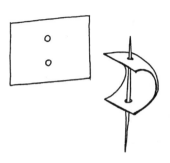

Figure 41. Sail for Loy Krathong-style boat.

To create a sail, affix a rectangle of construction paper to a toothpick. Poke two holes in the center of the paper, then slide the toothpick through, pressing down the paper to form a curved sail (see figure 41, page 195).

Incense: Lotus or gardenia.

Activities: Refer to the boat festival in early April for directions on making a wish boat at home (see page 51). If you can't make a boat, use the coins set around your circle as a component for your magic instead. Wish on them and toss them into a moving water source. Or, to divine information, focus on your question and skip the coin across the waters. The number of skips portends your answer either in days, weeks, or months, or by its symbolic associations. Here are some correlations to consider:

1 = harmony, health, logic and reason, personal matters;
2 = balance, relationships, compromise, or truce;
3 = symmetry, steadfastness, tenacity;
4 = goals, victory, success, and attainment;
5 = adaptability, comprehension, psychic awareness;
6 = commitment, finishing projects, loyalty;
7 = intuition, imagination, fruitfulness;
8 = energy, change, leadership;
9 = charity, kindness, compassion;
11 = nearing completion, just short of attainment;
10 = rationality, deduction, sagacity;
12 = productivity, endurance, end or start of a cycle;
13 = fidelity, tolerance, confidence.

Sample Incantation: Repeat this as you launch your boat or toss your coin:

Through the waters you shall go
Toward my wishes you shall flow.
Carry safe my heart's bequest
To the North, the East, the South, and West.

Through the waters you are bound
To land yourself on fertile ground.
Ride upon the current blue
To make my wishes all come true.

Alternative Timing: Boat Festival (early April, France)

Other Accents: For musical accompaniment, try *Wind in the Rigging* from Northstar records.[9]

November 10

CELEBRATION FOR THE GODDESS OF REASON
(FRANCE)

Magical Themes: Learning, knowledge, judgment, and rationality; liberty.

History/Lore: This holiday was observed in revolutionary France with parades through the streets of Paris. One woman was chosen to represent the goddess, and wore a blue robe and a red Phrygian hat (from Asia Minor). The processional moved to Notre Dame (an honored center of learning) where the woman received homage by being crowned with oak leaves.

Decorating Ideas: Books, eyeglasses, chalk boards, diplomas, a pair of scales, and other items symbolic of the logical, learning mind; highlights of gold, blue, and red should be predominant.

Garments: Follow the lead of the French: don a blue, graduation-style robe over your clothing with a red graduation cap. To create a robe for someone of average weight, begin with about 4¹/2 yards of fabric. Measure yourself from the base of your neck to the floor. Cut two pieces of fabric this length. Set one section aside. Cut the other in half length-wise for the front of your robe. Pin pleats in each side, moving away from the center, so that each piece has an equal number of pleats and measures 9 inches. This is for someone whose shoulder-to-shoulder

---

9. Otis Read, *Wind in the Rigging.* Northstar Records.

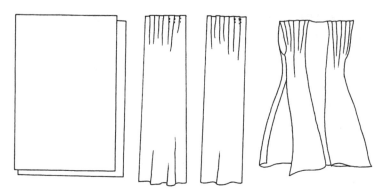

Figure 42. Graduation-style robe. Left: 4 1/2 yards of fabric cut into two pieces the length of a person of average height Center: one of the pieces is cut in half to create the front of the robe. Right: the finished robe with top seam and side seams with arm openings.

measurement is 17 inches. If your measurement differs, adjust the pleats outward or inward to allow a proper fit.

Repeat this procedure with the back piece so that, in finished form, the front and back are of even size. Then, place the panels with their right sides together to sew the shoulder seam. Make sure the two front pieces meet at the middle of the back so you have a centered opening in front (see figure 42). Turn down the edge around the neck and around the front opening twice for a finished look.

Ritual Cup: Grape juice or coffee for clear, concise thinking.

Ritual Foods: Fish is the traditional "brain" food, so start with that base and add herbs such as rosemary and dill. Here is one recipe to serve four people:

Consciousness Fish

    4 white fish fillets
    6 tablespoons olive oil
    2 tablespoons lemon juice
    1/4 teaspoon each dill, rosemary, basil, and garlic
    1/2 cup bread crumbs
    1/4 teaspoon dill and rosemary

Directions: Marinate the fish in lemon juice, oil, and the first set of herbs for 45 minutes. Mix together the bread crumbs, dill, and rosemary so they are well blended. Coat the fish completely with these, and bake in the oven for 15 minutes at 400 degrees. Time may vary slightly for thinner fillets.

Incense: Fresh, crisp spearmint to increase mental keenness.

Activities: A day for reconsidering any project that has been difficult to sort out, with strong emphasis on logic to guide your way. Take time out for studying anything about which you love to learn. Gather a group together for serious discussion on any subject (everyone should bring their research and ideas to share).

Also, make yourself an inspirational bookmark, scented with rosemary, to aid memory retention. Start with a sturdy piece of construction paper (yellow is a good choice). Arrange some small dried leaves, baby's breath, sprigs of rosemary, and pressed flowers over the surface in any pattern pleasing to the eye. Glue them with sturdy adhesive, adding a few drops of rosemary oil to the petals. Cover with a piece of clear, self-sticking film. Whenever the scent needs refreshing, just put the bookmark in a box with rosemary for a week.

Sample Invocation:

Goddess of reason,
We call and charge You!
Come, fill our minds with learning and truth.
Let our eyes be keen,
Our wits be sharp,
To discern the fullness of knowledge we seek.

From the East bring awareness;
From the South, renewed energy;
From the West, flowing insight;
And the North, cool comprehension.
Come, join us here and spark our conscious minds;
Be with us this night!

Alternative Timing: Just before returning to school after a vacation. Any time you are learning something new.

Other Accents: Items associated with the conscious mind or learning, including note pads, lightbulbs, computers, and the colors yellow or gold.

November 11

LUNANTISHEES (IRELAND)

Magical Themes: Fairy kinship.

History/Lore: Fairies are extremely important in Irish mythology and folklore. This day was set aside entirely to celebrate the fanciful wee folk. The types of fairies honored were plentiful, including nymphs, pixies, elves, flower sprites, and, of course, leprechauns.

Generally fairies are characterized in Ireland as more mischievous than nasty. According to old stories, they loathe lazy humans, but often reward a kind and generous heart. Even the frightening banshee had a special function as an ancestral spirit wailing to warn of impending death in the family.

Decorating Ideas: This is a day to give over to whimsy. Bright, lively decorations should fill the sacred space, especially any likenesses of fairy folk. Oh, and don't forget a pot of gold and rainbows!

Garments: Bright, light, and carefree. If you can find luminescent fabric (looking like gossamer), all the better. Another option would be to make a rainbow-colored headpiece or belt for yourself from macramé or other knot work.

Ritual Cup: Sweet cream is a favorite beverage of the fey.

Ritual Foods: Bake little wafer cakes using the following recipe and drench them in honey:

Fairy Cakes

1 cup flour
1 cup sugar
1 egg
3 tablespoons butter
2 teaspoons rose water
1 cup cream
1 teaspoon grated orange rind

Directions: Melt the butter. Mix the melted butter into the dry ingredients. Add milk slowly and blend until mixture is smooth. Let this stand at room temperature for an hour. Using a waffle iron or iron frying pan, pour out batter onto a well-greased surface. Turn to cook both sides evenly (about 4 minutes each). Lay out on a platter and drizzle with honey or powdered sugar. Remember to leave a few outside to entice fairies to visit you.

Incense: Oak, ash, and thorn wood chips with a bit of thyme.

Activities: Hold a fairy hunt! Take small gifts of nuts, berries, your honey cakes, etc., to a remote spot for the wee folk to find. Enjoy getting close to nature!

Sample Invocation: Before your expedition, gather those participating in a circle to send out a call to these elemental creatures:

Pixies and gnomes, brownies and elves,
Come to us, reveal yourselves!
Here within this enchanted dell
We've come to learn your stories well.
As bards of old, to us impart
A glimpse of gossamer to hold in our hearts.

Also this Date: Vinalia (Greece and Rome) in honor of Bacchus, the god of wine. Enjoy a little with your dinner or rituals on this day. The Christian version of this is Martinmas (same date), for the patron saint of vintners and tavernkeepers. A bright day on this day foretells an icy Winter, while frost before Martinmas is a sign of milder seasons ahead. For an invocation, look to Keats who wrote:

> *We follow Bacchus! Bacchus on the wing, a-conquering!*
> *Bacchus, young Bacchus! Good or ill betide, we dance*
> *before him through kingdoms wide.*[10]

November 14

ASKING FESTIVAL (ALASKA)

Magical Themes: Caring for those in need; thankfulness and the spirit of generosity; abundance.

History/Lore: Among Eskimos, it is considered bad for the local community if any one person has too many material possessions. Out of this ancient belief, the tradition of Asking Day was born. The youths of the village go out with their faces painted in patterns of dots and stripes, asking every home to donate food. These edibles are later brought to a great hall for a community feast.

While everyone enjoys the festivities, the man in charge sits in the center of the gathering and asks each man what he desires, from any given woman. Then the woman gets to ask for something in return. No matter what is requested (food, furs, etc.), it should be given to keep providence alive in the village. By the end of the night, a great deal of the village property has changed hands in the true spirit of sharing!

Decorating Ideas: Build a horn of plenty from large pieces of cardboard and fill it with gifts for coven members. Alternatively, have receptacles at the cardinal points to gather canned goods, clothing, etc. to donate to a good cause. Color the receptacles according to their element.

---

10. John Keats in Rev. J. Loughran Scott, ed., *Bullfinch's Age of Fable* (Philadelphia: David McKay, 1898), p. 208.

Garments: Nothing too flashy. A beggar's attire might be an enjoyable option.

Ritual Cup: For this I suggest something unique. Have each person participating bring a beverage. These can be exchanged with others at your site to kindle the energy of sharing.

Ritual Foods: A potluck feast is most fitting.

Incense: Add dry ash and oak leaves to your mixture for prosperity.

Activities: Make yourself an asking tool that can double as a ritual bowl or cup. For this you need a fairly large gourd with a naturally formed handle. Slice out a circle in the center of the largest area and clean out the gourd thoroughly (see figure 43). Let this dry completely, then apply a finishing spray. Ask your local art store about which sprays can be used safely on beverage containers.

Let the children of your group make a game out of painting each other as did the Eskimos with nontoxic, washable colors. Usually this deteriorates rapidly into finger painting, which is fine. Have large pieces of paper handy and let them make depictions of the things for which they are thankful.

Sample Verbal Components: Instead of an invocation or prayer, the Asking Festival is best honored by having each person in turn share something about their personal gratitude to the group or the gods. A slight variation on the Eskimo asking tradition would be to allow folks to go to each other and ask a small favor. These should be answerable within a year's time and should be nothing too outrageous. By so doing, you encourage continuing communication and support in your group.

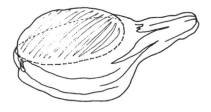

Figure 43. Ritual asking tool made of hollowed out half of a gourd.

Alternative Timing: Thanksgiving.

Other Accents: To have more of an Alaskan feeling, parkas could become part of your ritual attire. Decorate a portion of your space to the North with cotton and glitter to look like snow.

November 16

DIWALI, OR DIVALI (INDIA)

Magical Themes: New beginnings; prosperity; positive business ventures; beauty.

History/Lore: This is a five-day event marking the Hindu New Year. It is regarded as the best time to welcome Lakshmi, a goddess of wealth (and the queen of beauty) into your home, lighting her way with candles. Almost every activity is considered fortunate today, especially marriage, getting a new home, or starting a business.

Decorating Ideas: Use numerous candles, tiki torches, or other light sources leading up to, and around, your location. Also adorn the sacred space with plenty of gold, silver, and green, the colors of wealth.

Garments: Any garb that makes you feel more attractive and well-to-do; perhaps a tuxedo for men and an evening gown for women.

Ritual Cup: Ginger liqueur or tea for golden, flowing abundance. A half-gallon of the liqueur is made as follows:

Abundance Tea

2 ounces ginger root
1 lemon, sliced
1 small orange, sliced
4 oz. sweet almonds, mashed

> 1 inch vanilla bean
> 2 quarts brandy or vodka
> sugar

Directions: Slice and bruise the ginger root into 1/4 inch pieces. Place these with all other ingredients (except the sugar) in a 1/2 gallon jug. Leave in a dark area, shaking daily, for one month. Strain and add sugar to personal taste. Age or enjoy immediately.

Ritual Foods: Foods in which you might not normally indulge, like gourmet chocolates and coffee. Alternatively, edibles with strong associations with financial well-being, like saffron rice (the herb of kings), banana-bran bread, and lettuce salad.

Incense: To a base of cedar wood powder add a sprig of saffron, pine needles, grated orange peel, and a hint of nutmeg. Alternatively, use lotus to honor Lakshmi.

Activities: Follow the lead of tradition! Many people lay out a mixture of rice paste and earth pigments in sacred geometric patterns. This attracts luck to their residence during this festival (see figure 44). Cakes are left on crossroads to keep evil spirits busy elsewhere, and sweetmeats are placed on home altars for the gods to enjoy.

The Jains (a religious sect) pay special attention to their account books on this day. A Brahman comes to the home to place a lucky mark on the house leader, write "Sri" on a page of the books, and leave a rupee between the pages to bring good

Figure 44. Sacred geometric pattern created with rice paste and earth pigments.

luck. This coin must remain undisturbed for one year to tempt Sri (the spirit of wealth) to live in those pages. A more Western application would be to leave a blessed, lucky coin in your checkbook, wallet, or purse!

Sample Invocation:

Lakshmi, follow the flames!
Walk the path we have laid,
Filling the night with your radiance.
Bring with you good fortune and luck
To bless our homes, our loved ones, and our lives.
We have prepared the way
And welcome you among us.

Alternative Timing: Fortuna Redux, Good Luck Day.

Other Accents: Lily, ivy, and willow are all sacred to this goddess.

November 20 (approximate)

MAKAHIKI (HAWAII)

Magical Themes: Harvesting peace; safety; fertility.

History/Lore: This ritual commences when the Pleiades become visible in the night sky. Any type of war is forbidden during this season as a special gift to their god, Lono. This is the beginning of the Hawaiian harvest season.

According to legend, the Pleiades were the daughters of Atlas and the nymphs of Diana's train. When Orion became enamored of them, they prayed to the gods for aid. Jupiter (Zeus) turned them into pigeons and they flew to the skies, where they remain, still pursued across the sky by Orion.

Decorating Ideas: Any found pigeon feathers. A depiction of the Pleiades in silver on a black background hung from the ceiling.

Garments: Go with leis and Hawaiian shirts.

Ritual Cup: To honor Lono's fruitfulness, use peach or grape juice, served with passion flower garnishes.

Ritual Foods: Prepare a Hawaiian luau! Fresh pineapples, coconut, glazed meats, and fish in abundance.

Incense: For peace, use lavender and pennyroyal; for fertility, geranium or patchouli.

Activities: A time to put aside any bad feelings you have had toward another. Find a symbol of your anger and ritually burn or bury it, giving friendship (or love) a second chance. Alternatively, release a pigeon in keeping with the symbolism to free yourself of negativity and give flight to renewed dreams.

Sample Incantation: The first stanza of this is taken from Alfred Lord Tennyson:

> *Many a night I saw the Pleiades,*
> *Rising through the mellow shade*
> *Glitter like a swarm of fire-flies,*
> *Tangled in a silver braid.*

> *I saw my heart in their fires,*
> *Burning with an angry glow.*
> *Delivered into ritual pyres — [put the symbol in the fire]*
> *Let healing waters begin to flow.*

> *To the wind, to the flame,*
> *To the stars, and the ground*
> *I release all my pain,*
> *There to be forever bound.*[11]

Alternative Timing: Any ritual for forgiveness.

Other Accents: Timing this ritual so it coincides with a waning Moon will help "shrink" the anger.

Interesting Aside: Blackfoot Indians, ancient Peruvians, and the aborigines of Australia all worshipped the Pleiades. The latter group regarded them as givers of rain.

---

11. Alfred Lord Tennyson, in *Bullfinch's Age of Fable*, p. 257.

November 21

FESTIVAL OF KUKULCAN (MAYA)

Magical Themes: Time and the calendar; craftsmanship.

History/Lore: This festival lasts several days and honors the Maya god, Kukulcan. He appeared as a feathered water snake who had dominion over water. Later adopted into Quetzalcoatl, he is credited with creating the calendar and being the patron god of craftsmen.

Decorating Ideas: Any handicrafts made by yourself or others attending; a calendar; feathers; a vessel of water with a toy snake to honor Kukulcan.

Garments: Handmade outfits might be best in recognition of the crafts aspect of this holiday.

Ritual Cup: Water or a homemade beverage which accentuates creativity. One possibility is anything flavored with beechnut.

Ritual Foods: It was traditional to fast for this festival. If this is not possible because of dietary restrictions, arrange for a meal with twelve elements to honor the months of the year.

Incense: Creativity requires a fine balance between the intuitive nature and cognitive skills. For this, try rosemary mixed with thyme.

Activities: The Maya traditionally offered foods to the gods and had brilliant banners of colored feathers adorning their homes and ritual area. These can be made from construction paper shaped like a snake, to which feathers are glued. Hobby shops carry an incredible variety of colored feathers to suit your fancy.

The children of your home might enjoy making horsetail flutes to announce this celebration. According to lore, these will "call" snakes. Thus, the flutes bid Kukulcan to join the festivities. Cut the widest part of the horsetail in various lengths for different timbres. Slice out a triangular hole near one end, and a few small holes along the spine for an instrument which works like a flute (see figure 45). Alternatively, just leave the cuttings whole and blow evenly over one end to create the whistling sound.

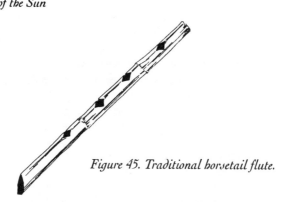

Figure 45. Traditional horsetail flute.

Sample Chant: This chant should naturally rise and fall as it moves around the circle. Afterward, anyone who wishes should go and work on a craft-related project, taking the magically inspired energy with them.

Creativity grow, inventiveness sow,
Round the circle, flow . . . flow.

Alternative Timing: Any holiday honoring a craftsman god.

Other Accents: Think in terms of terra-cotta and sandstone hues, Indian patterned blankets, etc.

November 26 (approximate)

INITIATION RITES (SENEGAL)

Magical Themes: Male mysteries; rites of passage for young men; the god aspect.

History/Lore: In the Basari villages of Senegal, 15-year-old boys are ushered into manhood with elaborate ritual. Months of preparation precede this, including many tests of the mind and body. After the ritual is complete, the young men are welcome to show off their talents to the entire community.

Decorating Ideas: Strong masculine symbolism in colors. Items which emblemize a change of state—for example a bowl of ice on one side of the room and water on the other.

Garments: Garments should be changed after the ritual. The clothes worn in by the young man should be something he is outgrowing. These can be ritually torn or destroyed during the observance as a way of breaking free of childhood.

Ritual Cup: I suggest beverages aligned with solar energy, such as grapefruit or pineapple juice.

Ritual Foods: Again, look to solar foods or those associated with Mars. Have an assortment of pretzels, carrots, olives, and radishes for finger foods. Add to this some asparagus with garlic butter for a side dish. The main dish is chosen by the young man/men participating.

Incense: Rosemary for good memories, strength, protection, and insight.

Activities: Some of the traditional tests include foraging for food for several days without provisions while away from home, or a time of total silence while maintaining other regular duties. If the young people are accomplished campers, the first test is feasible with certain prudent limitations. Take them to a known area and provide minimal equipment, such as a dagger or knife, some tarp for a lean-to, a flare for emergencies, and a good field guide to edible plants. Arrange a pick-up time three days later. During their outing, the teens should be instructed to spend considerable time contemplating their new roles and what it means to them.

A time of silence encourages reflection. It also builds self-discipline. This particular activity is more practicable than the first, as long as it doesn't interfere with school or work. A young boy can also do this alone, just like a young Native American boy does when he becomes a man.

Sample Invocation: As part of this rite, I suggest having the boy choose the masculine image on which he will call during the ceremony, and then write his own invocation accordingly. This will introduce him to his new role in your home or group. It will also afford an opportunity to consider what role magic will play in his life in the time ahead.

Alternative Timing: Feast of Banners and Kites (Japan).

Other Accents: Begin the ritual either just before dawn or at dusk. This way, as the Sun changes lighting, it will mark the occasion as a symbol of transition.

December

Early December
(approximately the first week)

DERVISH DANCING (TURKEY)

Magical Themes: Mystical knowledge; prophesy and divination; magical dance.

History/Lore: Dervishes belong to a Sufi religious order, among whom dance is used as a means to induce heightened spiritual awareness. In the Dervish tradition, dance is a form of worship that reunites individuals with the Divine and allows them to then act as channels for supernatural information. Many historians compare the Dervish techniques with those used by the prophets of ancient Israel.

At some point in early December, the Turks set aside an entire week to honor this tradition. Dervishes assemble in large cities and dance wearing their large, full skirts. Afterwards they forecast the future for those assembled.

Decorating Ideas: Any items which have fluid motion in their line or construction, especially those which have parts that move in circles. Examples: pinwheels, fans, wind-up music boxes.

Garments: Dervishes wear large circular skirts to accentuate their movements. As these billow out, the dancer literally

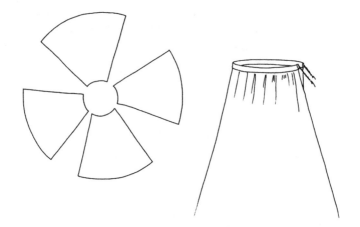

Figure 46. Dervish-style skirt. Left: four pieces of fabric cut as pictured so that the inner circle will easily fit your waist when gathered and sewn. The fabric is cut long enough to reach from your waist to the floor. Right: finished skirt with pleated waistband and ties.

becomes the central point of a magic circle! To make one for yourself, measure your body from the waist to the floor. Also measure just the front of your hips. Cut four pieces of material using those measurements and lay them on the floor (see figure 46). Next, using fabric chalk, outline a slight curve to the bottom edges. This gives the skirt a circular look when it is finished. Sew the pieces together, and pleat (or gather) the top of the skirt in a band which fits around your waist comfortably. Hold in place with a pin, snap, or ties.

Ritual Cup: In honor of the country of origin, how about Turkish coffee? Place one teaspoon of finely ground coffee into a sauce pan with 1/4 tablespoon sugar and 1/4 cup water for each person. Bring this to a boil and then remove from heat. Cool. Repeat this boiling process three times. Pour while still bubbly into small cups.

Ritual Foods: The Turkish people took Mohammed's teachings literally when interpreting the phrase, "The love of sweetmeats comes from faith." Some of the best candymakers in the world still live in Turkey. Here is one recipe for Turkish Delight to serve as an after-ritual snack:

Turkish Delight

2 cups sugar
1 cup water
1/8 cup corn syrup
1 envelope unflavored gelatin
1/8 cup lemon juice
3/4 cup cornstarch
1 1/2 teaspoons rosewater
1 1/2 teaspoons orange flower water
1/2 cup chopped nuts
confectionery sugar

Directions: Warm sugar, water, and syrup together until they reach 240 degrees. Set aside. Soak the gelatin in lemon juice. In a small saucepan, heat cornstarch with 1/8 cup water, then add the sugar mixture prepared earlier. Cook this over a low flame until it thickens, stirring constantly. Once thick, turn off the heat and add lemon juice with gelatin. Stir until well incorporated. Add flower waters and nuts, then pour into lightly greased pan. Sprinkle with confectionery sugar and let set. Cut in 1 inch squares. Yields approximately 1 dozen squares.

Incense: A mixture of rose and broom for prophetic insight.

Activities: A day to enjoy any ritual dancing or make divination efforts. Since most people will not wish to spin themselves in circles to obtain divine awareness, try using a top akin to the dreydl for oracular efforts. Simply determine in advance what each side of the dreydl represents, then focus on your question. Spin the top to receive your answer. Simple interpretations can be formulated, including:

Handle to the left, a negative response;
Handle to the right, a positive response;
Handle pointing directly away from you, look back to
    see what the past is teaching;
Handle pointing directly toward you, a new path or
    direction to follow;
Point at northeast — slow beginnings;

Point at southeast — an energetic undertaking;
Point at southwest — a passionate new relationship;
Point at northwest — cooling of anger.

Sample Incantation: Try adapting part of an old song like this one by S.S. Grossman.[12] Here are some of the verses:

ORIGINAL

I have a little dreydl.
I made it out of clay.
And when it's dry and ready,
Then dreydl I shall play.

My dreydl is always playful,
It loves to dance and spin;
A happy game of dreydl
Come play, now let's begin!

ADAPTATION

I have a little dreydl,
Made from out of clay
The future it will tell me
When it stops and lays.

Within this sacred circle,
It shall dance and spin,
'Round and 'round the power goes,
The magic to begin!

Also this Timing: In Japan, special reverence is given to the world's oldest tree, planted 288 B.C., on this day. This bower is thought to be a direct descendent of the fig under which Buddha gained enlightenment. Have you hugged a tree lately?

---

12. S. S. Grossman, "I Have a Little Dreydl," in Marguerite Ickis, *Book of Festival Holidays* (New York: Dodd, Mead & Co., 1964), p. 92.

December 8

BIRTHDAY OF AMATERASU (SHINTO — JAPAN)

Magical Themes: Solar energy; magical sewing projects.

History/Lore: Amaterasu is the most important goddess in Japan, because the royal family traces its lineage through her. Amaterasu is the Moon's sister who wove the garments of the gods. She and her brother are forever at odds, creating the division of night and day in the sky.

Decorating Ideas: Any items associated with Amaterasu including crows, cocks, kites, arrows, beads, mirrors, and the color gold.

Garments: Anything you have made yourself.

Ritual Cup: Something warm and solar, such as cinnamon tea.

Ritual Foods: Rice flavored with saffron and bamboo shoots; an Eastern-style stir-fry which honors the Sun in its components.

Incense: Dice up bits of leftover thread from sewing efforts to mix with a base of sandalwood powder.

Activities: If you enjoy sewing as a hobby, bless your machine and needles on this day, and make yourself a new robe. If someone else does your mending for you, consider giving them a small token of appreciation for their time and talents.

Sample Blessing:

Great goddess,
Let your light dance brightly [place in sunlight]
Upon these tools to cleanse and bless them.
Let my creativity shine through them, even
As You shine through the skies.

Alternative Timing: Any solar or fire festival is a good time to honor Amaterasu.

Other Accents: Best performed during daylight hours, possibly at noon when the Sun has reached its highest point.

December 14

Hopi Winter Ceremony (Native American)

Magical Themes: Welcoming Winter; gentle speech; offerings to the gods and prayer; health and happiness.

History/Lore: Eight days before the Winter Solstice, this ceremony begins, in honor of the Spider Woman and Hawk Maiden of Hopi legend. It celebrates creation and rebirth to insure the return of the Sun to the skies. Usually this festival takes place underground in a kiva that only tribal members or honored guests are allowed to enter.

Decorating Ideas: Any depictions of hawks and spiders. Cover any windows to give the appearance of being underground.

Garments: Either a dark robe which has a light-colored fabric lining, or two robes (one dark and one light), the dark one worn over the light.

Ritual Cup: Cranberry juice or wine for protection.

Ritual Foods: Young poke shoots steamed and eaten for safety through the Winter.

Incense: Mullein and juniper for health.

Activities: Every Indian makes a prayer stick with feathers to bring blessings on the home and symbolize the wish for gentle voice. There is also a ritual play performed by the holder of a Sun shield and an attacker to show that the golden disk will overcome the darkness. When the Sun wins, have everyone take off their darker robes so that the brightness fills the room (see section on garments, page 248).

To make a Sun shield, begin with cardboard, wood, or even the round lid to a plastic garbage can. Paint as shown in figure 47 (page 217). If made from cardboard, separate pieces can be cut out for the children to assemble like a giant puzzle. In this instance, it becomes a game where the children race to put the puzzle together before someone turns out the lights (or blows out the candles). A couple of the youths can act as "light" guardians to block the path of good-humored adults while the

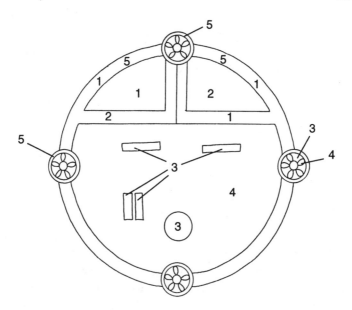

Figure 47. Ceremonial sun shield. The numbers represent the following colors: 1-red or orange, 2-white, 3-black, 4-yellow, 5-feathers.

other children work. Another lovely activity for this day is reciting prayers for all living things, as in the sample below.

Sample Prayer:

> *Great Spirit,*
> *From whom all life flows and returns,*
> *Extend now your blessings —*
> *To the creatures of sea, Earth, air, and land.*
> *Help them to forage through the months ahead,*
> *And live to see the Spring once more.*
>
> *Great Spirit,*
> *Also bless your people*
> *That we might learn wisdom from scant times;*
> *Teach us not to waste or to crave more than we need.*
> *Help us to live in harmony with your creation.*

Alternative Timing: Yule.

Other Accents: The Hopi plant beans on this day, which will be tended for two months and then given to each house to insure growth, new life, and Spring. Alternatives here would be giving out blessed dried beans or bean sprouts.

December 17—21

SATURNALIA (ROME)

Magical Themes: Plenty; magical gift-giving; freedom.

History/Lore: In remembrance of Saturn and Ops, this was a time to exchange gifts and charmed dolls for health and prosperity. Slaves were given a day of freedom to join in the revelry. No assemblies were held for public affairs, and no punishment for crime was given. Children received gaudy gifts and pictures. This celebration often lasted a month.

Saturn was the Roman god of seed sowing, believed to teach the people how to garden, and specifically how to grow olives. Ops is a god of fertility and prosperity.

Decorating Ideas: For Ops, have veils, lion images, or rice paper on the altar; for Saturn, garden knives, vines, and olives can be set out.

Garments: In his temple, woolen cloth was always seen wrapped around Saturn's feet, so wear something wool, like a sweater.

Ritual Cup: Saturn's favorite beverage was wine. You may want to warm it with some mulling spices, considering the season.

Ritual Foods: Anything you regard as a delicacy.

Incense: To a base of oak wood add some pine needles for abundance and productivity.

Activities: Work any spells or rituals related to ridding yourself of the things which enslave you. Magics pertaining to prosperity are also enhanced by this timing. Members of your gathering may wish to exchange little tokens of health and good fortune with each other too. For this, have each person bring one item and toss it in a grab bag. This is passed around the circle from east to west as each person retrieves renewed luck!

Sample Incantation: Add this chant/incantation to the movement of the gift pouch:

> *Sunward bound, 'round 'n 'round,*
> *Within our luck is surely found.*

Please note that the word "luck" can be changed to "health," "wealth," etc., as is appropriate to your needs.

The Winter Calendar

Winter's theme is well-deserved rest, coupled with a focus on the family, tending the hearth, and gradual change. The Earth has fallen into quiet slumber. Outwardly, most of the natural world seems dead, but this appearance is deceiving. Beneath the snows or furious rains, small saplings, seeds, and root crops are growing in preparation for Spring.

Winter was a season of conservation and sharing for our ancestors. Food was meted out with careful regard for the stores on hand. In the Victorian Era, families with meager reserves often found baskets of goods nestled on their porches; gifts from unnamed benefactors. This was one way villagers cared for each other, while allowing people to maintain their dignity. For your purposes, this corresponds to being aware of, and discreetly responsive to, your own community's needs. It also means not overextending your inner reservoirs, so you can stay healthy.

In northern climes, Winter was most feared because of sleet, hail, and the lack of proper protection against the elements. It is from this dread that the first stories of ice giants and other blustery creatures were born. These creatures were embodiments of the Storm Spirit, horrible and without pity. Conversely, many of Winter's festivals are the most elaborate and joyous of the year. The spirit of life was purposely venerated in these observances to defy the Storm Spirit, and hopefully overcome it.

Winter's hues are somber compared to the resplendence of Autumn. Brown, white, gray, and black exhibit themselves in mud or snow and dying foliage. Even so, this season does not leave us without hope. The evergreen still bears rich, green boughs and red berries to remind us that new life is just around the corner, while the glittering lights and colors of Yule dance before children everywhere.

The sacred space for Winter is generally sparser than other seasons. Pine branches and cones, bare twigs, melted snow for the water element, depictions of snow flakes, and icicles are all fitting. If you have dried flowers from earlier months, use these as heartening accents along with traditional holiday raiment. Scents for the season are all the aromas of holiday baking, including anise, cinnamon, and vanilla. In addition, frankincense, myrrh, and pine are popular around Yule. Divine entities to bless your efforts include:

Nix—Greek goddess of night;
Ida—Hindu goddess of dedication;
Fides—Roman goddess of promise;
Mithras—Persian god of friendship;
Fu-Hsing—Chinese god of happiness;
Samkhat—Babylonian goddess of joy;
Asclepius—Greek god of health;
Bridget—Irish goddess of well-being;
Kedesh—Syrian goddess of vitality;
Tien Kuan—Chinese god of fitness;
Bannik—Slavonic god of the home;
Hastehogan—Navajo god of the household;
Penates—Roman gods of the hearth and home;
Vesta—Roman goddess of domestic affairs;
Buddhi—Tibetan goddess of insight;
Deshtri—Hindu goddess of learning;
Gwion—Welsh god of perspicacity;
Sia—Egyptian god of wisdom;
Forseti—Scandinavian god of harmony;
Concordia—Roman goddess of restitution;
Syen—Slavonic god of safe homes;
Prometheus—Greek god of protection;

Aditi—Hindu goddess of safety;

Morgan—Breton goddess of courage;

Kunado—Japanese god of safe travel over roads;

Nike—Greek goddess of victory;

Vijaya—Hindu goddess of success;

Shekinah—Hebrew goddess of wisdom;

Buddha—Indian god of sagacity;

Holle—Teutonic goddess of snow;

Hadad—Babylonian god of storms;

Sadwes—Persian goddess of rain;

Sarama—Japanese goddess of wind.

Crystals associated with Winter include the garnet in January, for devotion, reliability, and affection; amethyst in February, for keeping the bearer free from intoxication, pain, sickness, and poison; bloodstone in March, its life-affirming color providing courage and longevity to its owner. Spiritual efforts enhanced by Winter timing include spells, rituals, and celebrations centering around reflectiveness, health, temperance, thrift, charity, strengthening relationships, and transitions of a gradual nature.

GENERAL WINTER CELEBRATIONS

Winter brought its own set of correspondences and associations which generated holidays and observances characteristic of the season. As in Spring, fire festivals were celebrated to coax the return of the Sun. These stood in direct contrast to festivals which celebrated the wintry elements and their own attendant pleasures. In Winter, the spirit of foraging and hunting replaced the summer and autumn images of sowing and reaping in many cultural traditions. Winter is also the season of the New Year, Yule and Christmastide, and various other religious festivals. Following are some representative examples.

FIRE FESTIVALS

To coax the Sun's return, or to give it sufficient strength to continue its journey, fire festivals abound in the Winter months. Instead of celebrating the mighty fire element, however, these rites focus on drawing the solar disk back into a position of power. Fires are also kindled to keep any malevolent beings of the night at bay.

The last day of the Chinese New Year, for example, is a lantern festival. Hundreds of lights are displayed to bid farewell to Winter, aid fertility, and increase the warmth of the Sun. Some lanterns are shaped symbolically, for instance a lantern shaped like a baby for couples wishing children. An alternative would be candles molded in similar fashion and brought into your sacred space. Some candle shops stock figurines. Otherwise, obtain a square candle and use warm cutting implements to carve your own image. In essence, the candle serves the same function as a poppet, which is also an option.

A slightly different approach to Winter fire observances is exhibited on Shetland Island. To honor their Viking heritage, the people come together and burn the image of a great longship, in a ceremony reminiscent of Viking funerals. In this case, the funeral is a figurative one celebrating the death of any evil spirits who plague the village or home. To follow this tradition, make the image of a longship out of cardboard or plywood and release it to the fires of your Winter cauldron. Let any negativity, sickness, or foreboding be lifted with the smoke.

Last, but not least, is the Winter Solstice itself. This is the shortest day of the year. With darkness taking its strongest stand, bonfires and candles are lit for protection. They also represent a kind of sympathetic magic, performed so days may again grow longer. With this in mind, Winter Solstice is a good time to put a fire under any project that has been lagging, perform spells for safety, and leave the past where it belongs—behind you. For a more potent impact, do this just prior to sunrise so that the emblem of light overcoming darkness prevails.

CHILSEONG-JE

Early in January, the Korean people perform a sacrifice to the Seven Stars. This ritual begins at midnight with an offering of water and rice bestowed upon Ursa Major (the Great Bear constellation). The god ruling this constellation in Korean lore also reigns over human undertakings. By leaving this offering, the people hope to win his favor for business and all other personal affairs.

For your purposes, this ritual works well just as it is. Wait until a night when you can see this constellation clearly, then set out your tokens with a prayer. Consult the Bear to provide strength and "hunting" skills for any goals you ardently seek.

Alternatively, consider the shamanistic symbolism behind the Great Bear. During the Winter, this powerful creature retreats to rest. Have you been getting enough sleep lately? Are you taking care of your spiritual and material resources? If not, let this constellation guide you. Meditate on the Bear and its lessons.

NEW YEAR'S FESTIVITIES

A variety of New Year celebrations take place throughout the Winter season, with some continuing nearly into Spring. Everything begins with a huge hurrah on January 1. Then, on the fifteenth day of Shebat (late January), the New Year of the Trees is observed in Palestine. Similar to Arbor Day in the United States, new trees are planted as monuments to beloved family members. The plants are placed in the ground with the wish, "Strength and courage to you."

I love this tradition, and can think of nothing more uplifting than planting a tree in the middle of Winter. Sow a seedling indoors so it won't die before spring. Name it after positive characteristics you want to grow in your life. When you transplant the tree in the Spring, continue to give it loving care so that those attributes endure.

Next comes the most elaborate New Year's celebration in the world—Chinese New Year. Based on the lunar calendar, this falls on the second New Moon after Winter Solstice (early February). Girls who are unmarried receive gifts of money in red envelopes for luck. Ancestral and household gods are venerated with incense, flowers, vegetables, and wine as offerings.

Any sharp items are banned from use on this day, lest they cut away good fortune. All debts are to be paid in full before the New Year arrives to insure prosperity to the house. These, and other traditions, are observed for as long as two weeks before regular business resumes.

A unique food for Chinese New Year is a rice dish with ten types of toppings (a perfect number). This dish is made with mandarin orange, five fruit seeds, garlic roots, juniper, meats, vegetables, and sprays of flowers. Ten chopsticks are placed on the dish and hold an almanac for the coming year. The dish is first offered to Heaven and Earth, then presented to the head of the household.

Each item in this elaborate meal has significance. The flowers are chosen for each season; lotus for Summer, olea for Autumn, orchid for Spring and almond for Winter. The chopsticks are a charm to keep the family together. Orange is for luck and the seeds for fertility. Finally the juniper bundle is an emblem of honor, which in China means long life to the recipient. Any or all of these symbols are perfectly fitting in your own New Year's observances.

To prepare this dish for the head of your house, start with a base of cooked white rice in the center of a platter. Around the perimeter, place mandarin oranges, dates, peanuts, filberts, and fresh vegetables. Add an appropriate silk flower at each compass point, using the rice to secure it. In the center, make a well to hold stir-fried meat spiced with ginger for prosperity. Before serving, lift this platter to the sky and invoke your chosen god/goddess. Offer the plate first to your house/coven leader, then share among the guests.

A third New Year's ritual, observed in Vietnam, is known as Tet. Celebrated around January 25, Tet is a holiday for good fortune. Carps are released to rivers, while offerings are made to gods and ancestors, similar to the Chinese festival. All households take care that their first visitor on this day has an auspicious name such as Kim (meaning gold). This way, the energy of that name is welcomed with the guest! So, if you have a friend with a felicitous name, be sure to invite them early to your celebration!

In Nigeria, ceremonies mark the opening of fishing season. On or around February 10, thousands of people line the river Sokoto with fishing nets. At the start of festivities, they all jump in with a huge splash, hoping that a startled fish will land in their nets. This is symbolic of God's favor. Also, the person catching the largest fish receives a prize. A version of this activity can be recreated for children using fruit pieces cut into the shapes of fish (various sizes) and a large bowl. Like dunking for apples, they dunk to capture the largest fish, and thus a little luck!

In Tibet, New Year takes place in mid-February and is known as Losar. The parades and archery competitions held on this day are the most spectacular of the year. Preceding the celebration, the old year is driven out, along with malevolent spirits, by monks performing devil dances. For these, bright colors and terrifying masks are donned to frighten away the old powers. Bearing this in mind, Tibetan New Year is an opportune time for spells pertaining to goals (targets) and banishing outmoded views or habits.

Ghanian New Year consists of a celebration which lasts thirteen days, the final day always falling just after Spring Equinox. The initial eleven days are given to dances which protect the people from evil, honor the dead, ensure bountiful harvests, and encourage luck. On the twelfth day, shrines are cleansed and prepared so that, the next morning, the New Year may be greeted without blemish. If you haven't purified your magical tools or altar lately, this is one date to remember for that purpose.

The Babylonians also observed the New Year close to the Spring Equinox (approximately March 19). Their rites lasted for ten days, during which Heaven and Earth were married. From this union, Spring was born, and with it new life.

Throughout these holidays, several themes recur. Wishes for luck and health, fruitfulness, triumph over evil or sickness, and remembering deceased loved ones all play important roles in New Year ceremonies. Since these exhibit themselves several times throughout the Winter months, finding a convenient date on which to hold personal observances should not be difficult.

ROMAN PLANTING FESTIVALS (LATE JANUARY)

To honor Tellus, the god of fertile Earth, and the goddess Ceres, who presides over farming, the Romans held two planting festivals. These celebrations took place around the end of January about one week apart. These were called the *feriae sementivae,* the feasts of sowing.

Other demi-gods were also remembered in this celebration, such as those governing ploughs, ingathering, and weeding. In an ardent effort not to overlook any aid, the Roman priests offered prayers to "any unknown gods, male or female," so none would be angered.

While it may be too early to consider sowing outdoor plants in your region, it is not too early to bless seeds. Gather those you plan to cultivate and place them in a sacred area of your home. Call on Tellus and Ceres to grant sturdy roots and bountiful harvests. Carry one or two kernels with you as a charm for grounding, fertility, and plenty.

CARNIVAL

Before the beginning of the lenten season, carnivals occur as a period of unbridled revelry, best exhibited by Mardi Gras in New Orleans. Since it is customary to eat all meat and fat before Lent starts on Ash Wednesday with a ritual fast, Mardi Gras literally means "fat Tuesday." In fact, the word *carnival* originates with two French words, *care* and *vale* that mean "farewell flesh or meat."

Numerous likenesses can be drawn between carnivals and the Roman Saturnalia, a rite that once announced Spring's arrival. The day is one of leisure, followed by a night of frolicking, costumes, candles, fortune telling, parades, music, and song.

Carnival's theme is one of flamboyance to offset the coming strictures of Lent.

In Venice, costumed people carry candles, sweetmeats, and flowers. They flirt outrageously from behind the masks until midnight. When the church bells toll, they blow out each other's candles and move silently homeward.

Austria has an unusual custom associated with Carnival known as the Dance of the Phantoms. This takes place on the third day of festivities, using masks which portray Spring's warmth or Winter's chill. One person portrays a good spirit who sweeps away evil with a broom. Other dancers toss grain and water toward the crowd as a blessing. To mimic this in your own circle, asperge the circle with dampened rice, oats, or wheat. Dance counterclockwise with brooms to clean away negativity, then turn sunward for good fortune.

FROST FAIRS (LONDON, ENGLAND)

Between the 16th and 19th centuries, frost fairs were held on the Thames as a diversion from Winter's chill. So popular was this activity that vendors came, setting up temporary booths to sell foods and beverages and offer games. Games of football were held at the shoreline, while huge pieces of lamb were roasted for everyone's eating pleasure. Apparently King Charles II openly visited these festivities!

Frost fairs are akin to snow balls, ice dances, and other blustery pleasures. These gatherings revel in the beauty of the season, rather than disdaining the cold. From a magical vantage point, the frost fair is a holiday to extol the element of water in all its forms. Employing ice and snow for components is particularly fitting, and exceedingly useful to binding spells.

One spell to halt gossip instructs us to write the name of the perpetrator on paper and freeze it, thereby freezing the negativity. Another country charm says that if you write something on ice in the Winter, you will never forget it! Finally, since both ice and snow melt, they are useful symbols for change and flexibility.

HODENING (WALES)

Taking place sometime during the Yule season, Hodening is an odd custom also known to other parts of the United Kingdom. It is probably a derivative of an ancient pagan ritual, but the actual origins are unknown. To begin, a wooden representation of a horse's head is placed on a pole bedecked with ribbons, the horse's mouth fashioned to open and shut on a hinge operated by its carrier. Young men ran in front of the creature ringing bells and shouting warnings.

As they arrived at various households, the men improvised poems demanding to be let in. The person at the door also had to reply with a rhyme. This competition of bardic skill went on until one party ran out of ideas. If the Hodeners won, they came in for cakes, ale, and a gift of money. Otherwise, they had to go on their way.

I believe this celebration may owe its roots to the worship of Epona, the horse-headed goddess, or possibly Rhiannon, who could ride her white horse more quickly than any man. Both goddesses embody the mother aspect, fertility, and composed leadership. If this is the case, then the Hodener's job was to collect tribute for the goddess.

Thus, if you wish to remember either of these divine ladies during this season, let your children play "horsey" to gather small tributes from other participants. Lay these on the altar with poetic incantations that express a wish. Visualize the image of a white horse, the emblem of communication and movement, and see what messages it holds for you.

This observance reminds me of the story of the Trojan Horse, which appeared to be an innocent gift, but carried danger. In this setting, the Hodener's message is one of caution. The horse snaps loudly at any caught unaware and demands a duty—the price we sometimes pay for negligence. Therefore, use this holiday as a gentle reminder to keep your senses keen. Be wary of those exacting high prices for spiritual gifts and listen closely to your intuition. Meditate and extend your awareness so that any warnings from your subconscious can come through.

JAPANESE TEA CEREMONY (CHANOYU)

I have placed this observance in Winter as a matter of preference. The Japanese performed this ceremony whenever it was appropriate. There is something about the chill of Winter months, though, that makes the thought of tea rituals more inviting.

The Chanoyu is a living art form, taking many years to perfect, and full of poise and grace. A formal tea ceremony can last as long as four hours, and is the embodiment of omnipresent truths; the connection of man to nature and the universe. It is also a model of decorum and propriety, each movement and section of the Chanoyu having specific meaning and import. The subtle undertones are changed only by the artistic impression of the individual.

The tearoom itself is an important aspect of the entire ceremony, quietly radiating an ambiance to the participants. It is designed to produce harmony from diversity through art, flowers, and subtle decor. The final effect is serene, liberating, and unintrusive.

To begin, all guests arrive a half-hour early to enjoy the gardens and meditate. The purpose of this time is to leave the outside world behind and prepare for fellowship. Next, the guests purify themselves by washing their hands and removing shoes. In ancient times, Samurai warriors left their weapons outside so nothing would mar the beauty of the ritual. Today it is simply unseemly to wear rings or watches, lest the timeless quality be marred.

The guests are ushered into the tearoom, the most honored of them sitting nearest the host. Normally, there are at least five people in attendance. The first part of the tea ritual, *kaiseki*, is a light meal including confections, followed by a brief intermission while the host prepares the tea utensils. All are carefully cleaned in advance; each step and tool which follows is ordained by rules meticulously followed. Many of these are family heirlooms.

Next comes the *koicha*, which means "thick tea." The koicha is announced by ringing a gong five or seven times to reassemble the visitors. Hot water is poured over green tea and whisked in a bowl for a cream-souplike texture. Visitors bow before taking the bowl, sip thrice, then turn to the next guest. This bowl is passed completely around the table once as a show of unity and trust.

There are many more details to the tea ceremony, but they are worthy of a lifetime of study, and cannot be contained by any one book. Instead, we adapt the spirit of the ritual in its hospitable, peaceful aspects by mirroring its movements and ideals.

Begin with a courteous invitation to friends, or people needful of renewed harmony. Set up an area for quiet contemplation, filled with small natural accents like dried leaves, pine needles, and flowers. This area will be a gathering place, and will set the tone for your entire ceremony. Also prepare a low table with floor mats from which to serve the beverage.

Next, create a tea which is tasty and magically attuned to your gathering. Let conversation be thoughtful while the bowl is passed, hand-to-hand, clockwise. This effectively develops a sacred space around the table. Let reconciliation have its way, along with the energy of fellowship.

Eastern import shops carry bowls, cups, and other utensils appropriate for such a gathering, at reasonable prices.

HANUKKAH

Celebrated near Yule, this is the Jewish Feast of Lights. Hanukkah commemorates the rededication of the Holy Temple in Jerusalem. When taken back from the Maccabeans in 165 B.C., the temple contained only enough oil to keep the lamps burning for one day. But, by a miracle, the lamps burned for eight days. To celebrate in modern times, eight are candles lit, one each day, on the traditional Menorah. This divine blessing in Jewish history preserved the religion.

In most homes, this is a festival for children, who receive small gifts each night. Dreydl games are played (the symbols mean "a great miracle occurred there") and potato pancakes are fried in oil by way of remembrance. Frequently the children will challenge each other to see who can best retell the story of Hanukkah using pantomime and masks. For the youths of a circle, this activity can translate into retelling the myths and legends of your guardian deities.

In addition, make some traditional potato pancakes as a side dish or main meal. Below is one recipe I enjoy. The olive oil adds a peaceful quality to the dish, potatoes are for grounding, and onion for zest. Combined, this is an excellent choice to bring improved harmony into your home:

Harmony Potato Pancakes

3 cups mashed potato
1 egg
$1/2$ cup milk
2 tablespoons flour
$1/4$ cup minced onion (optional)
2 tablespoons butter
olive oil

Directions: Beat together the potato, egg, milk, and flour so you get a smooth batter. Add a little extra milk if the mixture seems too dry. Blend in the onion. Heat the olive oil in a frying pan, then pour out in $1/3$ cup portions. Fry on both sides until golden brown. Dot the tops with butter. Yield: 9 pancakes.

December

December 19 (approximate)

HINDU AND CHINESE WINTER SOLSTICE FESTIVALS

Magical Themes: Redemption; prosperity; luck in relationships; weather divination; offerings to the gods and nature.

History/Lore: The Hindu version of Winter Solstice commemorates the awakening of gods who have slept for six months. Gifts of all types are exchanged between people, including butter, sugar, spices, combs, and mirrors. Brahmans receive the greatest tokens so that the giver is ensured of a prestigious life and a peaceful afterlife. It is also considered one of the most fortuitous days for weddings and engagements.

In southern India, special offerings of rice are given to the gods. Cows and oxen are anointed with water and bedecked with sacred greenery to move through the village. As they go, young children gather up the fruits jolted loose, taking them to the temple or home for luck.

In China, presentations to household gods are made by the family. Here, everyone gathers in the kitchen with red chopsticks, oranges, peony flowers, lotus, aster, and almond blossoms. Candles and incense are burned while the offering is made. Afterward, dumplings filled with pork are prepared by everyone to feast on the following morning. These are said to bring good fortune and health.

Decorating Ideas: Spicy potpourri, any of the traditional Chinese flowers, and lots of yellow trimmings to encourage plenty for yourself and your guests.

Garments: This is a festival centered around the home and family, so dress accordingly. Wear something festive, but comfortable for your environment.

Ritual Cup: Plum wine is my favorite Eastern beverage, and goes nicely with this celebration, having a light, pleasant taste. To prepare, gather, rinse, and dice 12 plums (one for each month of the year). Place these in a nonaluminum pan with 2 quarts water, 2 pounds sugar, 1/4 inch bruised ginger root, 1 tea bag, and a 1 inch slice of orange. Bring these to a low, rolling boil for 15 minutes. Remove from heat and cool. Meanwhile, mix 1/8 cup warm water with 1/4 package active yeast (wine yeast is best).

Once the plum juice is cool, strain it well. Pour in the yeast/water mixture and stir once. Cover with a thick towel for 48 hours. Strain and bottle with loose-fitting corks to age for 4 months, then cork tightly for 2-3 months before drinking. Makes 2 liters. If you don't like plums, substitute 12 *peeled* oranges.

Ritual Foods: Dien Hsing, from China, translates as "heart-toucher."

Heart-Toucher Noodles

BASIC NOODLES:

4 eggs
1/4 cup water
1/4 teaspoon salt
4 cups flour

FILLING:

1 1/2 cups minced beef
1/2 cup bamboo shoots
1/4 teaspoon ginger
1 tablespoon soy
3 cloves minced garlic
1/4 cup water chestnuts
4 chives, chopped
1/2 teaspoon sugar
1/2 cup Chinese cabbage
1/2 cup bean sprouts

Directions for noodles: Beat eggs, water, and salt until blended. Place the flour in a deep bowl, leaving an indentation in the center. Add egg mixture gradually until dough can be kneaded. Place this on a floured board and let stand for 20 minutes, kneading again until elastic. Divide this into quarters, rolling out the sections until paper thin, slicing into 3 x 3 inch squares. Layer these one on top of the other and place in the refrigerator, covered, until filling is prepared.

Directions for filling: The beef tastes best when marinated overnight in the refrigerator using soy sauce, 1/4 teaspoon ginger, 1/4 teaspoon onion powder, and a dash of garlic. This should be quickly stir-fried, set aside to cool, and shredded. In the meantime, chop all of the other ingredients finely, adding the beef with sugar and soy. Place 1-2 teaspoons of this into each wrapper. Fold the four corners of the noodle dough inward, sealing by dampening the edges with just a drop of water. Steam on a rack over a wok for 20-25 minutes, then fry the bottoms in oil for about 4 minutes or until golden brown. Serve with gingered soy sauce which has fresh chives floating in it, Chinese mustard, or duck sauce. Serves 6.

Incense: Sandalwood or lotus are favored in India and China.

Activities: The Chinese believe that sharing food with the trees brings happiness to the land. To follow this tradition, place cooked rice in the notches of trees around your home or your local park. Add a prayer or blessing of your choosing.

This is also regarded as a good day for weather forecasts, because Winter's night and Summer's day are evenly matched. The direction of the first breeze to greet you portends the disposition of the coming year. Those from the east bring mishaps, while the west wind speaks of providence. The southerly zephyr suggests difficulty in cultivating your efforts and the North wind brings munificence. If the north wind is accompanied by yellowish clouds, this is doubly fortunate, as they are a sign of abundance.

Sample Incantation: Use this before stepping outside to see what the changing winds are going to bring you:

> *Wind around me, Winds that blow,*
> *Winds that travel to and fro,*

Greet me truly, your message unfold;
Tell me what my future holds.

Also this Date: Day of the Dead in Egypt. Foods are left for the spirits of loved ones, along with window lamps to burn through the night. These guide wandering souls safely on their journey.

Other Accents: Wind-sensitive items hanging around your sacred space are helpful to the divinatory aspect of this holiday.

December 24 and 25

CHRISTMAS/YULE EVE AND DAY

Magical Themes: Rebirth; new beginnings; kindness and charity; hope and luck; divinatory efforts.

History/Lore: In northern Europe, a celebration honoring Odin known as *jolnir* occurred around December 25. This is how the modern term Yule originated. During this observance, special beers were brewed and offered to this chief god of the Norse pantheon.

To find the roots of Christmas, we have to explore history far before the birth of Christ. Many ancient civilizations watched the movements of the Sun carefully, hoping for its speedy return. Consequently we find the Mesopotamians celebrating *Sacaea*, the Greeks holding solar festivals, the Norse honoring dead heros, and the Druids harvesting their mistletoe, all on or about Yule Eve.

Christmas trees predate all Yule traditions, having started with animistic tree worshippers trying to appease the powerful spirit that defeated Winter's grasp—the pine! Holly and ivy, as plants that could protect the occupants from malevolent wandering spirits, decorated many medieval homes during late

Winter. Candles chased away the shadow of darkness, thereby hastening the Sun's return. Finally, our Yule ham may have originated with offerings of a boar's head to Frigga. In later history, King Henry VIII requested this menu for his annual Christmas dinner.

Decorating Ideas: Yule is a holiday filled with ancestral memory and tradition. As such, it's a great occasion to rummage through your family's attic for antique decorations. Return to old-fashioned popcorn-cranberry strings to mark the perimeter of your circle. The bright red of the berries honors the returning Sun! Set various colors of potted pointsettias at your cardinal points. And don't forget the mistletoe!

Garments: Reds, yellows, greens, and golds to honor the solar disk. Finery is the order of the day, but comfort shouldn't be forgotten either. Dress up for photographs and dinner, then change into comfortable attire for visiting friends, family, and neighbors.

Ritual Cup: Egg nog is my personal favorite. This can be made with or without alcohol to please children and adults alike. Another beverage to appear from wine cellars is fondly called "glögg." This is prepared by mixing equal quantities of brandy and port wine with cinnamon, ginger, nutmeg, cloves, and sugar to taste. This mixture should age, with raisins in the bottom of the bottle, for a month or two before serving.

Ritual Foods: This festival is the most lavish of all when it comes to food. Every type of confection adorns tables around the world. Cookies and candies are, by far, the favorites.

For a main meal, consider your family's country of origin for some hints. For example, a dinner in Norway would consist of pig, veal, or mutton. In Sweden, cod with white sauce, potatoes, braided bread loaves, and spiced brandy fill the board. The Finns enjoy prune tarts and seafood, and at my house we have roast beef!

Incense: Frankincense and myrrh; kitchen spices used in your holiday baking.

Activities: To keep your house full of food throughout the rest of Winter, sprinkle your doorways with grain as they did in

Old Russia. Bless the trees in your neighborhood by placing small pieces of sweet dough on bare branches. This tradition comes from Romania. Similarly, present sweet breads or those made from whole grain as gifts that carry the wish of prosperity to the recipient.

Serbians burn a Yule log with honey and wheat to guarantee food for their families. If you have, or can make, a Yule log, burn it and save the ashes to sprinkle around your home, garden (or window boxes) for blessings. If you don't have a fireplace, I suggest burning just a small bit of pine wood in a fireproof container instead.

It is also bad luck to let the Yule log burn away completely. A small section should be kept as kindling for the next year so good fortune will never leave your home. In this form, small shards of your Yule log can become components for good fortune spells.

Bohemians believe that if you cut an apple on this day and the pentagram within is perfect, you will have good health and happiness. Should this prove true, finely chop the apple and let it dry. In this form, you can add it to incense throughout the year to encourage well-being and joy. Another form of divination takes place in Germany. Here, if Christmas occurs on a Tuesday, it fortells a brutally cold Winter, a damp Summer, and a bad season for wine and beers. If Christmas is rainy, it means a rainy, damp year. If the Sun shines, however, this is a lucky sign.

For children, the Mexican piñata makes for marvelous fun. Fillable piñatas are available through import shops. If you don't want to stuff it with candy, try small bags of dried fruits and nuts instead. The piñata is hung out of reach and struck with the handle of a broom (move your breakables) by the children, who are blindfolded. Once the piñata breaks, all participating children run to gather up their treasures.

Another enjoyable tradition for children comes from Italy—the ceppo. This is made from plywood to resemble a tree, with several levels where tiny gifts can be left. Begin with a triangle 6 inches on each side for a base. Cut two smaller triangles, measuring 4 and 2 inches per side respectively. These are held in

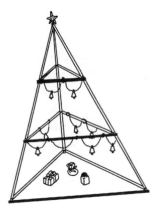

*Figure 48. Traditional Italian
ceppo — a gift tree.*

place by three slats of wood and tiny upholstery nails. The edges
should be well sanded, and then can be decorated by the children
(see figure 48).

The Scandinavians remember the harshness of Winter by
making a feeder of wheat and suet for the birds. This gift must
be put up before you partake of your own dinner to insure your
continued sustenance. To make such a feeder, buy some bird
seed and a block of fat at the supermarket. Skewer the fat on the
small end of a fallen branch and press the seed firmly into it. The
larger end of the branch is secured in a snow pile, set in the
ground, or hung in a tree for the birds to feast upon.

Sample Invocation: There is a lovely poem which celebrates the Sun in the Scandinavian *Eddas*, a collection of thirty-
seven poems which retell the stories of gods, legends, and
Scandinavian history. This can be used as part of your verbal ritual, specifically as you charge the southern point of the altar:

> *From the South the Sun shone on the walls;*
> *Then did the earth green herbs produce.*
> *The Moon went ahead, the sun followed;*
> *His right hand held the steeds of heaven.*[13]

Also This Date: Juvenalia (Rome) — Children's Day.
Wearing their best clothes and eating the best food, everyone

13. From the Scandinavian *Eddas*, *Bullfinch's Age of Fable* (Philadelphia: David
McKay, 1898), p. 410.

dedicated this day to children's enjoyment. The most treasured gifts were those considered lucky. This holiday's influence on your own Yule festivities is evident, so don't forget the youths in your life on this day! If there are no children around you, then celebrate your own inner child. Buy a toy you've always wanted, play a silly game, or watch cartoons.

Other Accents: Caroling didn't become popular until the 15th century, at which time carols were both sung and danced! Many old carols like *The Holly and The Ivy* have strong magical overtones to enjoy. Fill your home with uplifting music!

December 31, January 1

New Year's Eve and New Year's Day

Magical Themes: The spirit of hospitality; new beginnings; positive transformation; overcoming bad habits; luck, good health, and long life.

History/Lore: As mentioned earlier in this chapter, every civilization had its own timing for the New Year. The Egyptians and Phoenicians used the Autumn Equinox as a guide. Early Greeks employed the Winter Solstice.

It was not until the reformation of the Roman calendar that the first day of a new year was designated as January 1. Then, the date was dedicated to the god Janus, after whom January was named. This divine figure is sometimes portrayed with two heads, one facing the old year, and the other looking toward the future. With this in mind, the Romans felt January 1 was a particularly auspicious day for marriage.

In Japan, some people dress up as spirits to drive out misfortune for the coming year. Going house to house, they are greeted with offerings of sake and rice cakes. In Athens, this idea is mimicked with a slight difference. Young men go out with whips, rattles, and confetti to frighten away any ill fortune.

Decorating Ideas: Items which honor both the past and present, such as family photographs. Two candles, one to be lit at midnight to represent the new year while the other is blown out.

Garments: Personal choice.

Ritual Cup: Wassail, an Anglo Saxon beverage served on New Year's Day to insure good health to all who drink it. Literally translated *waes hael* means "Be well" or "Be hearty!" Here is one recipe:

Waes Hael Wine

> 1 cup water
> 1 teaspoon cardamom
> 1 teaspoon whole clove
> 1 teaspoon nutmeg
> 1 teaspoon powdered ginger
> 1 teaspoon coriander
> 1 bottle sherry
> 3 quarts ale
> 1 cup white sugar
> 6 eggs, separated
> 12 apples
> 1 cup brown sugar

Directions: Warm the water with all the spices until a dark tealike texture is achieved. Add this to the sherry, ale and white sugar, warming throughout. Separate the eggs, beating the yokes until thick and the whites to a froth. Fold these two together. Bake the apples, rolled in brown sugar, in a 400 degree oven for a half-hour.

When all is ready, pour the egg mixture into a punch bowl. Add the ale and sherry slowly, beating hard while pouring. Float the hot apples on top of the bowl. Yields 18 good-sized cups of beverage.

Alternatively, Scots enjoy a pint of hot ale on New Year's Eve for health.

Ritual Foods: In Europe, sweetcakes, cheese, and wine were favored. Small tarts known as "god cakes" were presented to children by their godparents. These were filled with spiced mincemeat or currants.

Residents of Norway enjoy fish, potatoes, rice pudding, and cardamom rolls. The Pennsylvania Dutch feast on coffee and buns. In my own home, we indulge in "luxury" foods for prosperity, especially shrimp.

During the Middle Ages, a popular confection and gift was marchpanes (marzipan). This is a sweet almond paste whose consistency lends itself to all manner of sculpting. One of the most exquisite carvings was one of St. Paul's Cathedral presented to Queen Elizabeth, appropriately on New Year's Day. Here is the recipe to try:

New Year Marzipan

> 1 cup almond paste
> 1 cup confectioners' sugar
> 2-3 drops of flavoring extract
> 1-2 drops food coloring

Directions: Mix your ingredients together then place them on a cold surface, kneading them for about 15 minutes. Afterward, shape the paste into any image desired. Marzipan can be iced using a thin white frosting, if desired, but is quite sweet by itself.

Incense: One possibility is vervain and oak. Vervain was ordered by Romulus to be offered with his gifts. Oak is sacred to the Druids, who presented people with gifts of mistletoe harvested from its boughs. Alternatively, create a mixture which represents your personal goals for the next year.

Activities: Reconcile any differences you have and pay all your debts. These actions assure you of a year full of peace and prosperity. Also, take care not to sweep your home, lest you sweep away your luck!

As at Christmas, weather divinations were quite popular at the New Year. One approach comes from Germany. Cut 6 onions in half and hollow out the center. Fill this area with salt, then lay the onions in a row in the attic on New Year's Eve. Name each half after a month of the year. The next day, look to see which onions are dry and which have dissolved the salt. The ones which are dry portend an arid month.

In England, it was believed that the first draught of water taken from a well after midnight would remain fresh all year.

Adapting this idea, go to your faucet right after the tolling of the New Year and pour out a goodly bottle of water. Use this in the months ahead as a tincture base to increase energy and creativity.

Armenian women bake bread on New Year's Day, filling it with almonds, nuts, and a lucky coin. This bread is enjoyed after midnight. The finder of the coin is assured of good fortune all year. In your own home, try modifying this slightly by purchasing some dairy-case sticky buns to cook just before midnight. Sneak a coin and other positive symbolic tokens into the center of each. Then, let people choose their future! Just warn everyone before hand about the tokens, so they are careful in biting.

Sample Invocation: This invocation is the essence of the New Year's holiday and of Janus himself.

> *Through your portals, come and go*
> *Opportunity, through them flow*
> *The years of life, beginnings and ends,*
> *Each of which a lesson sends.*
>
> *Count the time, measure true,*
> *Until my soul again joins you.*

Alternative Timing: Any other New Year's celebration.

Also this Date: Gamelia Festival (Greece). Named for Hera, this celebration honored marriages. Offerings of palm, bay, and sweetmeats were brought to the temple to insure a year full of happiness. Those who could afford it also gilded fruits for prosperity.

Other Accents: Take a little wassail from the bowl and carry it outside. Spill it a little at a time, in a clockwise direction, around your residence while singing "Here we come a-wassailing." This blesses the land and brings happiness to the home.

January

January 5 and 6

TWELFTH NIGHT AND TWELFTH DAY

Magical Themes: Informality; breaking social constraints.

History/Lore: In pre-Christian times, this was a holiday for reversing social strictures. Parodies of songs and rituals were performed specifically to breach taboos.

Twelfth day is slightly quieter, but no less filled with activity. In medieval France they observed a tradition known as "King of the Bean." The "King" was the individual fortunate enough to find a bean baked into his/her cake. This token entitled the person to large portions of food and a night of dominion over the feast hall.

Decorating Ideas: String sweet peapods around your altar to please providence.

Garments: Wear your clothes inside out, or wear clothes of the opposite sex, in keeping with the theme of the day.

Ritual Cup: Wassail is still enjoyed as it was on Yule. Apple cider is an appropriate alternative.

Ritual Foods: The English prepared a meal of beef, potatoes, and onions fried together. Magically, this is good for grounding.

Incense: Basil. The people of one region of Yugoslavia, Dalinatia, attached this to their nets to insure good catches, or put it under their pillows for visionary dreams.

Activities: According to tradition, it is best to have all your decorations cleared away by Twelfth Night so your year begins on a fresh note. Also, take notice of the weather through the twelve days of Christmas leading up to this date. The general pattern of each day portends that month's weather.

In rural England, blessing of the land accompanied the revelry, so consider taking time to sanctify your living or working space. Sometimes bits of cake were hung on trees or libations of cider poured to activate the magic. For your purposes, asperging with spring water and leaving bread around the perimeter of your home is more suitable.

Sample Invocation: As you bless your living space recite:

Clockwise round, blessings abound,
By bits of bread, we shall always be fed;
Where water fell, we shall always stay well.
The magic is free, so mote it be!

Alternative Timing: Beating the Bounds, Terminalia.

Other Accents: Throw caution to the winds. Hug someone on impulse, eat with your elbows on the table, and wait to do dishes until the next day. Find a way to feel liberated from anything which burdens you.

January 8

JUSTICA'S DAY (ANCIENT ROME)

Magical Themes: Promises and oaths; fairness and equity.

History/Lore: Justica was originally worshipped in the form of Themis, the Greek goddess of ethics and advisor to Zeus. Themis presided over the areas of sensible council and true justice, and was aptly represented by balanced scales.

Decorating Ideas: The color purple is sacred to these goddesses and to the realm of justice. Have some type of measures available as accents; even bathroom scales can suffice.

Garments: Any purple items or clothes which are very symmetrical in construction.

Ritual Cup: What fills the cup for this observance is not as important as how it is quaffed. In early history, specifically the Middle Ages, it was customary to drink from a common cup to seal a promise to the lips. This action was a sign of trust and unity.

Ritual Foods: This will vary depending on your specific goal for the day. Try a recipe with a marigold-petal garnish if your magic pertains to legal matters.

Incense: Celandine or hickory.

Activities: An excellent day to release magic to help in any matter of inequity. It is also a time when rededicating yourself to a cause or the goddess will be particularly potent. Consider the promises you have made lately. Have they been kept? If not, put some energy toward that goal.

Sample Spell: To create a portable charm which encourages fair dealings with everyone you meet, wrap a vanilla bean, 4 hematites, and 4 sunflower seeds or petals in yellow cloth. Leave this in the light of the Sun for 8 hours. This is best done when the sky is totally clear, so no clouds interfere with your perceptions. Empower the amulet by saying:

> *As shadows are chased by the light,*
> *Let dishonesty be revealed to my sight.*
> *In word or deed, discernment preside,*
> *Show me wherein untruth abides.*

Alternative Timing: Festival of Isis.

Other Accents: A gavel; law books; yin-yang symbol for symmetry.

Mid to late January

FESTIVAL OF SARASVATI (HINDU — ASIA)

Magical Themes: Wisdom and learning.
History/Lore: Hindus in southern Asia remember the god-

dess of learning with a sensible flourish. Being the personification of reason and sagacity, no giddy actions accompany her
observance. Instead, students fill the Katmandu Valley of Nepal
bearing flowers, food, and incense for Her temples. Books, pens,
brushes, and other writing utensils are placed on her altars to be
blessed.

Decorating Ideas: White flowers, especially the lotus;
magical books, the lute, and images of swans or peacocks, all
sacred to this goddess.

Garments: Students frequently wear saffron-colored robes
while offering marigolds upon the altar.

Ritual Cup: A marigold cordial. For this, place 1 quart of
vodka in a half-gallon jug. Add about 1^1/2 quarts of marigold
petals which have been well rinsed. Leave these to set in the
vodka for two weeks, shaking daily. Strain and warm over a low
flame, adding sugar until personally pleasing, and three pinches
of rosemary. Strain again and bottle, leaving to age in a dark
place for one month before serving.

Ritual Foods: To bring productivity to your efforts, make
eggs with marigolds. Beat 2 eggs with 1 teaspoon milk, 1 teaspoon water, salt, and pepper. Fry these lightly in ^{1}/2 tablespoon
butter. When almost done, add 1 washed, chopped marigold and
cook lightly. Serve with toast and a hint of nutmeg.

Incense: To strengthen your mind, use lily of the valley,
caraway, rosemary, or spearmint. For wisdom use iris, sage, or
peach.

Activities: Ancient people sometimes used walnuts to treat
mental difficulties because they resemble a brain. With this in
mind, you can make yourself a walnut ornament or scented ball
to adorn the area where you study. The ornament is simple to
make, requiring only small upholstery tacks, some cord, and tiny
silk flowers to complete. Begin by attaching a loop of yellow cord
to the top of the nut using tacks at each side. Then, glue on any
flowers you like at the top and hang it somewhere visible (see
figure 49, page 249).

For the nut ball, start with a base of foam. If you want to,
you can cut this to other symbolic shapes, such as that of an eye.

Figure 49. Walnut ornament.

Attach a circle of ribbon near the top using wire and glue. Then secure the nuts all around, using liberal amounts of epoxy. If there are any open spots when you are done, fill them with little flowers (see figure 50). Scent the bundle with oil of rosemary to encourage memory retention.

Sample Incantation: When putting the finishing touches on your ornament, add a verbal component such as:

> *Ribbon wound, 'round and 'round,*
> *Thus within is magic bound,*
> *With nuts entwined, by scent refined,*
> *So good memory will be mine.*

Alternative Timing: Celebration of the Goddess of Reason (Autumn).

Figure 50. Decorative nut ball. Left: ribbon attached with wire to a foam ball; Right: finished ball covered with nuts and flowers.

Other Accents: Students can set up their own altar to Sarasvati. Here they leave objects associated with school to be blessed. Afterward, books may be covered with yellowish-red paper (creativity/learning) and anointed with rosemary oil to further accent the magic.

January 20 (approximate)

FEAST OF THE KITCHEN GOD (CHINA)

Magical Themes: Hearth and home; thanksgiving to household guardians.

History/Lore: Taking place just before the end of the Chinese year, the Feast of the Kitchen God celebrates the robust caretaker of the family's virtue. The image of Tsao Wang is always round and smiling. He carefully watches the family, then, on the twenty-third night of the twelfth Moon, he returns to heaven and reports on their actions.

For this observance, all household members gather in the kitchen. Cakes, sweets, meat, and vegetables are laid out as offerings. In some regions, molasses is dabbed on the god's mouth so that only "sweet" messages will be conveyed to the great Jade Emperor.

Decorating Ideas: At one point in the ceremony, children throw beans over the roof to simulate the sound of Tsao Wang's horses. Therefore, any type of dried or fresh beans make appropriate accents to the sacred space.

Garments: Sandals or bare feet, both befitting the Chinese environment.

Ritual Cup: Something sweet so that your own words will be as kind as those of Tsao Wang to the emperor!

Ritual Foods: None; eat out! Give your hearth god/goddess a well-earned break.

Incense: Sandalwood or kitchen spices.

Activities: An activity which children will enjoy is imploring the Kitchen God for an answer to a secret question. To begin, the children should whisper their query into the god's ear, then firmly clasp their hands over both ears. Next, they go outside and listen. Since the Kitchen God is wise and helpful, the first sentence they hear clearly will be the response they seek.

Sample Invocation: Follow the lead of the Chinese, who recite this song as a paper image of the Kitchen God is burned, transporting him to heaven:

> *Go fit up to heaven;*
> *Begone in a trice;*
> *Forget all the bad*
> *And tell only what's nice!*[14]

Alternative Timing: Feast of the Kitchen Goddess (Autumn).

Other Accents: This is an excellent day to make or purchase special utensils for your kitchen and pantry. One such item is a scented kitchen mitt. Start with an inexpensive ready-made oven mitt. Using some sturdy material, cut a square which fits comfortably in the palm of the mitt. Iron down 1/4 inch on all sides of this patch, then sew on three sides, with the rough edges facing inward.

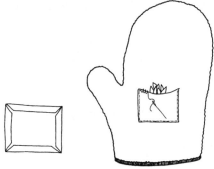

Figure 51. Scented kitchen mitt.

---

14. Traditional Chinese prayer quoted in Ruth Adams and Ruth Hutchison, *Every Day's a Holiday* (New York: Harper & Brothers Publishers, 1951), p. 20.

Fill the opening with a little dried lavender and mint. Take care that the pouch stays fairly flat so you can still handle pots and pans easily. Now stitch the final edge closed (see figure 51, page 251). Each time you use the mitt, heat will release the scents of peace and prosperity into your home.

January 30

FESTIVAL OF PAX (ROME)

Magical Themes: Peace and harmony; reconciliations, truces and agreements; serenity and composure.

History/Lore: The mighty Romans had at least three celebrations a year to honor Pax, the goddess of peace. These began with a parade at the center of the city. As people walked, they stoped at roadside shrines leaving pictures of their leaders at the feet of the goddess. Finally, on the steps of the temple, the names of individuals who were adversaries of accord were read by a priestess. To find your name on this list was akin to a curse.

Decorating Ideas: Pictures of world leaders, your boss, heads of the group or household, etc., over a white altar cloth.

Garments: Anything white, the color of armistice.

Ritual Cup: Anything with apple, apricot, or peach juice. As on Justica's Day, this should be served from a communal cup.

Ritual Foods: Make a lettuce, cucumber (without peels), olive, and white onion salad. Toss with any oregano-marjoram spiced dressing to sooth emotional wounds.

Incense: Violet or pennyroyal.

Activities: This should be a quiet day where an attempt is made to heal rifts between friends, family members, etc. If the war-hungry Romans could find time for peace, we should too!

Sample Invocation: Since white is the hue of peace and milk a beverage of the goddess, use milk as your libation during this invocation:

P oured out at this threshold, harmony;
E mitted from this vessel, serenity;
A t the edge of my windows flows unity;
C ircled around my home, accord;
E very one within to be blessed by fellowship;
    Pax, heed my prayer and answer!

Alternative Timing: Forgiveness rituals; after a divorce; Festival of Concordia (February 22, Rome)

Other Accents: Peace is not something that arrives with loud sounds or colors, so keep your ornamentation quiet and your music soft.

February

February 2

BRIDGET'S DAY (IRELAND); GROUNDHOG DAY (UNITED STATES); CANDLEMAS (EUROPE).

Magical Themes: Kindness to animals; omens and signs; weather divination; protection and prosperity.

History/Lore: The idea of Groundhog Day arrived in the United States with German immigrants, who believed that if any animal came out of its lair and saw the Sun on this day, Winter would last forty more days.

Candlemas may have received its name from the lighting of white candles that often accompanied the festival. Among modern Wiccans, it is a day to rid oneself of lingering shadows, and give strength to the slowly returning Sun.

In Ireland, this is called Bridget's Day, in honor of a Chieftan's daughter who lived in Kildare. Bridget dedicated her life to caring for forest creatures. Some people even speculated that she was really a fairy. Later, Bridget was revered as a triple goddess (maiden, mother, crone) among the Celts.

Decorating Ideas: Candles often burned all night on this holiday, so fill your sacred space with tapers, especially white ones. Depictions of young animals and rushes or sheaves of oat are also appropriate.

Garments: Use white sheets made into comfortable robes upon which you can paint depictions of burning candles.

Ritual Cup: Ale is traditional for Bridget's day.

Ritual Foods: Barmbreac, a bread made with raisins, currants, and candied citrus rinds. Here is one easy recipe:

Bridget's Bread

> 1 loaf frozen bread dough
> 1/2 cup mixed currants,
>   raisins, and candied rinds
> 2 tablespoons sugar
> 1 teaspoon cinnamon
> 1 egg, beaten
> 1 tablespoon butter, melted

Directions: Defrost and prepare the frozen dough according to the directions on the package. Set aside while it is rising. Mix together the fruits, sugar, and cinnamon and let stand. Knead these into the bread dough, then let it rise again in a warm place for 20 minutes. Put this into a greased bread pan, baking according to package directions. During the last 10 minutes, baste regularly with a mixture of beaten egg and butter. Cool and serve with a little honey.

Incense: Woodsy scents like pine, clover, and oak wood.

Activities: Make Bridget's Crosses out of any available material and hang them around your home. This protects against fire and lightning (see figure 52, page 255).

Another activity for the children in certain rural regions was to form a "Crios Bride." This is essentially a large rope loop with four Bridget's Crosses attached at the compass points. To gain the goddess' protection for the ensuing year, each child had to pass through the center of the loop.

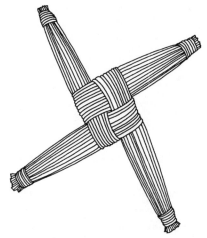

Figure 52. Bridget's Cross.

When everyone has passed through the center, take the crosses off, open up one end and allow your children to use it as a jump rope. In this form, it gives luck and health, as the jump rope makes complete circles around the children (even above and below them). Just check to be sure they move the rope clockwise for positive energy.

Sample Invocation: Bridget was known to be the patroness of poets, so any spells and invocations today are best performed in poetic form. Here's one example:

> *Light the tapers, one and all;*
> *Hearken to the Goddess' call.*
> *She who heals, She who's kind;*
> *She to whom our promise, we bind.*
>
> *See the tapers, heed the call;*
> *Come and fill this sacred hall.*
> *Lady of the wood and arts;*
> *Come and fill our waiting hearts!*

Alternative Timing: Initiation rites (Autumn or other). This is one time of the year when certain magical traditions welcome their initiates.

Other Accents: If anyone has a young pet they would like blessed, this is an exceptionally good occasion for it.

February 3 or 4

BEAN THROWING DAY (JAPAN)

Magical Themes: Banishing evil; attracting good fortune; memorials for those passed over.

History/Lore: Throughout Nara, Japan, this day is a day to litter the ground with beans, while bellowing "Fortune in — the devil out." The loud noise and the beans are both credited with scaring away any negative energies. Meanwhile, family members bring lanterns engraved with wishes to the Kasuga Shrine, devoting each lantern to a beloved ancestor. As the lantern burns, it provides hope to the living, and answers prayers for the dead.

Decorating Ideas: Candles, lanterns, tiki torches in abundance; dried or fresh beans on the altar.

Garments: Anything green to accentuate the lucky aspects of the day.

Ritual Cup: Whip 1/3 cup pineapple juice with 1/3 cup orange juice and 3 strawberries per person. To further enhance the fortunate magic, sprinkle with a little nutmeg.

Ritual Foods: Beans, of course! I like preparing homemade baked beans for this occasion so the oven can activate the serendipitous energy and the brown sugar can invoke sweetness. Here is my recipe for 4-6 people:

Banishing Evil Beans

2 16-oz. cans generic baked beans
3 tablespoons molasses
1 teaspoon minced garlic

1 small onion diced
3 tablespoons brown sugar
2 hot dogs per person, split
1/2 pound bacon

Directions: Mix the beans in a large bowl with the next four ingredients. Pour this into an ovenproof cake pan. Lay out the split hot dogs evenly, pushing them down into the beans slightly. Spoon a little sauce over top of them. Separate the bacon and arrange it on top of the hot dogs. Put this in a 300 degree oven for about 25 minutes until the bacon is fully cooked and the hot dogs are plump. Serve with sourdough bread or biscuits.

Incense: For banishing, use purgatives like frankincense and myrrh; for luck, try allspice.

Activities: Asperge the group by sprinkling small beans around them. Plant beans of various colors at the cardinal points of your circle for serendipitous energy.

Have some dried, variegated beans blessed with which to make a decorative luck charm for the home. For this, each person should bring a clear container with them. You will also need some decorative material, ribbon, and silk flowers (optional). Begin by filling your container with different colored beans in any manner pleasing to the eye. Once filled, cover the top with a circle of fabric which overlaps the edge by 1 1/2 inches. Tie this in place using ribbon, then add a few flowers at the knot for ornamentation (see figure 53).

Figure 53. Good luck bean charm.

Sample Invocation: While you prepare your charm, recite the following:

> *Beans a-many, bring me plenty.*
> *Each bean I pluck brings me luck.*
> *Beans which shine, good health be mine.*
> *With beans around, good fortune abounds.*

Alternative Timing: Good Luck Day.

Other Accents: This type of ritual is truly spectacular if held late at night. As the lanterns or candles are lit, they slowly change darkness into radiant light, shedding magic all around!

February 11

CAEDMON THE BARD (OLD ENGLAND)

Magical Themes: Visionary dreams; bardic talents and traditions; memory improvement.

History/Lore: Caedmon lived in the seventh century as a simple shepherd in England. The story goes that he attended a party one night in which a harp was passed to each guest that he might sing a song. Caedmon had no vocal skills or talent with poetry, so he returned to his sheep and fell asleep.

As the night progressed, Caedmon began to dream. The harp came to him once more and again he refused, saying he could not sing. The stranger holding the harp corrected him and bid him sing "the creation." In the vision, Caedmon shrugged in resignation and took the harp. Suddenly a beautiful voice came from him, along with words he'd never heard before.

Upon waking, Caedmon remembered each verse of the song in the dream. He took this knowledge to a near-by monastery to be recorded. According to legend, this song became known as the *Caedmonian Cycle*. Milton is said to have written *Paradise Lost* using this as inspiration.

Decorating Ideas: All musical instruments are welcome and encouraged in the sacred space, especially depictions of harps; a shepherd's crook.

Garments: Linen or cotton robes similar to those of a shepherd.

Ritual Cup: Caedmon was thought to drink wine this night, which inspired his dream. For minors, grape juice will suffice.

Ritual Foods: You can either prepare party-type foods, or edibles associated with unique dreams. Pizza with onions is one possibility.

Incense: Rose and jasmine to encourage visions.

Activities: Pass a staff or wand around the circle clockwise. As it reaches each person, have them share a story, poem, song, or musical piece. It would also be fitting for people to share recent dreams for interpretation by the group.

Sample Invocation:

Caedmon, with wine and song
Fill our circle all night long.
Bring to us the bardic arts,
With creativity, fill our hearts.
Bring to us a dream so pure
It fills our minds, our lips to stir.
Caedmon, with wine and song
Fill our circle all night long.

Alternative Timing: Eisteddfod (Summer).

Other Accents: Live performances of music, including background songs, are truly invigorating to this celebration.

February 13—21

PARENTALIA (ROME)

Magical Themes: Honoring one's parents, guardians or ancestors; memorials.

History/Lore: Unlike the usual wild revelry of Rome, this was a very quiet holiday. Marriage was forbidden, those in authority wore no insignia of rank, and the temples were closed. Instead, the entire week was given over to honoring ancestors and placating any family ghosts.

Decorating Ideas: Garlands of roses and violets are traditional, along with any representations of your parents, grandparents, etc.

Garments: Anything handed down to you from older family members. Try rummaging through a grandparent's attic!

Ritual Cup: Milk wine was sometimes brought to those being honored, along with honey for sweetness in this life or the next. I could not find a recipe for the former, but here is one for a milk cordial:

Memorial Milk Cordial

1/2 gallon whole milk
2 1/2 pounds sugar
1 quart grain alcohol (190 proof)
1/2 lemon, diced
1/2 orange, diced
2 vanilla beans

Directions: Pour the milk into a gallon-sized container with an airtight lid. Add the other ingredients and shake thoroughly. Let this stand for three weeks, then strain thoroughly. You may have to run it through cheesecloth several times to decant properly. If desired, other spices can be added at this point. Age the cordial another month, then serve.

Ritual Foods: Any recipes inherited from your family, or from the country in which your family originated.

Incense: Rosemary for good memories. Other good choices include frankincense and myrrh for protection, or lavender for peace.

Activities: Gather all the loose pictures you have of your family and other close associations. Put them in order and work on your scrap books. Anoint the edges of each page with rose oil for love, or rosemary to match your incense. Pray for those people you can't see frequently and visit those you can. This is an excellent day to hold a family reunion. Have everyone bring their memorabilia.

Sample Invocation: If you are having a reunion, one way to unify the gathering is through a group toast. This is begun by the host/hostess expressing his/her sentiments, ending with an uncompleted phrase. The person next to them continues the pattern, and so on around the group. This is like a progressive story, except that everyone adds their personal wishes and memories to the toast. When the entire circuit of the room is complete, all raise their glasses and affirm by saying, "Here, Here!"

Alternative Timing: Many Autumn festivals have similar themes.

Other Accents: If your family has been known for a particular pastime, craft, or art form, have everyone bring a sampling with them. This includes things like quilts, wine, woodworking, tatting, gardening, fishing, etc. The stories behind each item should be shared with the rest of the family.

February 14

ST. VALENTINE'S DAY (IRELAND)

Magical Themes: Love and romance in abundance!

History/Lore: Having its origins in the ancient Roman festival of Lupercalia, this was the holiday when young people drew names to discover their true love. When Valen was martyred on this day in A.D. 270, the feast for him replaced Lupercalia to discourage such pagan heresy. Despite the Church, however, divinations for love continued, and over time, St. Valentine became the patron of lovers everywhere.

Decorating Ideas: Lots of red and pink; hearts and flowers; bits of lace to ensnare love; Cupid and cherubic images.

Garments: Romantic, alluring, sexy, and fun.

Ritual Cup: A milk shake for two sipped from one glass, as the sweethearts of old used to do.

Ritual Foods: Heart-shaped chocolate cake with whipped cream frosting and strawberries. A candlelight feast featuring tomato salad (the love apple), glazed sweet potatoes, and meats spiced with rosemary and basil.

Incense: Rose with a hint of cinnamon for energy.

Activities: Pin five bay leaves to your pillow on this night to dream of a future love. Make a special valentine for someone you hold dear. Be sure to use traditional symbols like lace, two birds, ribbons, baskets (weave love together), and a hint of your own perfume or cologne. Let them know just how important they are!

Have a little fun with omen observation. Go outside and watch for any bird that flies overhead. Robins speak of marriage or close friendship with a sailor. Today this can equate to someone in the Marines or Coast Guard. Sparrows portend joyful relationships and a goldfinch foretells wealth.

Sample Incantation: Spells and rituals for love are best performed to strengthen relationships that already exist or to draw the right person into your life. They should not, however, be performed to manipulate feelings. Instead, release your energy to the god/goddess for guidance.

> *Cupid let your arrow fly*
> *Direct to where my true love lies.*
> *Let it safely find its mark*
> *Deeply in my lover's heart.*
>
> *Cupid let your arrow free,*
> *Yet one more to lodge in me,*

So love within my spirit lands
To freely share with heart and hand.

Alternative Timing: Allan Apple Day (Autumn) or Rosalia (Spring).

Other Accents: A bow and arrow; tools for Cupid's use.

February 15

BIRTHDAY OF THE PEARLY EMPEROR (CHINA)

Magical Themes: The way of Taoism: contemplation, reason, peace, and informality.

History/Lore: This day commemorates the Birthday of the Pearly Emperor who reigns in Taoist paradise over all his followers. Taoism was established 6 B.C by Lao Tse, and is regarded as the common peoples' faith in China. Taoists dislike violence and coercion, and have a general nonchalance about ritual and ceremony.

Decorating Ideas: See activities below.

Garments: Since Taoists have an aversion to formality, I suggest no real strictures on garments other than what makes you comfortable.

Ritual Cup: Mandarin tea.

Ritual Foods: Any edibles that have mandarin oranges, persimmons, peanuts, or dates as ingredients. One option is to make a nutty fruit salad using candied pineapple and raisins with the aforementioned fruits.

Incense: Again, keep things simple. Use plain scents that help you concentrate or encourage peaceful reflection. Jasmine and myrrh are two good options.

Activities: This day is observed by leaving offerings in a sunny place. Candles, flowers, three bowls of tea leaves, vermicelli, and biscuits shaped like peaches are all traditional. The noodles are symbols of long life, and the peaches denote immortality. If you desire children, leave a bowl of mandarin oranges with peanuts and melon seeds. This signals your wish to the emperor.

If there is anyone in your life with whom you have argued, this is a good time to extend the hand of peace. Contemplate your life, with reason and good judgment as your guide.

Sample Chant: This should be whispered like a round, moving clockwise around the circle. This will effectively surround all participants with gentle energy.

> *Contemplation, reason, and harmony,*
> *Both without and within, reside in me.*

Alternative Timing: Festival of Peace; Birthday of Buddha.

Other Accents: Candlelight and highlights of white throughout the space to underscore the theme of peacefulness.

February 16

CELEBRATION OF VICTORIA (ROME)

Magical Themes: Victory, success, overcoming, and mastery.

History/Lore: Originally a woodland goddess who was translated into a Roman military divinity, Victoria is everything her name implies. In Greece, she was known as Nike, and her dominion is that of accomplishment.

Decorating Ideas: Life-affirming colors; uplifting, positive images of yourself or the area in your life which needs a boost.

Garments: Choose your clothing colors according to the topic at hand. For success in a creative art, use yellow. For improved leadership, wear gold. For victory over sickness, choose bright red (for life) or green (for growth and change).

Ritual Cup: Steep lemon balm in warm water for a victorious tea.

Ritual Foods: Cinnamon-ginger sherbet, made with two potent herbs associated with success. This particular recipe is also very soothing to the stomach. This is enough for two quarts:

Success Sherbet

> 4 cups sugar
> 16 cups water
> 1/2 teaspoon powdered cinnamon
> 1/2 teaspoon powdered ginger

Directions: Place all the ingredients together in a large pot and bring to a boil. Stir constantly until a syrup is formed (about 5-7 minutes). Cool. Pour this into a flat pan and cover, placing the liquid in the freezer. Check this frequently. When the sherbet becomes slightly iced over the top, beat with a mixer. You will need to repeat this process every thirty minutes for the next four hours until the mixture is completely set. If you desire, add 1 cup of finely diced fresh peaches during the last mixing for a dessert filled with wisdom.

Incense: Red sandalwood.

Activities: Ritually destroy the image of anything that holds you back or binds you. Scatter the remnants to the winds or flowing water to move that negative energy out of your life. For example, if you have a passion for something unhealthy, use a torch as your focus. Discharge all your feelings into the flame, then extinguish it in a brazier of water. Pour the liquid to the earth and release your captivity with it.

Sample Chant: Let this chant rise slowly from your center until you sing it, shout it, move with it. Let the power of victory fill your being.

> *Victory in me, Victory be free;*
> *Goddess hear my urgent plea!*

Alternative Timing: St. George's Eve (Spring).

Other Accents: Have extra items available which are easily taken apart or removed by water, earth, air, or fire. This way, if you think of other areas where victory is needed, you can designate and destroy one of the "disposables" as part of your spell work.

February 23

TERMINALIA (ROME)

Magical Themes: Honoring or defining the boundaries in your life; protection of your home and land.

History/Lore: One of the early Roman kings named Numa decided that every citizen should mark the boundaries their land. This decree eventually evolved into Terminalia, a celebration honoring Terminus, the god of boundaries. Terminus is depicted without arms or legs because he is immoveable—staying to watch over all borders.

Decorating Ideas: Flower garlands draped over the four corners of your living space or land. Offerings on the altar of cake, fruit, honey, and grain.

Garments: A simple Roman toga is one possibility; any fabric with strict lines predominant in its pattern.

Ritual Cup: Wine was favored.

Ritual Foods: Anything with corn. Suggestions include corn chowder, corn bread, and corn on the cob. Corn was regarded as an acceptable gift to Terminus.

Incense: Choose strong protective herbs to burn in a brazier while you mark the boundary of your circle. Bay, clove, fennel, mint, and myrrh are all good options.

Activities: Walking the boundaries of your land while saying prayers was the main activity on this day. In your own home, this may equate to moving around each room with a smudge stick and invoking the blessings of your household guardian.

Terminalia was also a time to greet neighbors with good wishes. If someone has moved into your area lately, this might be a good opportunity to say hello and extend the hand of welcome. Don't forget a token gift for their hearth!

Sample Invocation:

I walk to the North of my sacred space;
Herein all negativity is erased.
I walk to the east where the magic winds dance;
Here I evoke the power of abundance.
I walk to the south where the fires burn bright;
There I shall banish, all evil, take flight!
I walk to the west, where clear waters flow;
The circle's completed, blessings bestow!

Alternative Timing: Festival of the Kitchen God; Festival of the Kitchen Goddess; Feast of the Guardian Angel.

Other Accents: Plant blessed crystals around your home to maintain a protective atmosphere or make a witch's bottle. This is devised by collecting reflective surfaces, sharp pieces of metal, nails, etc., and placing them all in a covered jar. The reflective surfaces bounce negative energy back to its source, while the rough edges "capture" haphazard energy which is not beneficial. Traditionally, this should be planted somewhere near your doorway. If you dwell in an apartment, use a large potted plant for this purpose.

February 26

HYGEIA'S DAY (AFRICA)

Magical Themes: Health and well-being; prevention and foresight.

History/Lore: Hygeia, as her name suggests, is the goddess of disease prevention and vitality. She appears as an older, wise woman wearing the traditional robes of a healer.

Decorating Ideas: Any depictions of snakes, especially the python, are appropriate, as this was an animal sacred to her. Snakes shed their skin in a kind of rebirthing process, making them powerful symbols for healing.

Garments: Check your region for African-American stores. They frequently carry beautifully colored, loose-fitting tops that are comfortable as ritual garb. Choose red and green hues to accentuate life and vitality.

Ritual Cup: Water for its cleansing, purifying qualities.

Ritual Foods: Chicken soup is one panacea. Any foods prepared specifically to improve your fitness, or those considered healthful, such as yogurt, oranges, and fresh vegetables.

Incense: Juniper, oak wood and thyme to maintain health.

Activities: Take the time to reflect on the way you have been caring for yourself. Do you eat right and get enough rest? Do you exercise regularly? Have you had a full checkup in the last few years? If the answer to any of these questions is "no," implore Hygeia for renewed enthusiasm in this area. Your physical state affects your spiritual nature and your magic. Don't overlook the temple of your soul.

Sample Spell: For any sickness, write the word abracadabra in descending form on a piece of paper. Make a hole in the base of a tree and spit in it, placing the paper therein. Bury the paper there to likewise bury your illness.

Another country charm to rid you of sickness is to take a glass of red wine with a gold coin therein (gold-colored is fine). Put this beneath the stars during a waning Moon for three nights. Each night, drink one third of the wine until it's gone, so that your sickness will shrink.

Alternative Timing: Fiesta of the Mother of Health.

Other Accents: The color of health is usually regarded as bright, vibrant green, like that of new spring sprouts. Use accents of this in and around the sacred space.

February 28

KALEVALA DAY (FINLAND)

Magical Themes: Myth, legend, symbolic stories, ritual drama and the honoring of one's heritage.

History/Lore: The Kalevala is an epic poem with twenty-two thousand verses. It is a folk tale, mingled with legends, history, and symbolism regarding the Finnish people and their lands. Until 1835, this poem was memorized and shared as part of the oral history of the Finnish people. Then Dr. Elias Lonnrot finished a complete transcription, taken from the traditional Finnish bards. This day marks the first time the Kalevala was ever printed. In honor of the occasion, a statue of the doctor is garlanded and surrounded by candles.

Decorating Ideas: Wreaths of spruce and pine are customary. To make one, take long bundles of the evergreens, placing the broader end of one at the base of the next. Secure them in place using florist wire. Continue in this manner until you have completed a large enough circle for your purposes. As a table centerpiece, this can be placed around a glass-enclosed candle. Around this central point, add any images you have of the founder(s) of your path, important individuals in your family's history, etc.

Garments: Anything blue and white, the colors of the Finnish flag.

Ritual Cup: A favored beverage in the northern climes, especially during the Winter months is glögg (see page 238 for recipe). This is a heavily spiced, fortified wine made with raisins and figs. It is usually drunk with a special toast which means, "Health to all." Just take care not to clank your pot when making this, as this indicates the presence of death.

Ritual Foods: Items which honor the heritage of your family or the traditions of their country of origin.

Incense: Pine.

Activities: Sit around a roaring fire recounting the sacred stories of your faith. If celebrating with the family, discuss the roots of your family tree and any tales you remember about your ancestors. People proficient in music or writing may want to try their hand at an epic poem or song which remembers family traditions.

Sample Invocation: This will have to be personalized to match the celebration.

Alternative Timing: Eisteddfod and Kermesse.

March

March 5

ANTHESTERIA (GREECE)

Magical Themes: The afterlife; immortality; honoring the dead.

History/Lore: This was a festival of flowers and a Day of the Dead all rolled into one. The reason for this was probably twofold: first, the scent of flowers is frequently linked to ghosts in folklore; and second, the Greeks believed that the spirits of the dead returned home when flowers began to blossom.

Decorating Ideas: Thorns draped over the lintels and doorways are traditional to keep any angry spirits caught up in their barbs. Pots of seeds were left out as offerings to the wandering ghosts.

Garments: Personal choice.

Ritual Cup: This festival also honors the death and resurrection of Dionysus, so wine or grape juice is most fitting.

Ritual Foods: Anything featuring grapes or figs.

Incense: Dried petals from early blooming flowers.

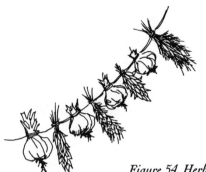

Figure 54. Herb and garlic garland.

Activities: It is customary to leave a place at your table for family members who have passed over for the next three days. The house should be decorated and blessed with protective items. Try making a decorative garland of garlic, intermingled with other dried herbs, for your kitchen (see figure 54).

If you are a brewer, the first day of this celebration is called "cask-opening day." The second is "pouring day." Therefore open up one of your bottles which has been aging to breathe, then serve it to guests the next eve!

Sample Invocation:

> *Dionysus, promoter of civilization,*
> *Lawgiver, and lover of peace,*
> *We raise our glasses in your presence.*
> *Let the wine which pours from our hands*
> *Remember those who are not among us*
> *And bless their spirits.*
> *Give to all who drink from this cup*
> *Good life, good health,*
> *And unity.*
> *Celebrate with us this night.*

Alternative Timing: Any observance for the dead; flower festivals like Rosalia.

Also this Date: Celebration of Isis (North Africa). Isis was the personification of nature, the Queen of the Dead, a protector of sailors, and the Queen Mother. If you can, toss a flower into running water for good fortune.

March 8

MOTHER EARTH DAY (CHINA)

Magical Themes: Giving honor to the Earth.

History/Lore: Dating back to the Sung dynasty, Mother Earth Day pays homage to the spirit of the ground itself. Having been called by many names in different civilizations, the spirit of Gaia receives tribute in China on this day. Here, this goddess rules over the productivity and fertility of the soil, as well as the wind and rain.

Decorating Ideas: Candles are placed in an area as offerings along with rice, water chestnuts, and white almonds. Traditionally these are left in three bowls, each bearing a stick of incense to carry the gift to the goddess.

Garments: Yellow, green, and brown hues should highlight your robes to mirror the colors of a flourishing world.

Ritual Cup: Celebrate the fruits of the Earth with a mixed fruit punch.

Ritual Foods: Any items with dates, grains, beans, or peanuts. These are also fitting offerings.

Incense: Sandalwood.

Activities: Usually the married daughter of each family takes gruel to the goddess, along with condiments to gently remind the lady of abundant harvests. If there are no married children in your home, let the eldest perform this rite.

Another enjoyable activity for children is making a model Earth out of papier-mâché. Use a small ball or piece of fabric for the center. As they lie on each piece of paper, the children should voice their wishes for Earth's future. I highly recommend that the adults of your home observe this project. You will be amazed by how touching their concerns and feelings are.

Sample Prayer:

Earth Mother, Gaia, Ishtar, Ge,
We thank you.
The blessings you provide fill our lives

To overflowing.
Tonight we serve your spirit.
Let our energy be guided to heal the wounds
You bear so sustenance may continue.
Forgive us for our neglect and
Accept now our grateful offering.

Alternative Timing: Earth Day.

Other Accents: In China, Mother Earth is regarded as the wife of the god of wealth. Therefore, leave some coins in the sacred space to welcome him and to bring a little extra prosperity among you.

March 9

TIBETAN BUTTER FESTIVAL

Magical Themes: Divination; destiny; the movement of time; kindness, prosperity, and reflective prayer.

History/Lore: Buddhists believe that all things are transient and changeable with time. This central conviction is remembered in the Tibetan Butter Festival where figures of heroes and gods are carved in butter. The preparation for this observance is long and laborious. Monks make the figures by mixing twenty dyes into iced butter over a period of months. Some of the effigies are two stories high!

Come the time of the festival, the figures are mounted with lanterns and taken down the streets parade-style. Afterward, the monks toss them into a river to allow the images to "melt away."

Decorating Ideas: The favorite depiction is that of the god of wealth who wears gold armor, and purple and green robes, bears a silver spear, and wears golden sandals. Any decorations around him are done in blue, pink, and yellow against black wool, with green scallops. This last configuration would be appropriate as a covering for the altar, using pastel flowers or candles, and a woolen cloth over the surface. The area of the celebration may also be lit with thousands of lanterns.

Garments: Wear yellow garb, the color of creamy butter.

Ritual Cup: Hot buttered rum is one choice, or anything with a golden hue to maintain congruity.

Ritual Foods: As many buttered dishes as you can think of. Begin with hot bread and butter to whet the appetite. Freshly steamed vegetables with butter, and poultry basted with an herb-butter sauce for prosperity are all fitting. For the latter add basil, dill, ginger, mint, or dry onion to the butter.

Incense: Lotus.

Activities: Divination by butter lamps is a very old and venerable tradition in Tibet. You can accomplish this by placing a wick in softened butter which is shaped emblematically according to your question. Let this harden again.

Place the finished butter candle on a plate or in a bowl to collect the melted liquid. Light the wick while focusing on your question. If the flame grows larger, it is a positive sign. If the flame shortens or smolders, the omen is negative. Sparking, leaping light portends change and increased energy. Split flames indicate detached or divided attention to the matter at hand. Broad, fat flames mean growth and fertility.

Sample Invocation: Before lighting the candle, use a verbal charge to empower your divination:

> *My question moves from darkness to light; [light the candle]*
> *Let the flames tell true, grant second-sight.*

Alternative Timing: Any festival of lights.

Other Accents: At your feast table, have an image of your goal carved out of butter. Before eating, have everyone at the table join hands and direct positive energy toward the emblem. Then manifest the magic by eating!

March 13

BALINESE PURIFICATION FEAST

Magical Themes: Spells for cleansing and protection.

History/Lore: According to local legend, this is the time of year when the lord of hell cleans out his home and the demons are left to roam Bali freely. Because of this, the natives purify the island with elaborate spells and offerings.

Decorating Ideas: The best and most beautiful fruits, flowers and leaves are left on the altar to appease Brahma and invoke protection. Each aspect of life is represented with coins, tools, wines, meats, etc. These items are laid out decoratively in an eight-pointed star which the Balinese call the Rose of the Wind. It is so named because each compass direction and the point midway between each direction is symbolically represented. Such a radiant display is believed to attract the demons to a central point from which the can be cast out.

Garments: To please the gods, wear your best robes. The Balinese wear body paint (akin to wode) to frighten away the evil spirits.

Ritual Cup: Wines and liqueurs are traditional.

Ritual Foods: Calf meat and goose are both featured foods.

Incense: Something tropical like mimosa and coconut, both of which are also protective in nature.

Activities: Dust off all your favorite spells and incantations for protection and put them to work to reinforce your home or neighborhood. Bright fires of any type and noisemakers are also customary to help keep the wandering spirits away.

Sample Spell: Make the following anointing oil for your living space: Take 6 teaspoons dried mint, 6 cloves, and 6 frankincense and myrrh tears and place them in 1 cup of warm almond oil. Allow this to soak in bright sunlight to empower it for 6 days before your celebration. Place dabs of the mixture on all your windows, doors, and other openings around the home during the observance. As you anoint the area, add a brief charm such as, *Where there is light, darkness may not dwell.* Envision each anointed

area as being bound together by a network of white-light webs
to strengthen this spell.

Alternative Timing: The cleansing lily; Kallyntaria and
Plynteria.

Other Accents: Take out all your mundane tools for cleaning and bless them to purify your sacred space or home.

March 19

QUINTARIA; FEAST OF ATHENA (GREECE)

Magical Themes: Physical and mental ability; artistic talents.

History/Lore: Every town or village in Greece held annual observances for Athena. Athens, however had special celebrations. This feast was most notable during the years of 500-300
B.C., and lasted for five days. The first day included a footrace;
the second, gymnastic competitions; the third, a festival of song;
the fourth, poetry; and the fifth day was dedicated to satire.
Laughter was regarded as a great gift from Athena!

At the end of the festivities, Athena would receive a new
tunic (peplus) in the Acropolis along with libations. The tunic
was always presented by the youth who had woven it.

Decorating Ideas: Wheels, musical instruments, needles
and thread, artistic tools, shields or spears, depictions of owls,
oak and olive leaves are all sacred to Athena. Make a garland of
the leaves and place it around the perimeter of the sacred space
or altar. Place your musical instruments and artistic implements
in the center of the circle to be blessed.

Garments: The robes made for Athena were white with
gold trim. Consider maintaining this theme.

Ritual Cup: Use fruit juices, particularly mulberry, which
is sacred to Athena. Juice enhances your physical and mental
energy.

Ritual Foods: Any items with olives (perhaps an olive salad) or coconut (a pie which is also lunar in nature).

Incense: Musk, geranium, or lily.

Activities: Celebrate your arts and sports. Hold special competitions and games which focus on both. Consider making yourself a new robe that, when donned, will allow you to take on Athenic qualities. Tell jokes to lift any burdens you bear away.

Sample Charm: To encourage a good sense of humor, make the following amulet. Find an amusing picture of yourself. To this, apply feathers, a small agate, oil scented with catnip, and a toy. As each is applied to the picture, add your verbal charge — something like:

> *Feathers for fancy, agate for smiles,*
> *Oil smooths all the wrinkles, catnip for whiles.*
> *Then comes a trinket to remind me to play.*
> *Humor tomorrow, humor today!*

Keep this amulet near your clothing so that it draws energy into items you use regularly.

Alternative Timing: Festival of Minerva (Spring); Hilaria.

PART III

The
Days of
Our Lives

The holiest sanctuary is the home.
The family altar is more venerable
than that of a cathedral.
The education of the soul for eternity
should begin and be carried on at the fireside.
—Richard Baxter

Personal Celebrations and Observations

Read nature;
Nature is a friend to truth.
—Edward Young

The most important days of our lives are rarely those noted on any calendar. In devising your personal Wheel of the Year, the memories closest to your heart become paramount. Traditional holidays hold significance, but they do not affect you as intimately as the changes you experience firsthand.

In this hurry-up world, sometimes we gloss over these transitions, never really taking the time to incorporate their significance into our lives. Part of the purpose of your annual observance calendar is to do just that. Here, you stop your rushing for a moment and reassess your place, purpose, and perspectives. This examination is vitally important to spiritual and emotional growth. Without it, you get lost in a haze of "doing" that never acknowledges what it means to *be*.

Being is a verb that denotes active, participating energy. This means that the central character in each Season of the Sun is *you*. With this in mind, living a magical reality is extended herein to include each important plateau you reach. I am certain I haven't begun to think of them all, but this section should provide you with ideas with which to work.

RITES OF PASSAGE

I have had to be more general with these celebrations than the others previously covered because of the splendid diversity of humankind. You are a wholly unique and beautiful creation whose celebrations will mirror that singularity. My words can only give you the outlines within which to work. The crayons must be supplied by your imagination, your faith, and a little tenacity. I wish you good fortune in the process of discovery.

BIRTHDAYS

On this day you traveled to this planet to begin a new cycle of learning. What a tremendous blessing! Today is your special day, so treat yourself accordingly. Consider performing a ritual of rededication, go out to dinner, take a luxurious bath, get a massage, or participate in a favored hobby.

Enjoy the fellowship of those who count you as a friend or loved one. Let these people give you renewed energy and hope for the coming year. Take time out to meditate on the lessons life has given you over the past months and how to put that learning to good use. Set some goals (within reason) for the coming year to provide motivation and the promise of opportunity.

Finally, don't forget to make a wish when blowing out the candles on your cake. Let the smoke carry those desires to the gods with a prayer for health, long life, and happiness.

ENGAGEMENTS, WEDDINGS, AND ANNIVERSARIES

The celebration of love and its proclamation is something that has always been done with a flourish. Today you honor your emotions and your willingness to commit your life to another in partnership. This is no small decision, and if driven by love, it is one of the most powerful learning experiences you will ever have.

All of us tend to have sentimental ideals about relationships that prove a little too rosy. Today, however, put the rose-colored glasses back on and celebrate the spirit of romance! Put aside any bad feelings or talk them out, making efforts to tend the garden of love tenaciously. If weeds have grown, pull them out. Saturate the soil of your hearts with patience, communication, and understanding to keep that love alive.

Today should be a private occasion. Take time to *be* with each other. Wear each other's favorite outfit, make preferred foods, and talk about the things you would not have time for otherwise. Go out and enjoy all the activities you have in common. Celebrate your oneness and the tremendous strength that comes from unity.

PREGNANCY, CHILDBIRTH, AND ADOPTION

You have decided to extend your love yet again. Now a small spirit joins your home and family unit. Whether this occurs naturally or through the adoptive process, your life is about to be changed forever and you are bound to have certain doubts.

Talk with other families that you know and respect. Gather ideas about childcare and childrearing that can help you find your way. Perform a ritual for conception (or smooth adoption proceedings) to invite Divine blessings on your efforts.

Once that child is home, listen closely to the tiny soul which is visiting you. I have yet to figure out who learns more from childrearing, the child or parent! Introduce them to all parts of the house and the beings within (including animals). Set up a specially prepared protective sphere around their bed so that peaceful sleep will always be at their pillow.

Finally, hold a celebration in gratitude for this gift. Invite friends and loved ones to witness the naming or welcoming of the child. Bless the child with each of the elements, then enjoy an afternoon of fellowship with a heart full of thanksgiving.

GRADUATION AND COMING OF AGE

Parents don't realize what a transformational experience graduation or coming of age is for *them,* let alone the children in their lives. Suddenly, the spiritual being you have nurtured is an adult—fully responsible and fully aware. You find yourself reflecting on their upbringing. Were you a good parent? If you extended love and support, and provided the basic lessons for them to become good people, then your answer is "yes."

This plateau is not an ending. It is the beginning of a new relationship; one more mature and balanced. Mark this occasion in some special way which is meaningful to both yourself and the teenager. Perhaps provide them with more trust and responsibility at home. If they have chosen a magical path, let them assume adult roles in your circle and give them suitable tools to fulfill that function.

Many tribal cultures use this as an opportunity to instruct their new adults in matters of sexuality, family tradition, and ancestry. They also share wise observations from the elders of the group. Considering the confusing times in which we live, this is not a bad idea. These children are facing some of the most difficult decisions of their lives. The sagacity of those more experienced may not always be heeded, but the support will be appreciated.

HOMECOMINGS AND REUNIONS

You know that old saying, "You can never go home again"? In a sense, it's true. Once you leave your hometown, when you return, your experiences have created a new person. The time away has been a kind of rebirth where you have defined yourself outside of familiar, safe surroundings. You have grown and suddenly feel a little out of place in those "old shoes."

First, don't let people's expectations mold you into outmoded habits and thoughtforms. Instead, surprise them! I remember how enjoyable my class reunion was. Everyone expected the same skinny, awkward, insecure girl to come strolling in. Instead, a self-possessed, elegant lady showed up (thanks to a little make-up and ego-boosting by my husband). By the end of the evening, I found this wasn't just a role that I'd assumed. I really had changed, and it was a tremendous relief to find myself at ease with the new *me*!

Some ways to avoid feeling like a "kid" again are to stay at a hotel instead of in your old bedroom. Your parents may not understand, but they usually respect the decision. Wear new clothes, bring pictures of what you've been doing, and take the initiative in planning activities. You are not a child anymore and have every right to act like the mature, responsible adult you've become. Enjoy it!

PROMOTIONS AND EMPLOYMENT TRANSITIONS

We all have guises in life. At work we wear one set of clothes. At home and circle we often don something completely different. As these roles change, we sometimes need to stop and reevaluate how they affect the other portions of our lives. Employment is a major part of this consideration.

When you start a new job, lose a job, or change positions within a company, insecurities often come to the forefront. You hope that your talents will be accepted, and will provide enough income to live on. Each person you meet in a professional capacity causes you to reflect on your place and abilities yet again. This is not necessarily bad, but you need to keep it in perspective.

In the business world, sometimes you need to see yourself through other people's eyes to succeed. This is where visualization can be very helpful. Imagine your job (or job search) from the perspective of an observer. Watch how you sit, stand, and present yourself. Are you assured, knowledgeable, reliable, and competent? If not, consider positive steps toward effecting change. Visualize yourself performing your job (or interview) to your best ability. See yourself as successful, then act upon that new assurance!

SPECIAL RECOGNITION

You have set yourself apart somehow and been recognized as a leader. The reasons can be many, but this is an occasion to pat yourself on the back for a job well done. Pride in your accomplishments is only a bad thing when it is puffed up. Revel in this moment of self-esteem and confidence. Enjoy tasting the fruit of your efforts!

If you have been given a commemorative plaque, hang it somewhere readily visible to bring back these warm feelings in the future. Let this moment inspire you to even greater things. Delight in the knowledge that somehow you have made a real difference, not only in the world, but in yourself.

DRASTIC LIFE CHANGES,
ELDERSHIP, AND CRONING

Ritual helps you to accept and incorporate drastic life changes. It brings the verity of change to your attention and focuses your spirit on coping with those changes. While there are many occasions which could be listed in this section, moving into your elder years with nobility is something a greater number of people face every day. Our society has lost sight of age as an honorable thing. Today, old means useless, ineffective, or unproductive. Nothing could be further from the truth.

Westerners should take some cues from the East and the Native Americans in this regard. Just as with a beautiful antique whose artistic value grows with time, age shapes and molds your awareness. You become the sum of your experiences. When the time comes that you are recognized among others as an elder, you should rejoice instead of cringe. This is but another Season of the Sun. Now you have the chance to teach those who will fashion the future!

Greet your age with dignity. Recognize it as a natural part of life and a great gift. You have already lived and learned. Use your eldership or croning rites to accept this new role, and spend time with those who look to you for guidance.

ENDINGS

As confusing and uncertain as is the first part of the circle, the ending is no less filled with questioning. Be it a relationship or a life, we meet endings with an array of questions and thoughtful reflections. Positive Endings are but the dawning of a new day. The old way of life is now behind you, so look to the future. Here or in the afterlife, the Sun rises to illuminate your heart with hope. Yes, the season has changed once more and the wheel moves on. You are part of that movement, as is your magic. So let it be.

Bibliography

FOLKLORE/SUPERSTITION/MYTH

Alexander, Marc. *British Folklore*. New York: Crescent Books, 1982.

Baker, Margaret. *Folklore and Customs of Rural England*. Totawa, NJ: Rowman & Littlefield, 1974.

Boland, Margaret. *Old Wives' Lore for Gardeners*. New York: Farrar, Straus & Giroux, 1976.

Budge, E. A. Wallis. *Amulets and Talismans*. Hyde Park, NY: University Books, 1968.

Complete Book of Fortune. New York: Crescent Books, 1936.

Cooper, J. C. *Symbolic & Mythological Animals*. London: Aquarian Press, 1992.

Cunningham, Scott. *The Magic in Food*. St. Paul, MN: Llewellyn, 1991.

Felding, William J. *Strange Superstitions & Magical Practices*. New York: Paperback Library, 1968.

Graves, Robert. *The Greek Myths*. London: Penguin, 1983.

Hendricks, Rhoda. *Mythologies of the World*. New York: McGraw Hill, 1979.

Leach, Maria, ed. *Standard Dictionary of Folklore, Mythology and Legend*. New York: Funk & Wagnall, 1972.

Loewe, Michael, ed. *Oracles and Divination*. Boston: Shambhala, 1981.

Lorrie, Peter. *Superstition*. London: Labyrinth, 1992.

New Larousse Encyclopedia of Mythology. London: Hamlyn, 1959.

Opie, Iona and Moria Tatem, eds. *Dictionary of Superstition*. London: Oxford University Press, 1989.

Scott, Rev. J. Loughran. *Bulfinch's Age of Fable*. Philadelphia: David McKay, 1898.

Skinner, Charles M. *Myths and Legends of Flowers, Trees, Fruits and Plants*. Philadelphia: Lippincott, 1925.

Telesco, Patricia. *Folkways*. St. Paul, MN: Llewellyn, 1995.

_____. *Kitchen Witch's Cookbook*. St. Paul, MN: Llewellyn, 1994.

_____. *Victorian Flower Oracle*. St. Paul, MN: Llewellyn, 1994.

Tuleja, Tad. *Curious Customs*. New York: Harmony Books, 1987.

Whitlock, Ralph. *A Calendar of Country Customs*. London: B.T. Batsford, 1978.

Wootton A. *Animal Folklore, Myth & Legend*. London: Blanford Press, 1986.

GODS AND GODDESSES

Carlyon, Richard. *A Guide to the Gods*. London: Heinemann/Quixote, 1981.

Conway, D.J. *Ancient Shining Ones*. St. Paul, MN: Llewellyn, 1993.

Farrar, Janet, and Stewart. *The Witch's God*. Custer, WA: Phoenix, 1989.

_____. *The Witch's Goddess*. Custer, WA: Phoenix, 1987.

Hendricks, Rhoda. *Mythologies of the World*. New York: McGraw Hill, 1979.

Leach, Maria, ed. *Standard Dictionary of Folklore, Mythology, and Legend*. New York: Funk & Wagnall, 1972.

Lyttleton, Margaret. *The Romans: Their Gods & Their Beliefs*. London: Orbis Press, 1984.

Monaghan, Patricia. *The Book of Goddesses & Heroines*. St. Paul, MN: Llewellyn, 1981.

New Larousse Encyclopedia of Mythology. London: Hamlyn, 1959.

Scott, Rev. J. Loughran. *Bulfinch's Age of Fable*. Philadelphia: David McKay, 1898.

HERBALISM

Beyerl, Paul. *Master Book of Herbalism*. Custer, WA: Phoenix, 1984.

Black, William George. *Folk Medicine*. New York: Burt Franklin, 1883.

Chase, A. W. *Receipt Book and Household Physician*. Detroit, MI: F. B. Dickerson, 1908.

Clarkson, Rosetta. *Green Enchantment*. New York: McMillan, 1940.

Culpepper, Nicholas. *Complete Herbal and English Physician*. Greenwood, IL: Meyerbooks, 1991. Originally published 1841.

Cunningham, Scott. *Encyclopedia of Magical Herbs*. St. Paul, MN: Llewellyn, 1988.

Digby, Kenelm. *The Closet Opened*. London: E.L.T. Brome, 1696.

Fox, William, MD. *Family Botanic Guide*, 18th edition. Sheffield, England: William Fox & Sons, 1907.

Lousada, Patricia. *Cooking with Herbs*. London: Bloomsbury Books, 1988.

Palaiseul, Jean. *Grandmother's Secrets*. New York: G. P. Putnam's Sons, 1974.

Plat, Hugh. *Delights for Ladies*, London: Humfrey Lownes, 1602.

Rodale's Complete Illustrated Encyclopedia of Herbs. Emmaus, PA: Rodale Publishing, 1987.

Skinner, Charles M. *Myths and Legends of Flowers, Trees, Fruits, and Plants*. Philadelphia, PA: Lippincott, 1925.

Williams, Judith. *Judes Home Herbal*. St. Paul, MN: Llewellyn, 1992.

HISTORY (GENERAL)

Ainsworth-Davis, James R. *Cooking through the Centuries*. London: Jim Dent &Sons, 1931.

Arnold, John P. *Origin and History of Beer and Brewing*. Chicago: Wahl-Henius Institute of Fermentology, 1911.

Attenborough, David. *Journeys to the Past*. England: Butterworth, 1981.

Broth, Patricia and Don. *Food in Antiquity*. New York: Praeger, 1969.

Brown, Peter. *The World of Late Antiquity*. London: Thames & Hudson, 1971.

Everyday Life Through the Ages. London: Reader's Digest Association Limited, 1992.

Harlan, William. *Illustrated History of Eating & Drinking through the Ages*. New York: American Heritage, 1968.

Hearn, L. *Japan*. London: MacMillan, 1905.

Hern, Gerhard. *The Celts*. New York: St. Martin's Press, 1975.

Kakuzo, Okakura. *The Book of Tea*. Tokyo: Charles E. Tuttle, 1956.

Magnall, Richmal. *Historical & Miscellaneous Questions*. London: Longman, Brown, Green & Longman, 1850.

Tannahill, Reay. *Food in History*. New York: Stein & Day, 1973.

HOLIDAYS, FESTIVALS, AND CELEBRATIONS

Adams, Ruth and Ruth Hutchison. Adams. *Every Day's a Holiday*. New York: Harper, 1951.

Bauer, Helen. *Japanese Festivals*. Garden City, NY: Doubleday, 1968.

Bodde, Derk. *Festivals in Classical China*. Princeton, NJ: Princeton University Press, 1975.

Budapest, Z. E. *Grandmother of Time*. New York: HarperCollins, 1989.

Campanelli, Pauline. *Ancient Ways*. St Paul, MN: Llewellyn, 1991.

_____. *Wheel of the Year*. St Paul, MN: Llewellyn, 1989.

Cooper, Gordon. *Festivals of Europe*. London: Percival Marshall, 1961.

Cooper, J. C. *Aquarian Dictionary of Festivals*. London: Aquarian, 1990.

Gaer, Joseph. *Holidays Around the World*. Boston: Little, Brown, 1953.

Ickis, Marguerite. *Book of Festival Holidays*. New York: Dodd, Mead, 1964.

James, E.O. *Seasonal Feasts & Festivals*. London: Thames & Hudson, 1961.

Joy, Margaret. *Days, Weeks & Months*. London: Faber & Faber, 1984.

Kieckhefer, Richard. *Magic in the Middle Ages*. Melbourne, Australia: Cambridge University Press, 1989.

Linton, Ralph and Adelin. *Halloween through Twenty Centuries*. New York: Henry Schuman, 1950.

Murray, Keith. *Ancient Rites & Ceremonies*. Toronto: Tudor Press, 1980.

Mystical Rites & Rituals. London: Octopus, 1975.

Mystical Year. Mysteries of the Unknown Series. Alexandria, VA: Time-Life Books, 1992.

Nakamura, Julia V. *The Japanese Tea Ceremony*. Mt. Vernon, NY: Peter Pauper Press, 1965.

Rosen, Mike. *Autumn Festivals*. E. Sussex, England: Wayland Press, 1990.

Snelling, John. *Buddhist Festivals*. Vero Beach, FL: Rourke Enterprises, 1987.

Spicer, Dorothy Gladys. *The Book of Festivals*. New York: Woman's Press, 1937.

Starhawk, *The Spiral Dance*. New York: HarperCollins, 1979.

Telesco, Patricia. *Urban Pagan*. St. Paul, MN: Llewellyn, 1993.

Van Straalen, Alice. *The Book of Holidays around the World*. New York: E. P. Dutton, 1986.

MAGIC AND MAGICAL HISTORY

Adler, Margot. *Drawing Down the Moon*. New York: HarperCollins, 1987.

Ancient Wisdom & Secret Sects. Mysteries of the Unknown Series. Alexandria, VA: Time-Life Books, 1989.

Browne, Lewis. *The Believing World*. New York: MacMillan Company, 1959.

Cavendish, Richard. *History of Magic*. New York: Taplinger, 1977.

_____. ed. *Man, Myth & Magic*. London: Purnell, 1972.

Cunningham, Lady Sara. *Magical Virtues of Candles, Herbs, Incense and Perfume*. Glendale, CA: Aleph Books, 1979.

Cunningham, Scott. *The Magic in Food*. St Paul, MN: Llewellyn, 1991.

Drury, Nevill. *Dictionary of Mysticism & the Occult*. New York: HarperCollins, 1985.

Hall, Manly. *Secret Teachings of All Ages*. Los Angeles: Philosophical Research Society, 1977.

Loewe, Michael, ed. *Oracles & Divination*. Boston: Shambhala, 1981.

Murray, Keith. *Ancient Rites & Ceremonies*. Toronto: Tudor Press, 1980.

Mystical Rites & Rituals. London: Octopus, 1975.

Singer, Charles J. *Early English Magic and Medicine*. London: British Academy, 1920.

Starhawk, *The Spiral Dance*. New York: HarperCollins, 1979.

Telesco, Patricia. *Urban Pagan*. St. Paul, MN: Llewellyn, 1993.

RECIPES

Belt, T. Edwin. *Flower, Leaf & Sap Wines*. London: Mills & Boons Ltd., 1971.

Better Homes and Gardens New Cookbook. New York: Bantam Books, 1979.

Chase, A.W. *Receipt Book & Household Physician*. Detroit, MI: F.B. Dickerson, 1908.

Cheng, Rose & Michelle Morris, *Chinese Cooking*. Los Angeles: Price, Stern, Sloan, 1981.

Clifton, C. *Edible Flowers*. New York: McGraw Hill, 1976.

Compleat Anachronist Guide to Brewing. Milpitas, CA: Society for Creative Anachronism, 1983.

Digby, Kenelm. *The Closet Opened*. London: E.L.T. Brome, 1696.

Doorn, Joyce V. *Making Your Own Liquors*. San Leandro, CA: Prism Press, 1977.

Encyclopedia of Creative Cooking. Charlotte Turgeon, ed. New York: Weathervane Press, 1982.

Flower, Barbara and Elizabeth Rosenbaum, trans. *The Roman Cookery Book*. London: George G. Harrap, 1958.

Frere, Catherine F., ed. *A Proper Newe Booke of Cokery*. Cambridge, England: W. Heffer & Sons, 1913.

Harlan, William. *Illustrated History of Eating and Drinking through the Ages*. New York: American Heritage, 1968.

Hechtlinger, Adelaide. *The Seasonal Hearth*. New York: Overlook Press, 1986.

Hiss, Emil. *Standard Manual of Soda & Other Beverages*. Chicago: G. P. Englehand & CO, 1897.

Jagendorf, M.A. *Folk Wines*. New York: Vanguard Press, 1963.

MacNicol, Mary. *Flower Cookery*. New York: Fleet Press, 1967.

Napier, Mrs. Alexander. *Noble Boke of Cookry*. London: Elliot Stock, 1882.

Plat, Hugh. *Delights for Ladies*. London: Humfrey Lownes, 1602.

Roden, Claudia. *A Book of Middle Eastern Foods*. New York: Random House, 1968.

Spayde, Jon. *Japanese Cooking*. Secaucus, NJ: Chartwell Books, 1984.

Stafford, Edward Lord. *The Form of Curry*. London: J. Nichols Co., 1780.

Telesco, Patricia. *Kitchen Witch's Cookbook*. St. Paul, MN: Llewellyn, 1994.

QUOTATIONS

Bartlett, John. *Familiar Quotations*. Boston: Little, Brown, 1938.

Edwards, Tyron D.D. *New Dictionary of Thoughts*. New York: Standard Book Co., 1934.

MISCELLANEOUS

Cristiani, R. S. *Treatise on Perfumery*. London: Baird & Co., 1877.

Delsol, Paula. *Chinese Astrology*. New York: Warner, 1969.

Laver, James. *Costume*. London: Jr. Heritage Books, 1956.

Oesterley, W.O.E. *The Sacred Dance*. Cambridge, MA: Cambridge University Press, 1923.

Riotte, Louise. *Sleeping with a Sunflower*. Pownal, VT: Garden Way, 1987.

Sheen, Joanna. *Flower Crafts*. London: Salamander Books, 1992.

Walker, Barbara. *Women's Dictionary of Symbols and Sacred Objects*. San Francisco: HarperCollins, 1988.

Index of Holidays and Celebrations

Index of Holiday Recipes

General Index

atricia Telesco is a trustee for the Universal Federation of Pagans, a professional member of the Wiccan Pagan Press Alliance, and an ordained pagan minister. From 1988 to 1992 she produced the *Magi Newsletter*, a Wiccan Pagan New Age newsletter. Her activities include historical herbalism, antique restoration, and singing. In addition, Telesco is the Creative Advisor for MAGIC (Metaphysical Artists for Gala), a networking cooperative of spiritually-centered writers and artists. She is the author of *Folkways, Brother Wind, Sister Rain* [children's], *A Witch's Brew, A Kitchen Witch's Cookbook, The Victorian Grimoire, Urban Pagan, The Victorian Flower Oracle*, and will soon publish *A Healer's Handbook* (Weiser 1997). She lives in western New York with her husband, two children, four cats, a dog and a bunny, welcomes doing lectures, and looks forward to hearing from her readers.